AAT

Level 4

Business Tax

Professional Diploma in Accounting

Course Book

For assessments from
September 2022 to December 2023

First edition 2021

ISBN 9781 5097 4337 7
ISBN (for internal use only) 9781 5097 4080 2

British Library Cataloguing-in-Publication Data
A catalogue record for this book is available from the British Library

Published by

BPP Learning Media Ltd
BPP House, Aldine Place
142-144 Uxbridge Road
London W12 8AA

www.bpp.com/learningmedia

Printed in the United Kingdom

Your learning materials, published by BPP Learning Media Ltd, are printed on paper obtained from traceable sustainable sources.

Contents

		Page
Introduction to the course		iv
Skills bank		vii

1	Tax framework	1
2	Computing trading income	15
3	Capital allowances	33
4	Taxing unincorporated businesses	59
5	Partnerships	73
6	National insurance	87
7	Computing corporation tax	95
8	Losses	109
9	Self-assessment for individuals	131
10	Self-assessment for companies	147
11	Chargeable gains for companies	159
12	Share disposals	173
13	Business disposals	185
14	Tax planning for businesses	209

Activity answers	221
Test your learning: answers	263
Tax reference material	293
Bibliography	301
Index	303

Introduction to the course

Syllabus overview

This unit introduces the student to UK taxation relevant to businesses. Students will understand how to compute business taxes for sole traders, partnerships and limited companies. They will also be able to identify tax planning opportunities while understanding the importance of maintaining ethical standards.

In learning how to prepare tax computations, students will gain the skills required to apply the tax treatment of capital expenditure and the adjustment of accounting profits for tax purposes. Students will allocate profits to tax years for ongoing businesses as well as in opening and closing years. In addition, students will allocate profits between partners in a partnership and will calculate National Insurance (NI) contributions for the self-employed, advising clients on the tax implications of making losses.

Students will understand the administrative requirements of UK tax law, including the implications of errors in tax returns, late filing of returns, late payment of tax and not retaining records for the required period. Students will compute tax on the sale of capital assets by companies and will understand the capital gains implications of the sale of a business and the tax reliefs available to businesses.

Tax advice is an important part of many accountancy roles in recognising tax planning opportunities for businesses. Students will discuss the ethical issues facing business owners and managers in reporting their business tax and the responsibilities that an agent has in giving advice on tax issues to business clients.

Business Tax is an optional unit.

Test specification for this unit assessment

Assessment method	Marking type	Duration of assessment
Computer based assessment	Partially computer/partially human marked	2 hours

	Learning outcomes	Approximate weighting
1	Prepare tax computations for sole traders and partnerships	25%
2	Prepare tax computations for limited companies	15%
3	Prepare tax computations for the sale of capital assets by limited companies	15%
4	Understand administrative requirements of the UK's tax regime	15%
5	Understand the tax implications of business disposals	10%
6	Understand tax reliefs, tax planning opportunities and agents' responsibilities in reporting taxation to HM Revenue & Customs	20%
Total		100%

Assessment structure

2 hours duration

Competency is 70%

Analysis of the practice papers

The two **practice assessments each** consisted of 11 tasks as follows:

Task	Expected content	Max marks	Chapter ref	Study complete
Task 1	Adjusting accounting profits and losses for tax purposes	8	2	
Task 2	Capital allowances	12	3	
Task 3	Basis period rules	6	4	
Task 4	Analysing profits and losses of a partnership and calculating NICs	8	5, 6	
Task 5	Chargeable gains and allowable losses of companies	6	11	
Task 6	Chargeable gains and allowable losses in company disposal of shares	9	12	
Task 7	Calculating taxable profits and corporation tax payable	6	7	
Task 8	Administrative requirements of UK tax law	15	9, 10	
Task 9	Tax planning and the responsibilities of the business and agent	12	1, 14	
Task 10	Trading losses	8	8	
Task 11	Business disposals	10	13	

*Note that the number of tasks and the number of marks per task will remain as per the practice assessments. The practice assessments demonstrate how the unit content may be assessed using as many of the question types that may be used in an assessment as possible. However, this does not mean that the live assessments will use the exact same question types as in the practice assessments. The marking type for a Task position will always be the same. For example, Task 6 will always be fully human marked, and the number of human marked marks will be comparable across the assessment.

Skills bank

Our experience of preparing students for this type of assessment suggests that to obtain competency, you will need to develop a number of key skills.

What do I need to know to do well in the assessment?

This unit is one of the optional Level 4 units.

To be successful in the assessment you need to:

- Calculate business taxation and understand how tax has an impact on the running of a business for sole traders, partnerships and limited companies.

- Apply the tax rules to scenarios given to calculate tax due, be knowledgeable with regard to the administration of tax, the implications of errors, late payment of tax, late filing of returns and also ethical issues facing business owners.

Assumed knowledge

Business Tax is an **optional** unit which requires no assumed knowledge. The Level 4 unit, *Personal Tax*, is associated with this unit, although these units can be taken separately. Knowledge developed in either of these units will be useful in the later study of the other unit.

Assessment style

In the assessment you will complete tasks by:

1   Entering narrative by selecting from drop-down menus of narrative options known as **picklists**

2   Using **drag and drop** menus to enter narrative

3   Typing in numbers, known as **gapfill** entry

4   Entering **ticks**

5   Entering **dates** by selecting from a calendar

6   Writing written explanations in a very basic word processing environment which has limited editing and no spelling or grammar checking functionality

7   Entering detailed calculations in a very basic spreadsheet environment that has limited editing functionality. In some circumstances there may be a pre-filled autosum formula to total figures for you, but these sums will not earn marks. They are there to assist you with presenting your answer.

You must familiarise yourself with the style of the online questions and the AAT software before taking the assessment. As part of your revision, login to the **AAT website** and attempt their **online practice assessments**.

Answering written questions

In your assessment there will be written questions. The main verbs used for these type of question requirements are as follows, along with their meaning:

- Identify – analyse and select for presentation
- Explain – set out in detail the meaning of
- Discuss – by argument, discuss the pros and cons
- Define – state or describe exactly the meaning

Analysing the scenario

Before answering the question set, you need to carefully review the scenario given in order to consider what questions need to be answered, and what needs to be discussed. A simple framework that could be used to answer the question is as follows:

- Point – make the point
- Evidence – use information from the scenario as evidence
- Explain – explain why the evidence links to the point

For example if an assessment task asked us to explain which three of the fundamental ethical principles are most threatened in the following situation:

You are working on a company's corporation tax return, and notice some errors in the previous year's return which has already been filed. Your manager is concerned about the implications for their own career if the errors are disclosed, and has said that you would be considered for promotion if you agreed to keep quiet about the errors.

We could answer as follows:

1   Point – state which principles are most threatened – objectivity, integrity, professional behaviour

2   Evidence – use information from the scenario – the manager is asking me to keep quiet about an error and offered to consider me for promotion if I keep quiet

3   Explain – explain why the evidence links to the point – the manager is trying to influence my behaviour (objectivity), the manager wants me to act in a way that is not straightforward and honest (integrity), the manager wants me to behave in a way that is not legal and may discredit the profession (professional behaviour)

Introduction to the assessment

The question practice you do will prepare you for the format of tasks you will see in the *Business Tax* assessment. It is also useful to familiarise yourself with the introductory information you **may** be given at the start of the assessment.

You have **2 hours** to complete this practise assessment.

- This assessment contains **11 tasks** and you should attempt to complete every task.

- Each task is independent. You will not need to refer to your answers in previous tasks.

- The total number of marks for this assessment is 100.

- Read every task carefully to make sure you understand what is required.

- Where the date is relevant, it is given in the task data.

- Both minus signs and brackets can be used to indicate negative numbers **unless** task instructions say otherwise.

- You must use a full stop to indicate a decimal point. For example, write 100.57 **not** 100,57 or 10057

- **You may use a comma to indicate a number in the thousands, but you don't have to.** For example, 10000 and 10,000 are both acceptable.

- If your answer requires rounding, apply normal mathematical rounding rules **unless** the task instructions say otherwise.

1   As you revise, use the **BPP Passcards** to consolidate your knowledge. They are a pocket-sized revision tool, perfect for packing in that last-minute revision.

2   Attempt as many tasks as possible in the **Question Bank**. There are plenty of assessment-style tasks which are excellent preparation for the real assessment.

3   Always **check** through your own answers as you will in the real assessment, before looking at the solutions in the back of the Question Bank.

Key to icons

 Key term
A key definition which is important to be aware of for the assessment

 Formula to learn
A formula you will need to learn as it will not be provided in the assessment

 Formula provided
A formula which is provided within the assessment and generally available as a pop-up on screen

 Activity
An example which allows you to apply your knowledge to the technique covered in the Course Book. The solution is provided at the end of the chapter

 Illustration
A worked example which can be used to review and see how an assessment question could be answered

 Assessment focus point
A high priority point for the assessment

Open book reference
Where use of an open book will be allowed for the assessment

Real life examples
A practical real life scenario

BPP LEARNING MEDIA

AAT qualifications

The material in this book may support the following AAT qualifications:

AAT Level 4 Diploma in Professional Accounting

AAT Diploma in Professional Accounting at SCQF Level 8

Supplements

From time to time we may need to publish supplementary materials to one of our titles. This can be for a variety of reasons, from a small change in the AAT unit guidance to new legislation coming into effect between editions.

You should check our supplements page regularly for anything that may affect your learning materials. All supplements are available free of charge on our supplements page on our website at:

www.bpp.com/learning-media/about/students

Improving material and removing errors

There is a constant need to update and enhance our study materials in line with both regulatory changes and new insights into the assessments.

From our team of authors BPP appoints a subject expert to update and improve these materials for each new edition.

Their updated draft is subsequently technically checked by another author and from time to time non-technically checked by a proof reader.

We are very keen to remove as many numerical errors and narrative typos as we can but given the volume of detailed information being changed in a short space of time we know that a few errors will sometimes get through our net.

We apologise in advance for any inconvenience that an error might cause. We continue to look for new ways to improve these study materials and would welcome your suggestions. If you have any comments about this book, please use the review form at the back.

These learning materials are based on the qualification specification released by the AAT in September 2021.

Tax framework

Syllabus learning outcomes / objectives

6.4   Ethical guidelines

Learners need to understand

- The definitions of:
    - Tax planning
    - Tax avoidance
    - Tax evasion
- Ethical implications of tax avoidance and tax evasion
- The requirement to report suspected tax evasion
- The ethical principle of confidentiality

Assessment context

This chapter provides you with important background to your syllabus and helps you to distinguish between illegal and legal tax measures as well as ethical and unethical behaviour.

You will not have to calculate income tax payable in your assessment but you need to know how this works so you can understand other parts of the syllabus (eg loss relief).

Qualification context

You will not see these areas again unless you study the Personal Tax unit.

Business context

A tax practitioner needs to know the duties and obligations the taxpayer owes to HMRC.

A tax practitioner needs to know and understand the detailed tax rules.

A tax practitioner needs to adhere to AAT's ethical standards when giving tax advice and dealing with clients.

Chapter overview

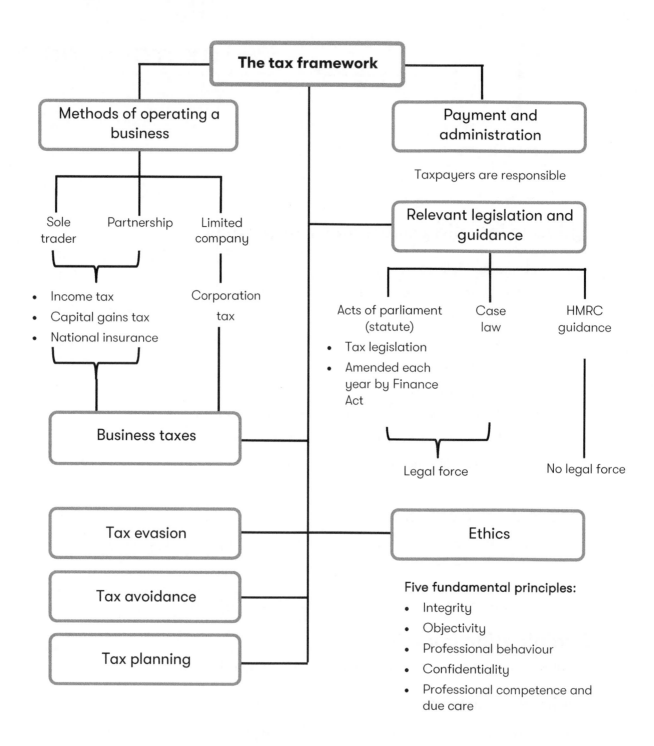

The tax framework

Methods of operating a business
- Sole trader
- Partnership
- Limited company

Income tax, Capital gains tax, National insurance (Sole trader, Partnership)

Corporation tax (Limited company)

Business taxes

Payment and administration

Taxpayers are responsible

Relevant legislation and guidance
- Acts of parliament (statute)
  - Tax legislation
  - Amended each year by Finance Act
- Case law → Legal force
- HMRC guidance → No legal force

Tax evasion

Tax avoidance

Tax planning

Ethics

Five fundamental principles:
- Integrity
- Objectivity
- Professional behaviour
- Confidentiality
- Professional competence and due care

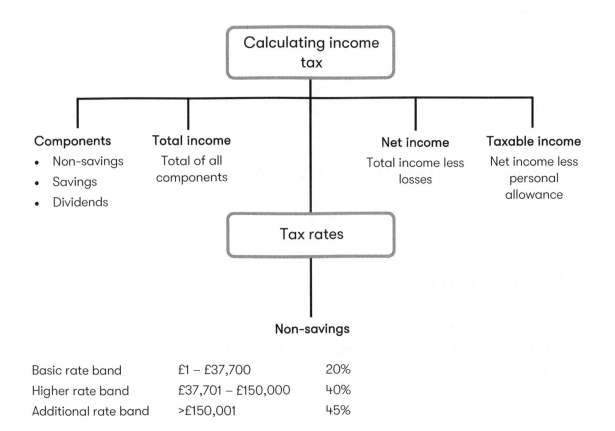

Calculating income tax

Components
- Non-savings
- Savings
- Dividends

Total income
Total of all components

Net income
Total income less losses

Taxable income
Net income less personal allowance

Tax rates

Non-savings

Basic rate band	£1 – £37,700	20%
Higher rate band	£37,701 – £150,000	40%
Additional rate band	>£150,001	45%

1 Introduction

In this opening chapter, we consider the various methods by which a business can operate. The method of operation affects how the business is taxed. We then see that the tax law governing businesses is included in Acts of Parliament and in a body of law known as case law. We will also look at ethics and the fundamental differences between legal and illegal tax planning.

Finally, we briefly consider the basics of how to calculate an individual's income tax liability. You may need to be aware of this when dealing with business losses.

2 Method of operating a business

- **Sole trader** – self-employed individual
- **Partnership** – self-employed individuals working together
- **Limited company** – incorporated body legally separate from owners

3 Business taxes

Income is a receipt that is expected to recur (eg trading income) while a **gain** is a one-off profit on the disposal of an asset (eg a factory).

Sole traders and **partnerships are unincorporated businesses.** This means that there is no legal separation between the individual(s) carrying on the business and the business itself.

As a result the individual(s) concerned must pay:

- Income tax on trading income
- Class 2 and Class 4 national insurance contributions (NICs)
- Capital gains tax on disposal of assets

Companies are incorporated businesses. This means they are taxed as separate legal entities independently of their owners.

Companies must pay corporation tax on all profits, including gains on disposal of assets.

4 Payment and administration

Taxpayers who are required to perform self-assessment have a legal responsibility to pay their tax on time and submit a tax return before the deadline.

Employees have tax deducted at source by their employer so, for most people other than the self-employed, there is no need to submit a tax return.

5 Relevant legislation and guidance from HMRC

5.1 Statute law

Most of the rules governing income tax, capital gains tax and corporation tax are laid down in **statute law**, which consists of:

- **Acts of Parliament** (the tax legislation), which are created directly by the Government and amended annually by that year's Finance Act. This text includes the provisions of the **Finance Act 2021.**

- **Statutory Instruments,** which are detailed rules created on behalf of the Government by civil servants to amend/alter an act without parliament having to pass a new act.

5.2 HMRC guidance

To help taxpayers, **HM Revenue & Customs (HMRC)**, which administers tax in the UK, publishes a wide range of guidance material on how it interprets the various acts. Much of this information can be found on HMRC's website **www.hmrc.gov.uk.**

None of this guidance material has the force of law.

5.3 Decided tax cases

A taxpayer and HMRC may disagree over the interpretation of the legislation.

Either party may appeal to the tax tribunal. The tax tribunal is independent of the Government and will listen to both sides of the argument before making a decision.

A judge will rule in favour of one party.

Cases decided by the courts provide guidance on how legislation should be interpreted, and collectively form a second source of tax law known as **case law.**

You will not be expected to quote the names of decided cases in your assessment but you may need to know the principle decided in a case. Where relevant, this will be noted within this Course Book.

6 AAT guidelines on professional ethics

A member shall comply with the following five fundamental principles: (AAT, 2017)

Fundamental principle	What it means
Professional competence and due care	You must maintain professional knowledge and skill (in practice, legislation and techniques) to ensure that a client or employer receives competent professional service.
Integrity	You must be straightforward and honest in all professional and business relationships.
Professional behaviour	You must comply with relevant laws and regulations, and avoid any action that may bring disrepute to the profession.
Confidentiality	You must not disclose confidential professional or business information or use it to your personal advantage, unless you have explicit permission to disclose it, or a legal or professional right or duty to disclose it.
Objectivity	You must not compromise professional or business judgment because of bias, conflict of interest or the undue influence of others.

7 Tax avoidance, tax evasion and tax planning

7.1 Tax evasion

Tax evasion is always illegal. It is when people or businesses deliberately do not declare and account for the taxes that they owe. It includes the hidden economy, where people conceal their presence or taxable sources of income or over-state their expenses.

Tax evasion can result in fines/imprisonment.

BPP
LEARNING
MEDIA

7.2 Tax avoidance

Tax avoidance involves bending the rules of the tax system to gain a tax advantage that Parliament never intended. It often involves contrived, artificial transactions that serve little or no purpose other than to produce this advantage. It involves operating within the letter – but not the spirit – of the law. Most tax avoidance schemes simply do not work, and those who engage in it can find they pay more than the tax they attempted to save once HMRC has successfully challenged them.

7.3 Tax planning

Tax planning involves using tax reliefs for the purpose for which they were intended. For example, claiming tax relief on capital investment, or saving via ISAs or for retirement by making contributions to a pension scheme. However, tax reliefs can be used excessively or aggressively by others than those intended to benefit from them or in ways that clearly go beyond the intention of Parliament. Where this is the case, it is right to take action, because it is important that the tax system is fair and perceived to be so. (HMRC, 2015)

Typical tasks in the assessment might ask you to define any of the above and to decide whether a particular scenario is an example of tax evasion/ tax avoidance or tax planning.

Activity 1: Tax avoidance and tax evasion

The following acts have been committed by one of your clients.

Action 1: A customer invoice was omitted from their business accounting records in order to push the income into the taxable profits of the following tax year.

Action 2: The client has transferred income generating assets into her husband's name as he pays a lower rate of tax on the investment income.

Required

Which of these actions amounts to tax evasion?

- Action 1 only
- Action 2 only
- Both actions
- Neither action

7.4 Reporting suspicions

A practicing accountant often acts for taxpayers in their dealings with HMRC and situations can arise where the accountant has concerns as to whether the taxpayer is being honest in providing information to the accountant for onward transmission. They must use their professional judgement and uphold the ethical standards of the AAT.

If a client evades tax, for example by making a material error or omission in a tax return, the accountant must first try to make the client change it and disclose their error or omission. If the client does not correct the error, omission or failure when advised, the accountant should cease to act for the client, inform HMRC of this cessation (without informing them of the reason in order to maintain client confidentiality) and consider making a money laundering report to their firm's money laundering reporting officer (or the National Crime Agency if the accountant is a sole practitioner).

Accountants who suspect, or are aware of, tax evasion by a client may be committing an offence if they do not report their suspicions. Furthermore, the accountant must not disclose to the client or a third party that a money laundering report has been made. Doing so would constitute a criminal offence of 'tipping-off'.

8 Calculating an individual's income tax liability

8.1 Types of income

An individual may receive different 'components' of income which are taxed at different rates depending on whether they are non-savings income, savings income or dividend income. For the purposes of your assessment trading income, employment income and property income are taxed as non-savings income (NSI), interest income is taxed as savings income (SI) and dividends as dividend income (DI).

We prepare an income tax computation for a **tax year** (or fiscal year) which runs from 6 April to 5 April. The 2021/22 tax year is the tax year on which you will be assessed so we will consider the income an individual receives between 6 April 2021 and 5 April 2022.

All income is added together to produce **total income**.

Some items, such as loss relief, are deducted from total income to give **net income**.

Often a taxpayer will have no deductions from total income so here the terms total income and net income can be used interchangeably.

A personal allowance is then deducted from net income to give **taxable income**. This represents the amount of income they are allowed to earn tax free.

- Taxpayers are entitled to a personal allowance of £12,570.
- However, individuals with net income in excess of £100,000 will have their personal allowance reduced or removed completely. Tasks will not be set in your assessment which involve knowledge of this.

Open book reference

The personal allowance is given in the Tax reference material available to you in your assessment.

Illustration 1: Income tax computation for fiscal year (6.4 – 5.4)

	Non-savings income £
Trading income	22,750
Less carry forward loss relief	(5,000)
Employment income	15,200
Property income	3,400
Total income	36,350
Less carry back loss relief	(2,000)
Net income	34,350
Less personal allowance	(12,570)
Taxable income	21,780

Activity 2: Taxable income

An individual has the following gross income in 2021/22.

	£
Trading income	16,000
Property income	2,500

Required

His taxable income is:

£	

8.2 Income tax liability

Once we have taxable income, we can then tax it. Any non-savings income is taxed first, then savings income and finally any dividend income. The rate of tax paid on each type of income is different and increases as the individual's taxable income increases:

Illustration 2: Calculation of tax liability

This gives us **tax liability** ie the total amount of tax that should be paid on our income.

Non-savings income is taxed in three bands:

1 Basic rate at 20% for income up to £37,700
2 Higher rate at 40% for income over £37,700 up to £150,000
3 Additional rate at 45% for income over £150,000

Once non-savings income is taxed we then tax any savings income. The rate of tax depends on whether there is any room left in any of the earlier bands of tax:

1 Basic rate at 20%
2 Higher rate at 40%
3 Additional rate at 45%

Finally, any dividend income is taxed as the top slice of the individual's taxable income. The rates of tax are:

1 Basic rate at 7.5%
2 Higher rate at 32.5%
3 Additional rate at 38.1%

Open book reference

The tax rates for the different types of income are given in the Tax reference material available to you in your assessment. The £37,700 and £150,000 figures, however, are not given. This is because you will not be expected to prepare a full computation in your Business Tax assessment. Tasks will be written so that it is clear whether an individual is a basic, higher or additional rate taxpayer.

Some basic illustrations showing how an individual's income tax liability would be calculated are given below to help you understand the calculation, however, remember that you will not be required to prepare an income tax computation in your assessment. The differing rates of tax on different types of income may be used in tax planning questions which we will cover later in this Workbook.

Illustration 3: Calculating tax liability

Zoë has taxable income (after the deduction of the personal allowance) of £40,000. This is all non-savings income.

Zoë's income tax liability for 2021/22 is calculated as follows:

Non-savings income	£
£37,700 × 20%	7,540
£2,300 × 40%	920
£40,000	
Tax liability	8,460

Illustration 4: Additional rate taxpayer

Clive has taxable income of £190,000 which is all non-savings income.

Clive's income tax liability for 2021/22 is calculated as follows:

Non-savings income	£
£37,700 × 20%	7,540
£112,300 × 40%	44,920
£40,000 × 45%	18,000
£190,000	
Tax liability	70,460

Activity 3: Calculation of income tax liability

Arthur has a salary of £17,000.

Required

Calculate the income tax liability for 2021/22.

BPP
LEARNING
MEDIA

Solution

	Non-savings income £

Assessment focus point

You will not be expected to produce a large income tax computation in your assessment. It is included here for background knowledge and will be useful when you come to study the chapter on Losses. Knowledge of the different rates of tax applying to different types of income could be used in tax planning tasks.

Chapter summary

- A business may be operated by a sole trader, partnership or company.

- Individuals trading as sole traders or in partnerships pay income tax, capital gains tax and NICs.

- Companies pay corporation tax.

- Companies and individuals must submit regular tax returns.

- It is important to be able to distinguish between tax evasion (illegal) and tax planning/avoidance (legal).

- If an accountant is concerned that a client is evading tax they should ask the client to disclose the error or omission. If the client refuses they should cease to act for the client, notify HMRC that they are ceasing to act (without giving a reason) and consider making money laundering report.

- When working in tax one should adhere to the AAT's five fundamental ethical principles of:

  - Confidentiality
  - Integrity
  - Objectivity
  - Professional behaviour
  - Professional competence and due care

- All of an individual's components of income for a tax year are added together to arrive at total income.

- Trading losses are deducted from total income to arrive at net income.

- A personal allowance is deducted from net income to arrive at taxable income.

- Taxable income is taxed at different rates, depending on which rate band it falls into.

Keywords

- **Confidentiality:** Respecting the confidentiality of client information, and keeping it confidential unless there is a legal or professional obligation to disclose it

- **Integrity:** Being straightforward and honest in all business relationships

- **Net income:** Total income minus, for example, trading losses

- **Objectivity:** Refusing to allow bias, conflicts of interest or undue influence to override professional judgements

- **Professional behaviour:** Compliance with relevant laws and regulations to avoid discrediting the profession

- **Professional competence and due care:** A professional accountant has an obligation to keep their knowledge and skills at a level that enables clients to receive a competent professional service, and to act diligently when providing those services

- **Tax avoidance:** Making use of loopholes in tax legislation in order to reduce tax liabilities. It is currently legal

- **Tax evasion:** To deliberately mislead the tax authorities in order to reduce a tax liability. Tax evasion is illegal

- **Tax planning:** Making use of tax planning opportunities to legally reduce a tax liability

- **Tax year:** The period for which personal tax computations are prepared which runs from 6th April to 5th April

- **Taxable income:** An individual's net income minus the personal allowance

- **Total income:** The total of an individual's components of income for a tax year, from all sources

Test your learning

1   You work in the tax department of a large company. You have prepared the tax return for the quarter, and submitted it to your Finance Director for her review. On reviewing your draft return, she has asked you to amend it to include some expenditure which was incurred shortly after the start of the next year in order reduce the profit for the year. She mentioned at the end of the conversation that your annual performance appraisal was due.

Which fundamental principle(s) could be breached if you agreed to her request?

Tick THREE boxes.

	✓
Integrity	
Objectivity	
Professional competence and due care	
Confidentiality	
Professional behaviour	

2   Tax avoidance is illegal and can lead to fines/imprisonment.

Show whether this statement is true or false.

Tick ONE box.

	✓
True	
False	

3   A company pays income tax on its total profits.

Show whether this statement is true or false.

Tick ONE box.

	✓
True	
False	

4   **Complete the following statement.**

Each tax year all of an individual's components of income are added together, then a personal allowance is deducted to arrive at:

[▼]

Picklist:

Net income
Taxable income
Total income

5   Arun (aged 35) has the following gross income in 2021/22:

Trading profits   £25,000
Property income   £12,000

Calculate Arun's income tax liability for 2021/22. Show your answer in whole pounds.

£	

Computing trading income

Syllabus learning outcomes / objectives

1.1 and 2.1 **Adjusting accounting profits and losses for tax purposes**

Learners need to understand:
- How to identify deductible and non-deductible expenditure
- How expenditure is classified as either revenue or capital

Learners need to be able to:
- Adjust accounting profits and losses for tax purposes

6.2 **Badges of trade**

Learners need to understand:

- How to identify if clients are trading through the application of the badges of trade

Assessment context

Adjustment of profits is highly examinable.

Qualification context

You will not see these areas again in your qualification.

Business context

Adjusting trading profit is one of the core tasks a tax adviser will have to perform for their client.

Chapter overview

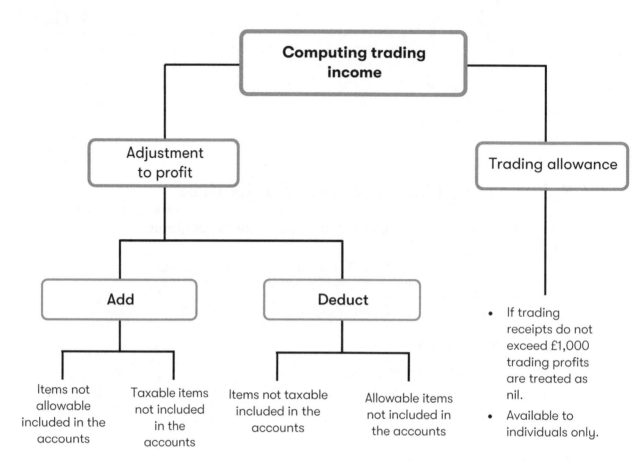

- Items not allowable included in the accounts
- Taxable items not included in the accounts
- Items not taxable included in the accounts
- Allowable items not included in the accounts

- If trading receipts do not exceed £1,000 trading profits are treated as nil.
- Available to individuals only.

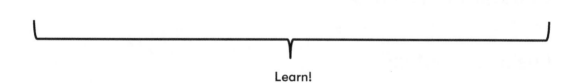

Learn!

BPP
LEARNING
MEDIA

1 Introduction

In this chapter, we will look at how to calculate a taxable trading profit figure on which an individual will pay tax if they are trading.

2 Is a trade being carried on?

It is important to know whether profits of an individual or company should be assessed as trading income.

For example, a person who buys and sells stamps may be trading as a stamp dealer. Alternatively, stamp collecting may be a hobby of that person. In this case, he is probably not trading.

If a trade is not being carried on, any profit arising from selling items could be exempt from tax or chargeable to capital gains tax. If a trade is being carried on, then we will need to calculate the taxable trading profit on which the individual will be taxed.

To make this decision we use some tests known as the 'badges of trade' to determine whether an individual is trading or not. These tests are covered later in the course book in the tax planning for businesses chapter.

In this chapter we assume that the individual is considered to be trading and we look at how we calculate the profits on which they are taxed.

3 Adjustment of profits

Whether the business is unincorporated (sole trader or partnership) or incorporated (limited company) the tax computation will usually always start with the **adjustment of profits. This is a vital area for all business types**. Many of the rules are the same for unincorporated businesses and for companies, with some differences highlighted in this chapter.

The exception to using an adjustment to profit approach is if a sole trade business has trading receipts during a tax year of less than £1,000 when the **trading allowance** will be used. This is covered in more detail in Section 4 below.

3.1 Taxable trading profits

Taxable trading profits are not the same as accounting profits. The trader arrives at the profit for the year in the accounts by taking income and deducting various trading expenses. However, the trader is unlikely to follow tax rules in arriving at this profit as, for example, there are some costs for which tax legislation does not allow a tax deduction, even though the taxpayer quite legitimately deducts them for accounting purposes.

Profits before tax from the financial statements need adjusting in accordance with tax legislation as follows:

		£
Net profit before tax per accounts		X
Add back:		
(a)	Items charged in the accounts but not deductible for trading profits purposes (eg depreciation)	X
(b)	Income taxable as trading profits which has not been included in the accounts (eg goods taken by owner for own use)	X

	£
Deduct:	
(a) Items included in the accounts but not taxable as trading profits (eg profit on disposal of fixed assets)	(X)
(b) Expenditure which is deductible from trading profits but has not been charged in the accounts (eg capital allowances)	(X)

Activity 1: Adjustment of profits (i)

Pratish trades as a car mechanic. His most recent accounts show a profit of £38,000. In arriving at this figure, he deducted entertaining expenses of £2,000 and depreciation of £4,000. These amounts are not allowable for tax purposes. Capital allowances of £3,500 are available for tax purposes.

Required

Using the proforma layout provided, calculate the taxable trading profit.

The starting figure has already been entered for you.

Solution

	£
Profit for the year in the accounts	38,000

3.2 General rule for disallowed expenditure

Expenditure incurred not **wholly and exclusively** for business purposes is disallowed.

3.3 Specific disallowed expenses:

3.2.1 Capital expenditure including depreciation

Open book reference

Disallowed expenditure

Capital expenditure is one-off expenditure leading to the creation or improvement of an asset (eg a piece of plant).

Revenue expenditure is regular ongoing expenditure required in the day to day running of the business (eg paying the gas bill).

Usually, revenue expenditure is allowable: it can be deducted from income before tax is calculated.

Capital expenditure is not allowable so must be added back if it has been charged in the statement of profit or loss. This includes any purchase cost of an asset which has incorrectly been charged to the statement of profit or loss (including any associated legal fees), depreciation and any profit/ loss on disposal of a fixed asset. **Capital allowances** (see later) may sometimes be claimed on capital expenditure.

Repair expenditure can cause problems:

- Maintaining an asset (ie keeping it in its current condition) is allowable.
- Improving an asset is not allowable as this is, in fact, capital expenditure.

However, where a repair is made which brings an asset up to date with what would now be considered industry norm this is considered to be a repair and is an allowable expense. An example of this would be replacing a single-glazed window with a double glazed equivalent.

There are special rules where assets are repaired following acquisition:

- If the repairs are to make the asset usable, they are not allowable (eg repairs to an unseaworthy ship).
- If the repairs merely improve the appearance of an asset, they are allowable (eg refurbishing a cinema).

Activity 2: Capital versus revenue

Identify whether the following expenses are revenue or capital in nature by ticking the relevant box.

Solution

	Revenue ✓	Capital ✓
Paying employee wages		
Paying rent for premises		
Buying machinery		
Buying a van		
Building an extension to shop		
Paying for repairs to car		

3.2.2 Adjustments to general provisions/general allowances for doubtful debts

Only irrecoverable debts incurred wholly and exclusively for the purposes of the trade are deductible for taxation purposes. Thus, loans to employees written off are not deductible unless the business is that of making loans, or it can be shown that the write-off was earnings paid out for the benefit of the trade.

Increases or decreases in a general provision are not allowable and an adjustment is needed.

Illustration 1: Irrecoverable debts account

The account below results in a credit to the statement of profit or loss of £124. What adjustment should be made to the profit for the year when calculating taxable trading profits?

2021	£	£	2021	£	£
			1 January		

2021	£	£	2021	£	£
			Provisions b/d		
			General	150	
			Specific	381	
					531
Provisions c/d					
General	207				
Specific	200				
		407			
Statement of profit or loss		124			
		531			531

The only adjustment you need to consider is the increase in general provision from £150 to £207. Thus £57 is added to the accounts profit to arrive at taxable profit.

3.2.3 Private expenditure of the owner

Open book reference

Disallowed expenditure

Strictly, expenditure incurred partly for private purposes and partly for business purposes has a dual purpose and is not deductible. However, HMRC sometimes allows taxpayers to apportion the expenditure between the part that is wholly for business purposes, and therefore deductible; and the part that is wholly for private purposes, and therefore not deductible.

If the owner has taken any 'salary' from the business and has incorrectly deducted this in their accounts it must be added back as it constitutes drawings and is not tax deductible. In addition, the owner's Class 2 and Class 4 national insurance contributions and any personal legal and professional fees are not tax deductible.

If the owner pays a salary to a family member then only the reasonable salary is allowable. Any excess salary over a reasonable amount must be added back.

Goods taken from stock by the proprietor of a business should be treated as if they had been sold for their market value. If correctly accounted for as drawings, this will require an adjustment for the profit, whereas if the cost is still reflected in cost of sales, the full selling price will need to be added back. The AAT have confirmed that a question would specifically state if an adjustment to cost of sales for the goods taken has been made so, if a question does not make it clear, the selling price should be added back.

Illustration 2: Private use expenditure

A sole trader who runs his business from home incurs £500 on heating and lighting bills. 30% of these bills relate to the business use of his house. £500 has been deducted in arriving at the accounts profit. How much should be added back in the calculation of taxable trading profits?

The 30% relating to business use is allowable. Therefore, 70% × £500 = £350 must be added back to the accounts profit as disallowable expenditure.

Assessment focus point

In the CBT you may need to calculate adjusted profits for a sole trader/partnership (unincorporated business) or a company (incorporated business).

The calculation is basically the same; however, there are no private adjustments for a company.

Everybody who works for a company (including a director) is an employee, so any benefit they receive is taxed on them as part of their employment income (rules examinable in Personal Tax).

The cost is part of the company's cost of employing the workforce it needs to perform its trade, and is therefore allowable.

3.3 The treatment of various other items

Open book reference

Disallowed expenditure

The table below details various types of allowable and **disallowable expenditure**, with mention of any differences between unincorporated businesses (sole traders and partnerships) and incorporated businesses (companies) where necessary.

Allowable expenditure	Disallowable expenditure	Comments
	Fines and penalties	HMRC usually allows parking fines incurred in parking an employee's car whilst on the employer's business. Fines relating to the owner of the business are, however, never allowed. Similarly, a company would not be able to deduct fines relating to directors
Costs of registering trademarks and patents		This is an exception to the rule of 'capital' related expenditure being disallowable
Incidental costs of obtaining loan finance		This deduction does not apply to companies because they get a deduction for the cost of borrowing in a different way. We look at this in Chapter 4 of this Course Book
	Depreciation or amortisation	In specific circumstances, a company can deduct these amounts, but this is outside the scope of this assessment
	Any salary or interest paid to a sole trader or partner	
	The private proportion of any expenses incurred by a sole trader or partner	The private proportion of a director's or employee's expenses is, however, deductible

Allowable expenditure	Disallowable expenditure	Comments
Irrecoverable debts incurred in the course of a business. Specific provisions for irrecoverable debts	General provisions for irrecoverable debts (and other general provisions)	Loans to employees written off, despite being specific, are not allowable
Patent and copyright royalties		Patent and copyright royalties paid for trade purposes are deductible
Staff entertaining	Non-staff (eg customer/supplier) entertaining	
Gifts for employees Gifts to customers as long as they: • Cost no more than £50 per donee per year • Carry a conspicuous advertisement for the business; and • Are not food, drink, tobacco or vouchers exchangeable for such goods Gifts to a small local charity if they benefit the trade	All other gifts including donations to national charities. Charitable gifts by companies are referred to as 'qualifying charitable donations (QCDs)'.	QCDs are charitable gifts by companies on which tax relief is given. These are covered in Chapter 7 of this Course Book. The similar scheme relevant to individuals is not assessable in this *Business Tax* assessment Small gifts to a local charity will only be examined in unincorporated business tasks in this assessment.
Subscriptions to a professional or trade association	Political donations	
Legal and professional charges relating directly to the trade	Legal and professional charges relating to • Capital items • Purchase/ renewal of a long lease • Purchase of short lease (50 years or less) • Breaches of law/ regulations	Deductible items include: • Charges incurred defending the taxpayer's title to non-current assets • Charges connected with an action for breach of contract • Fees on renewal of a short lease

Allowable expenditure	Disallowable expenditure	Comments
	Accountancy expenses relating to specialist consultancy work	Deductible items include: • Expenses for the renewal (not the original grant) of a lease for less than 50 years • Charges for trade debt collection • Normal charges for preparing accounts and assisting with the self-assessment of tax liabilities
Interest on loans taken out for trade purposes	Interest on overdue tax	These rules are for unincorporated businesses. Companies have different rules for interest. We look at these in Chapter 7 of this Course Book
Costs of seconding employees to charities or educational establishments		
Expenditure incurred in the seven years prior to the commencement of a trade		Provided expenditure is of a type that would have been allowed had the trade started. Treat as an expense on the first day of trading
Removal expenses (to new business premises)		Only if not an expansionary move
Travelling expenses on the trader's business	Travel from home to the trader's place of business	
Redundancy payments		If the trade ceases, the limit on allowability is 3 × the statutory amount (in addition to the statutory amount)
	15% of leasing costs of car with CO_2 emissions in excess of 50g/km	

Activity 3: Calculation of add back

A sole trader charged the following expenses in computing his accounts profit:

	£
Fine for breach of Factories Act	1,000
Cost of specialist tax consultancy work	2,000
Redundancy payments	10,000
Salary for himself	15,000
Leasing cost of car (CO_2 emissions 55g/km)	3,000

The redundancy payments were made for trade purposes as a result of reorganisation of the business. The trade is continuing.

Required

Calculate how much must be added back in computing taxable trading profits.

Tick ONE box.

Solution

Amount to add back	✓
£17,450	
£16,000	
£18,450	
£11,450	

Activity 4: Entertainment and gifts

Decide whether each of the items in the entertainment account below should be added back in computing taxable trading profits.

Expenditure	£	Add back ✓
Staff tennis outing for 30 employees	1,800	
2,000 tee shirts with firm's logo given to race runners	4,500	
Advertising and sponsorship of an athletic event	2,000	
Entertaining customers	7,300	
Staff Christmas party (30 employees)	2,400	

Activity 5: Adjustment of profits (ii)

Hugo Drax, a sole trader, has the following statement of profit or loss for the year ended 31 December:

	£
Sales	100,000
Cost of sales	(50,000)
Gross profit	50,000
Add other income	
Bank interest	4,000
Less expenses	
Depreciation	(5,000)
Entertaining clients	(100)

	£
Office costs	(2,000)
Staff wages and salaries	(15,000)
Hugo's personal council tax bill	(1,000)
Net profit	30,900

Salaries include £5,000 paid to Hugo and £10,000 paid to his wife. His wife's salary is reasonable in respect of the work she performs in the business.

Required

Complete the table below showing the calculation of adjusted trading profits before capital allowances. Complete the narrative by using the items in the picklist below the table.

Solution

Adjustment to profit	£	£
Net profit per the accounts		
Add back		
▼		
▼		
▼		
▼		
Total added back		
Deduct		
▼		
Adjusted profits before capital allowances		

Picklist:

Bank interest
Cost of sales
Council tax
Depreciation
Entertaining
Gross profit
Office costs
Sales
Staff wages

4 Trading allowance

From 2017/18, the trading allowance was introduced to simplify the calculation of trading profits for smaller sole traders.

If a sole trader has trading receipts (under the accruals basis) for a tax year which do not exceed the trading allowance of £1,000, the trading profits are treated as nil and there is no charge to income tax as a result of the trade. An election can be made for the trading allowance rules not to apply if, for example, the deduction of allowable costs would instead give rise to a trading loss.

If the sole trader has trading receipts exceeding the £1,000 trading allowance, then the usual adjustment to profits approach will be used to calculate trading profits as explained in Section 3 above. If the sole trader would prefer, perhaps if allowable costs were small, then an election can be made to deduct the £1,000 trading allowance from trading receipts in order to calculate the taxable trading profits instead of deducting allowable expenses.

Assessment focus point

Please refer to the reference material at the end of this Course Book to see which elements of this chapter will be available to you as a pop-up in the live assessment.

Chapter summary

- Revenue expenses are generally allowable expenses for computing taxable trading profits but capital expenses are not (unless relieved through capital allowances – see later chapter).

- The main disallowable items that you must add back in computing taxable trading profits are:

  - Entertaining (other than staff entertaining)

  - Depreciation charges (deduct capital allowances instead)

  - Increase in general provisions

  - Fines

  - Legal fees relating to capital items

  - Wages or salary paid to a business owner

  - The private proportion of any expenses for a sole trader/partner (not applicable to a company)

- Deduct non-trading income/capital profits included in the accounts from the accounts profit to arrive at taxable trading profits.

- If a sole trader has trading receipts for the tax year not exceeding the trading allowance of £1,000, the trading profits are treated as nil.

Keywords

- **Adjustment of profits:** The adjustment of the accounting profits to comply with tax legislation

- **Disallowable expenditure:** Expenditure that cannot be deducted in computing taxable trading profit

- **Expenditure wholly and exclusively for trade purposes:** Expenditure that is incidental to the trade and that does not have a dual purpose

- **Trading allowance:** An allowance of £1,000 which allows sole traders with trading receipts not exceeding the allowance to set their trade profits as nil and avoid the need for an adjustment to profit calculation.

Test your learning

1   Which of the following expenses are allowable when computing taxable trading profits?

	Allowable ✓
Legal fees incurred on the acquisition of a factory to be used for trade purposes	
Heating for factory	
Legal fees incurred on pursuing trade receivables	
Acquiring a machine to be used in the factory	

2   A sole trader incurs the following expenditure on entertaining and gifts.

	£
Staff entertaining	700
50 Christmas food hampers given to customers	240
Entertaining customers	900
	1,840

How much of the above expenditure is allowable for tax purposes?

£ [   ]

3   For each of the following expenses, show whether they are allowable or disallowable by ticking the relevant boxes.

	Allowable ✓	Disallowable ✓
Parking fines incurred by the owner of the business		
Parking fines incurred by an employee while on the employer's business		
Parking fines incurred by the director of a company while on company business		
Legal costs incurred in relation to acquiring a 10-year lease of property for the first time		
Legal costs incurred in relation to the renewal of a lease for 20 years		
Gifts of calendars to customers, costing £4 each and displaying an advertisement for the company		
Gifts of bottles of whisky to customers, costing £12 each		

4   Herbert, a self-employed carpenter, makes various items of garden furniture for sale. He takes a bird table from stock and sets it up in his own garden. The cost of making the bird table amounts to £80, and Herbert would normally expect to achieve a mark-up of 20% on such goods.

Identify the adjustment Herbert needs to make to the accounts for tax purposes, assuming he has reflected in the accounts the deduction for the cost of making the table.

Tick ONE box.

	✓
£80 must be deducted from the accounts profit	
£80 must be added back to the accounts profit	
£96 must be deducted from the accounts profit	
£96 must be added back to the accounts profit	

5   Set out below is the irrecoverable debts account of Kingfisher, a sole trader:

Irrecoverable debts

	£	1.4.21	£
		Provisions b/d	
		General	2,500
		Specific (trade)	1,875
31.3.22			
Provisions c/d			
General	1,800		
Specific (trade)	4,059	Statement of profit or loss	1,484
	5,859		5,859

Insert the amount that needs adjusting and tick whether it should be added to, or deducted from, Kingfisher's accounts profit to arrive at taxable trading profits.

£ [   ]

Added back ✓	Deducted ✓

6   Trude works from home as a self-employed hairdresser. She incurs £450 on heating and lighting bills and this amount is deducted in her accounts. 20% of this expenditure relates to the business use of her home.

How much of the expenditure is disallowable for tax purposes?

£ [   ]

7   Calculate the taxable trading profits for the following sole traders, assuming they make any beneficial claim available to them. Their income and expenditure for 2021/22 is stated below:

	Zack	Mythili	Rohan	Arthur
Trading receipts	800	800	1,500	1,500
Allowable expenses	200	900	800	1,100

	Taxable trading profits
Zack	
Mythili	
Rohan	
Arthur	

3

Capital allowances

Syllabus learning outcomes / objectives

1.2   Prepare capital allowances computations for sole traders and partnerships

Learners need to understand:

- Which capital allowances apply to different assets:
  - Plant and machinery
  - Structures and buildings

Learners need to be able to:

- prepare capital allowance computations for accounting periods:
  - Longer than 12 months
  - Shorter than 12 months
  - Equal to 12 months
  - Including adjustments for private usage

2.2   Prepare capital allowances computations for limited companies

Learners need to understand:

- Which capital allowances apply to different assets:
  - Plant and machinery
  - Structures and buildings

Learners need to be able to:

- prepare capital allowance computations for accounting periods:
  - Longer than 12 months
  - Shorter than 12 months
  - Equal to 12 months

Assessment context

All the rules in this chapter are highly examinable and could be examined in a variety of different combinations. Make sure you can deal with any scenario the assessment throws at you. Some students find the task on capital allowances quite challenging, so you must make sure you practise plenty of tasks to feel comfortable with applying your knowledge of this topic. In addition, you must ensure you know what information is available in your reference material.

Qualification context

You will not see these rules outside of this unit.

Business context

In practice, capital allowances are a significant form of tax relief for reducing a taxpayer's tax liability.

The government often uses capital allowances to encourage people to invest in new plant and machinery.

Chapter overview

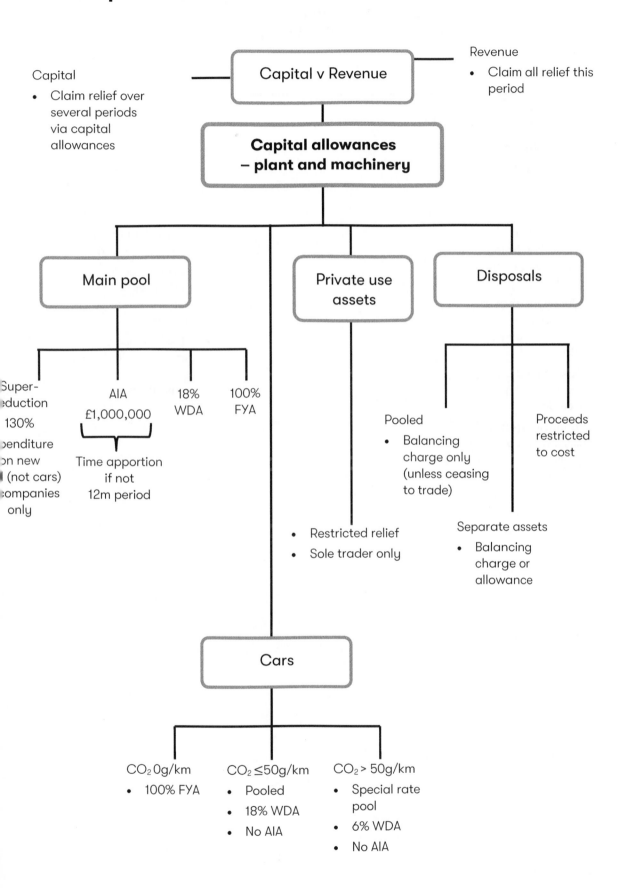

Capital v Revenue

Capital
- Claim relief over several periods via capital allowances

Revenue
- Claim all relief this period

Capital allowances – plant and machinery

Main pool

Super-deduction
- 130%
- expenditure on new (not cars)
- companies only

AIA
£1,000,000

Time apportion if not 12m period

18% WDA

100% FYA

Private use assets
- Restricted relief
- Sole trader only

Disposals

Pooled
- Balancing charge only (unless ceasing to trade)

Proceeds restricted to cost

Separate assets
- Balancing charge or allowance

Cars

CO_2 0g/km
- 100% FYA

$CO_2 \leq 50$g/km
- Pooled
- 18% WDA
- No AIA

$CO_2 > 50$g/km
- Special rate pool
- 6% WDA
- No AIA

```
                    ┌─────────────────────────────┐
                    │     Capital allowances       │
                    │   – structures and buildings │
                    └─────────────────────────────┘
                                   │
                ┌──────────────────┴──────────────────┐
      ┌──────────────────┐                  ┌──────────────────┐
      │   Qualifying     │                  │  Writing down    │
      │   expenditure    │                  │   allowance      │
      └──────────────────┘                  └──────────────────┘
```

Qualifying expenditure

- Construction/ acquisition from builder of qualifying assets
- Qualifying property includes offices, shops, factories, bridges
- Cost of land and acquisition expenses excluded
- Enhancing/renovating existing property can qualify

Writing down allowance

- 3% straight line once brought into use
- Apportioned in periods of acquisition and disposal
- SBAs claimed are added to seller's sale proceeds in gain computation

1 Introduction

This chapter looks at the difference between capital and revenue expenditure; and how to get tax relief for the different types of expenditure by either treating them as an expense, or **plant and machinery or a structure or building** for capital allowances.

2 Capital and revenue expenditure

Capital expenditure is one-off expenditure that will bring benefits to the business over a number of years (eg purchase of machinery).

Revenue expenditure is regular ongoing expenditure that only brings benefit in the period in which the expenditure is made (eg payment of electricity bill).

Revenue expenditure, generally, may be deducted against taxable profits before they are taxed (but we saw in the previous chapter that not all revenue expenditure is automatically allowable).

It may be possible to claim **capital allowances** on some capital expenditure. Capital allowances are just the tax version of accounts depreciation. They are calculated to replace the depreciation charged in the accounts.

Both individuals (sole traders and partners) and companies may claim capital allowances.

3 Expenditure qualifying for capital allowances

Plant and machinery is something which has a **function** within the trade as opposed to being part of the **setting** where the business takes place. Essentially, plant and machinery is any capital item used in the business other than buildings. For example, equipment, furniture, machinery and vehicles are all examples of plant and machinery.

> ### Assessment focus point
>
> There is much law determining what is allowable as plant and machinery and what is not. The AAT have confirmed that the very detailed rules on this do not form part of your syllabus but, for information, some examples include:
>
> - Moveable office partitions are plant – but fixed partitions are not.
> - Decorative items (eg paintings) in hotels are plant.
>
> The more common items you will see in the assessment are:
>
> - Cars, vans and lorries
> - Furniture
> - Computers
>
> You may also be provided with a list of capital expenditure which includes costs incurred in altering premises. You are expected to understand that this forms part of the setting for the business and that therefore capital allowances on plant and machinery will not be available.

Capital expenditure on buildings (part of the setting of a business) did not historically qualify for any type of capital allowances. However, a structures and buildings allowance is now available for qualifying expenditure on new commercial structures and buildings for contracts entered into on/after 29 October 2018.

We will first consider the capital allowances available on plant and machinery and then, later in this chapter, we will consider the capital allowances available on structures and buildings.

4 Allowances on plant and machinery

4.1 When and how capital allowances are given

Allowances are computed by reference to the period for which accounts are drawn up.

They are deducted from the taxable profits of the period.

They include all additions and disposals occurring in the relevant accounting period. Expenditure must be of a capital nature.

4.2 General pool for capital allowances

Most expenditure on plant and machinery is put into a 'pool' of assets known as the **general (or main) pool**. This includes expenditure on cars with CO_2 emissions of 50g/km or less.

4.3 Annual investment allowance

Capital allowances

Open book reference

A business can claim an **annual investment allowance (AIA)**, giving 100% tax relief on its expenditure on plant and machinery.

A business can claim AIA on the first £1,000,000 of expenditure on plant and machinery in a 12-month **period of account**.

The AIA is not available for expenditure on cars.

The amount of the AIA is scaled up/down for long/short periods of account.

Note. Companies cannot have a corporation tax period that is longer than 12 months.

Activity 1: Annual investment allowance

Delson starts a business on 1 January 2022. In the nine-month period to 30 September 2022, he incurs the following expenditure:

		£
15 January 2022	Manufacturing equipment	650,000
16 January 2022	Computer equipment	60,000
7 May 2022	Office furniture	30,000
13 May 2022	Delivery vans	20,000
20 June 2022	Car	19,000

Required

Delson can claim an annual investment allowance of £ [   ] .

Workings (on-screen free text area provided in the CBT as part of larger question)

4.4 First year allowances (FYAs)

These are special allowances given in addition to the AIA.

First year allowances (FYAs) are available at 100% on expenditure incurred on:

- Zero emission cars

You must give FYAs at 100% to the assets that are eligible for them. Do not use the AIA against them.

FYAs are **never** time apportioned for short or long accounting periods.

Open book reference

Capital allowances

The capital allowances section of your reference data, which you can access in your assessment, reminds you of the assets on which the FYA is available and the CO_2 emissions for cars and their respective capital allowance treatment.

4.5 Writing-down allowances

Open book reference

Capital allowances

A **writing-down allowance (WDA)** is given on the general pool at the rate of 18% per year (on a reducing balance basis). The WDA is calculated on the value of pooled plant, after adding current period additions and taking out current period disposals (as explained shortly).

The additions will include:

(a) Expenditure that qualifies for the AIA but is in excess of the maximum AIA available for the period.

(b) Cars with CO_2 emissions of between 0g/km and 50g/km. These are cars that do not qualify for 100% FYA and do not go into the special rate pool (see later). The emissions are stated clearly in the capital allowances section of your reference material, which you can access in your assessment.

Illustration 3: Basic proforma for calculating WDAs

	General pool £	Allowances £
TWDV b/f	X	
Additions (not eligible for AIA/FYA)	X	
Less disposals	(X)	
	X	
WDA @ 18%	(X)	X
TWDV c/f	X	

Note. TWDV = Tax Written-Down Value: this is the value of the pool of assets for tax purposes.

The total allowances for the accounting period can then be deducted in the adjustments to profit working.

WDAs are time apportioned for short/long accounting periods ($\frac{n}{12} \times 18\%$).

Activity 2: Writing-down allowances in the general pool

Jamie draws up his accounts to 31 March. At 1 April 2021, he has a balance of £10,000 on his general pool.

In his period of account to 31 March 2022, he has the following transactions:

		£
13 June 2021	buys a car (CO_2 45g/km)	18,000
31 August 2021	buys a van	29,000
30 October 2021	sells plant for	2,000
20 November 2021	buys manufacturing plant	1,030,000

Required

Complete the capital allowances computation for the year ended 31 March 2022.

	AIA	General pool	Total allowances

	AIA	General pool	Total allowances

4.6 WDA for small pools

Open book reference

If the balance on the general pool or special rate pool (before WDA) is less than the small pool limit at the end of the chargeable period, a WDA can be claimed up to the value of the small pool limit. This is known as a 'small pools allowance.'

This means that the pools may be written down to nil, rather than a small balance being carried forward.

The small pool limit is £1,000 for a 12-month period (pro rata for short and long chargeable periods). Note that this does not apply to any assets which are kept separate and not included in the pools.

5 Disposals

When an asset is sold in the year, we deduct the proceeds from the tax written down value of the pool brought forward. Note that if a zero-emission car on which a 100% FYA was claimed is sold, the proceeds are deducted from the general pool.

The proceeds deducted will usually be the proceeds received on sale of the asset, however, if an asset is sold for more than its original cost, we only deduct the original cost from the pool.

Illustration 4: Disposal proceeds

On 6 April 2021, a sole trader had a balance on his general pool of £47,000. Plant that had cost £7,000 was sold in the year for proceeds of:

(a)   £14,000
(b)   £4,000

In (a) proceeds are more than original cost and so only £7,000 would be deducted from the general pool balance of £47,000.

In (b) the actual proceeds are less than original cost and so the proceeds of £4,000 would be deducted from the general pool balance of £47,000.

6 Periods that are not 12 months long

The AIA limit and WDA are adjusted by the fraction: months/12.

The FYA is never adjusted.

A sole trader or partnership may have a period shorter or longer than 12 months. AIA and WDA can therefore be scaled up or down.

A company may have a corporation tax period shorter than 12 months but not longer than 12 months. AIA and WDA could therefore be scaled down but not up.

> ### Assessment focus point
>
> Note that the Chief Assessor has commented that short or long accounting periods are one of the scenarios which students find most challenging in this Task and so you must make sure you fully appreciate the consequences of the length of the accounting period on the calculation.

Activity 3: Short period of account

Edward has been in business a number of years, drawing up accounts to 31 March.

In 2021, Edward decided to change his year end to 31 December.

In the period ended 31 December 2021, Edward had the following additions:

		£
13 April	Car (CO_2 emissions 30g/km)	7,000
15 April	Plant	1,046,750

Edward sold a van for £2,000 on 7 July that had cost £3,000.

TWDV b/f at 1 April 2021 was £12,000.

Required

Complete the capital allowances computation for the period ended 31 December 2021.

	AIA	General pool	Total allowances

	AIA	General pool	Total allowances

7 Cessation of a business

When a business ceases to trade, no AIAs, FYAs or WDAs are given in the final period.

Additions in the final period are added to the pool in the normal way. Similarly, any disposal proceeds (limited to cost) of assets sold in the final period are deducted from the balance of qualifying expenditure. If assets are not sold, they are deemed to be disposed of on the final day of trading for their market value. For example, a sole trader may keep a car from the business that has just ceased trading and so must deduct the market value from the pool.

If, after the above adjustments, a positive balance of qualifying expenditure remains in the pool, then a **balancing allowance** equal to this amount is given. **The balancing allowance is deducted from taxable trading profits**. If, on the other hand, the balance on the pool has become negative, a **balancing charge** equal to the negative amount is given. **The balancing charge increases taxable trading profits**.

Balancing allowances on the general pool and the special rate pool (see below) can only arise on cessation of trade, whereas balancing charges on these pools, although most commonly happening on cessation, can arise whilst trade is still in progress.

Assessment focus point

This is another scenario which the Chief Assessor has said that students find challenging.

Activity 4: Cessation of a business

Baxter normally has a June year end. On 1 July 2021, he has a TWDV in the pool of £12,000. He ceases to trade on 31 January 2022. His additions and disposals in his final period are as follows:

		£
5 September	Buys plant	2,000
12 October	Sells plant	See below

(a) **Required**

If Baxter sells his plant for £15,500 then he will have a

| ▼ | of | £ | |

Picklist:

balancing allowance
balancing charge

Workings

(b)   Required

If Baxter sells his plant for £11,500 then he will have a

[▼] of [£   ] .

Picklist:

balancing allowance
balancing charge

Workings

Notes.

1   A balancing allowance only arises in the general pool on the cessation of trade.
2   A balancing charge may arise on the general pool at any point in the business's life.

8 Assets that are not included in the general pool

We have seen above how to compute capital allowances on the general pool of plant and machinery. However, some special items are not put into the general pool. A separate record of allowances must be kept for these assets.

These assets are:

- Cars with CO_2 emissions greater than 50g/km

- Assets not wholly used for business purposes in **unincorporated businesses** (such as cars with private use by the proprietor)

8.1 Cars with CO_2 emissions greater than 50g/km

Open book reference

Capital l
allowances

Cars with CO_2 emissions in excess of 50g/km are put in a pool known as the **special rate pool**. The **WDA rate on the special rate pool is 6% for a 12-month period** calculated on the pool balance (after any additions and disposals) at the end of the chargeable period.

Activity 5: Special rate pool

Myles Ltd prepares accounts to 31 March each year and incurred the following transactions for the year ended 31 March 2022.

1.7.21	Bought car for £17,000, CO_2 emissions of 40g/km
1.10.21	Bought car for £8,000, CO_2 emissions of 60g/km

On 1 April 2021, the TWDV of plant and machinery were as follows:

	£
General pool	25,000
Special rate pool	10,000

Required

Complete the capital allowance computation for the year ended 31 March 2022.

	General pool	Special rate	Total allowances

8.2 Assets used partly for private purposes

If a proprietor of a sole trader business or a partner in a partnership uses a business asset for private purposes, the following treatment applies:

- The asset is put in a separate column.

- TWDV is reduced by **full amount** of AIA/FYA/WDA calculated as normal.

- A balancing allowance or charge will arise at the date of disposal.

- Only the business proportion of the allowance/charge is transferred into the allowances column.

We refer to these as **private-use assets**.

An asset with some private use by an employee (not the business owner) suffers no restriction. The employee may be taxed on the private use as a taxable benefit, so the business is entitled to full capital allowances on such assets. This means **there is never any private use restriction in a company's capital allowance computation**, whether the asset is used by an employee or a director.

> ### Assessment focus point
>
> The Chief Assessor has noted that making private use adjustments when they are not required is a common mistake, so please ensure you check who you are calculating capital allowances for.
>
> - If it is a sole trader or partnership - make the adjustment **IF** it is the sole trader or partner who is using the asset privately.
>
> - If it is a company – **do not** make the adjustment.

Activity 6: Private-use assets

At 1 January 2021, Sweeney has two cars used within his business: a car he uses himself with a TWDV b/f of £20,000 (20% private use, CO_2 emissions 80g/km); and a car used by his employee, Doris, with a TWDV b/f of £16,000 (35% private use, CO_2 emissions 40g/km). He draws up his accounts to 31 December 2021.

Sweeney has no other assets.

Required

(a) Calculate the capital allowances available to Sweeny for the year ended 31 December 2021.

	General pool	Private use asset	Total allowances

Required

(b) What capital allowances would Sweeney claim if the business instead ceased in this period and both cars were sold for £15,000 each?

| | ▼ | of | £ | | .

Picklist:

balancing allowance
balancing charge

Workings (on-screen free text area provided in the CBT as part of larger question)

9 Differences between unincorporated and incorporated businesses

We have seen in this chapter that, broadly, the rules on capital allowances are the same for unincorporated businesses (sole traders and partnerships) and incorporated businesses (companies).

However, three important differences in the calculation of capital allowances are as follows:

(a) There is never a **private use asset** column in a company's capital allowance computation.

- The director or employee may suffer a taxable benefit instead and so the company can deduct the allowance in full.

- If a sole trader or partner uses a business asset for private purposes, then we restrict the capital allowances claimed on this asset.

(b) Long **period of account** (accounts that have been made up for more than 12 months).

- If a sole trader/partnership has a period shorter or longer than 12 months, we would scale down or scale up the calculation.

- If a company has a long period of account, we perform two capital allowances computations (see Chapter 4).

Assessment focus point

Both of these points are ones which the Chief Assessor has noted students find challenging in this task, so make sure you feel comfortable with these points.

(c) Companies are able to claim enhanced capital allowances, otherwise known as a super-deduction, on new plant and machinery purchases. These are explained in more detail in the next section.

10 Enhanced capital allowances for companies

From 1 April 2021, companies can benefit from enhanced capital allowances, known as a super-deduction, on new plant and machinery purchases. These allowances are:

- Available to companies only (not sole traders or partnerships).
- Available only on new plant and machinery (not second hand).
- Not available on cars.

The enhanced capital allowance available is a 130% first year allowance and is known as a super-deduction. These will be preferable to the 100% AIA for companies on any qualifying purchases.

Assessment focus point

The super-deduction is only available on expenditure incurred prior to 1 April 2023 and there are special rules for accounting periods which straddle this date and for disposals of assets on which the super-deduction has been claimed. The AAT has confirmed that these will not be examinable in your assessment.

Activity 7: Enhanced capital allowances for companies

Backwell Ltd makes up accounts for the 6 months to 30 June 2021. The brought forward value on its general pool on 1 January 2021 was £81,000. The following assets were bought and sold during the period:

		£
11 January 2021	Plant	41,000
16 March 2021	Car for salesman	
	(CO_2 emissions 49g/km)	11,000
8 May 2021	Car for finance director	
	(CO_2 emissions 62g/km)	50,000
31 May 2021	Machinery	36,000
1 June 2021	Disposed of plant (cost £30,000)	32,000

Required

Calculate the capital allowances claim that Backwell Ltd can make for the period ended 30 June 2021.

Solution

	AIA	FYA	Super deduction	General pool	Special rate pool	Private use asset	Total allowances

	AIA	FYA	Super deduction	General pool	Special rate pool	Private use asset	Total allowances

Assessment focus point

It is very important in an assessment capital allowance task that you spot whether the business is a company or not. You must only consider the super-deduction rules if the business is a company.

Activity 8: Calculation of capital allowances

Oscar, a sole trader, makes up accounts for the 18 months to 30 June 2022. The brought forward value on his general pool on 1 January 2021 was £481,000. He bought and sold the following assets:

		£
10 July 2021	Plant	1,410,000
10 August 2021	Car for salesman	
	(CO_2 emissions 0g/km)	11,000
12 September 2021	Plant	550,000
1 June 2022	Disposed of plant (cost £30,000)	32,000

Required

Calculate the capital allowances claim that Oscar can make for the period ended 30 June 2021.

Solution

	AIA	FYA	General pool	Total allowances

11 Structures and buildings allowances

A structures and buildings allowance (SBA) is available for qualifying expenditure on new commercial structures and buildings for contracts entered into on/after 29 October 2018. Qualifying expenditure is expenditure on the construction of the building or structure itself (or the acquisition cost if bought from a developer), but not the cost of land, nor the cost of planning permission, fees and stamp taxes.

Where an existing building is renovated or converted, this expenditure may qualify (even if the underlying property was constructed prior to 29 October 2018).

Commercial structures and buildings include:

* Offices
* Retail and wholesale premises
* Factories
* Warehouses
* Walls
* Bridges
* Tunnels

Residential property or any part of a building which functions as a dwelling does not qualify for SBAs.

The allowance is given at 3% straight line, over a 33 ⅓ year period.

Each building or structure is treated separately, and enhancement expenditure is treated separately to the underlying building.

For SBAs to be claimed, the relevant asset must be in qualifying use, for example used in a trade or property letting business.

The allowance is pro-rated for accounting periods which are not 12 months in length, or where the structure of building is brought into use or sold during the period. This is in contrast to plant and machinery allowances which are given in full in the period of acquisition (with no WDA at all in the period of disposal).

There is no balancing adjustment on the sale of an SBA asset; however, an adjustment is made to the chargeable gain or capital loss arising, by adding the SBA claimed to the seller's disposal proceeds.

The new purchaser takes over the remaining allowances (based on the original cost) over the remainder of the 33 ⅓ year period. The seller and buyer both time apportion up to the date of disposal.

Activity 9: SBAs

Rose Ltd purchases a newly constructed office building from a developer for £2,050,000 (excluding land) on 1 July 2021 and brought it into use immediately. The purchase price of £2,050,00 includes £50,000 relating to solicitor's fees and other acquisition costs.

Rose Ltd prepares accounts to 31 December each year.

Required

What are the maximum SBAs available to Rose Ltd in the year ended 31 December 2021?

£

Rose Ltd continued to use the office building for its trade until 30 June 2024, when it was sold to Petal plc for £2,500,000 (excluding land). Petal immediately started using the office for trading purposes.

Petal plc prepares its accounts to March each year.

Required

Which **TWO** of the following statements are correct regarding the implications of the disposal?

1. Rose Ltd will not be entitled to any SBA on the building for its year ended 31 December 2024

2. Rose Ltd's chargeable gain will increase by £180,000 due to the SBAs claimed

3. Petal plc will claim £75,000 pa structures and buildings allowances on the office

4. Petal plc will time apportion its SBA by 9/12ths in its year ended 31 March 2025

Solution

Assessment focus point

In the live assessment, you will be provided with reference material that can be accessed through pop-up windows. The content of this reference material has been reproduced at the end of this Course Book.

Chapter summary

- Assets that perform a function in the trade are generally plant. Assets that are part of the setting are not plant.

- Most expenditure on plant and machinery goes into the general pool.

- An annual investment allowance (AIA) of £1,000,000 is available on expenditure other than on cars. The limit is pro-rated for periods of more or less than 12 months.

- FYAs at 100% are available on zero emission cars.

- There is a writing-down allowance (WDA) of 18% on the balance of the general pool in a 12-month period and 6% on the special rate pool.

- WDAs are time-apportioned in short or long periods.

- FYAs are never time-apportioned for short or long periods.

- If the WDV on the general or special rate pool is £1,000 or less, an election can be made to write off the pool balance, known as a 'small pools allowance'.

- Balancing allowances or balancing charges will be given when the trade ceases, and when an asset is disposed of, which is not included in the general pool or special rate pool.

- Private use of assets by sole traders and partners restricts capital allowances.

- Cars are dealt with according to their CO_2 emissions:

  - 0/km – FYA at 100%

  - up to 50g/km – general pool with WDA of 18%

  - Over 50g/km – special rate pool with WDA 6%

- A 130% super-deduction is available to companies only purchasing new plant and machinery (not cars) after 1 April 2021.

- Qualifying buildings constructed since October 2018 are entitled to a 3% straight-line structures and buildings allowance on cost (excluding land).

Keywords

- **Annual investment allowance (AIA):** Available in a period in which expenditure is incurred on plant and machinery

- **Balancing allowance:** Given when a positive balance remains at cessation or disposal of certain assets

- **Balancing charge:** Given when a negative balance remains at cessation or disposal of certain assets

- **Capital expenditure** is one-off expenditure that will bring benefits to the business over a number of years (eg purchase of machinery)

- **First year allowance (FYA):** Available at 100% on zero emission cars

- **Period of account:** The period for which a business prepares its accounts

- **Plant and machinery:** Apparatus that performs a function in the business. Apparatus that is merely part of the setting is not plant

- **Private-use asset:** Has restricted capital allowances but does not apply to companies

- **Revenue expenditure** is regular ongoing expenditure that only brings benefit in the period in which the expenditure is made (eg payment of electricity bill)

- **Writing-down allowance (WDA):** A capital allowance of 18% per annum, given on the general pool of plant and machinery, or 6% per annum on the balance in the special rate pool

Test your learning

1   An item of plant is acquired for £2,000 and sold five years later for £3,200.

The amount that will be deducted from the pool as proceeds when the disposal is made is:

£ [   ]

2   Nitin, who prepares accounts to 30 September each year, had a balance on his general pool of £22,500 on 1 October 2021. In the year to 30 September 2022, he sold one asset and bought one asset as follows:

Addition (eligible for AIA) 1.12.21   £171,250
Disposal proceeds on sale on 1.8.22 (less than cost)   £7,800

The amount of capital allowances available for the year ended 30 September 2022 is:

£ [   ]

3   A company starts to trade on 1 July 2021, making up accounts to 31 December 2021 and buys a car with CO_2 emissions of 45g/km costing £18,000 on 15 July 2021. The company also buys a car with CO_2 emissions of 0g/km for £5,000 on 1 September 2021.

The capital allowances available in the first period of account to 31 December 2021 are:

£ [   ]

4   Abdul ceased trading on 31 December 2021, drawing up his final accounts for the year to 31 December 2021.

The following facts are relevant:

General pool balance at 1.1.21   £12,500
Addition – 31.5.21   £20,000
Disposal proceeds
   (in total – proceeds not exceeding cost on any item) – 31.12.21   £18,300

Identify whether the following statement is true or false. Tick ONE box.

There is a balancing charge of £14,200 arising for the year to 31 December 2021.

True	
False	

5   Raj, a sole trader who makes up accounts to 30 April each year, buys a Volvo estate car, with CO_2 emissions of 60g/km, for £30,000 on 31 March 2021. 60% of his usage of the car is for business purposes.

The capital allowance available to Raj in respect of the car for y/e 30 April 2021 is:

£ [   ]

6   Barry ceased trading on 31 December 2021, having been self-employed for many years. On 1 January 2021, the tax written down value of his plant and machinery general pool was £7,200. On 10 November 2021, Barry purchased a computer for £1,600. All of the items of plant and machinery were sold on 31 December 2021.

(a) **Required**

If Barry sells all the plant and machinery for £10,000 then he will have a

[▼] of £ [   ].

Picklist:

balancing allowance
balancing charge

Workings

(b) **Required**

If Barry sells his plant for £6,000 then he will have a

| | ▼ | of | £ | | .

Picklist:

balancing allowance
balancing charge

Workings

7   Peter is a sole trader who started to trade and acquired a car for both business and private purposes on 1 July 2021. He prepared his first set of accounts for the 9 months to 31 March 2022. The car purchased has CO_2 emissions of 60g/km and cost £19,000. The private mileage for the nine months ending 31 March 2022 represented 20% of his total mileage for that year.

Required

Peter can claim capital allowances for the 9 month accounting period ending 31 March 2022 of

£ [   ] .

Workings

8   Xeon Ltd purchases a newly-constructed office building from a developer for £1,875,000 on 1 March 2021 and starts using it on 1 April 2021. The purchase price includes acquisition costs of £75,000. Xeon Ltd has a 31 December year end.

What are the maximum SBAs available to Xeon Ltd in the year ended 31 December 2021?

£ [   ] .

9   A Ltd is building a new factory for £1,000,000 including £200,000 for land. A Ltd prepares its accounts to 31 December.

Identify which of the following statements are true or false.

	True ✓	False ✓
If the contract for the factory is signed in 2021 and the factory brought into use in that year, an SBA will be available for the year ended 31 December 2021.		
If the factory is constructed by 1 March 2021 and brought into use in A Ltd's trade on 1 July 2021 then an SBA of £24,000 is available as SBAs are claimed in full in year of construction/ purchase.		
The eligible cost qualifying for the SBA is £1,000,000.		

10   Nailsea Ltd makes up accounts for the 9 months to 30 September 2022. The brought forward value on its general pool on 1 January 2022 was £123,000. The following assets were bought and sold during the period:

		£
11 January 2022	Zero emission car	41,000
16 April 2022	Machinery	60,000
8 July 2022	Car for managing director	
	(CO_2 emissions 42g/km 10% private use)	38,000
31 August 2022	Plant	36,000
1 September 2022	Disposed of plant (cost £20,000)	15,000

Required

Calculate the capital allowances claim that Nailsea Ltd can make for the period ended 30 June 2021.

How would the allowances be calculated differently if Nailsea Ltd was a sole trader?

Solution

	AIA	FYA	Super deduction	General pool	Special rate pool	Private use asset	Total allowances

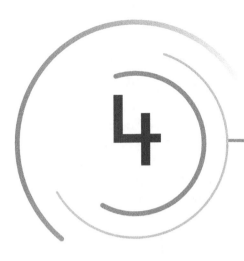

Taxing unincorporated businesses

Syllabus learning outcomes / objectives

1.3 Application of basis periods

Learners need to understand:
- the basis periods using current year basis, opening and closing year rules
- the advantages and disadvantages of different accounting dates

Learners need to be able to:
- calculate taxable profits using the basis period rules
- determine overlap periods and calculate overlap profits using the basis period rules

Assessment context

Basis period rules are highly examinable and need a lot of practice to ensure you are familiar with the different rules that apply in each circumstance.

Qualification context

You will not see these areas again in your studies.

Business context

Taxpayers need to know which tax year their profits fall into so they can determine when their tax is due. These rules will often influence when a taxpayer chooses to have his accounting period end.

Chapter overview

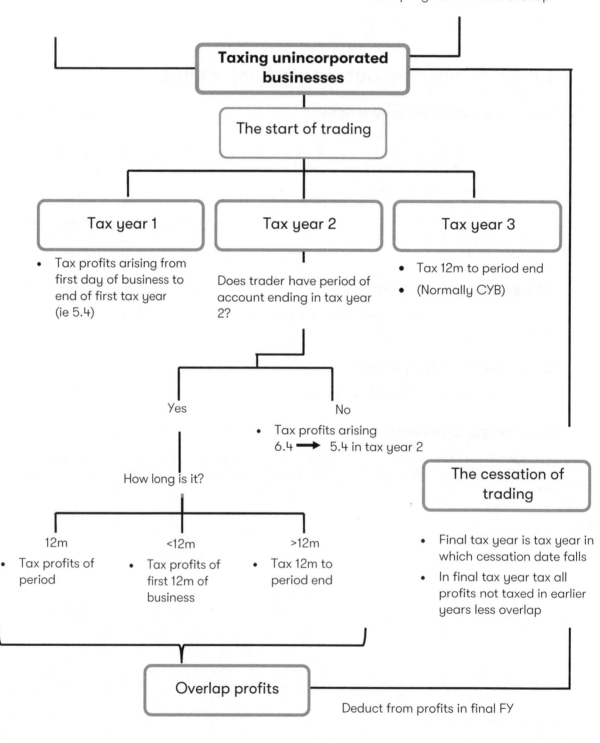

Choice of accounting date

- 30 April (ie early in tax year) delays time between profits being earned and taxed
- Dates earlier in tax year also give more time for tax planning
- 31 March/5 April avoids overlap profits whereas 30 April gives 11 month overlap

Continuing business

- Current year basis (CYB)
- Tax profits of period of account ending in current tax year

Taxing unincorporated businesses

The start of trading

Tax year 1

- Tax profits arising from first day of business to end of first tax year (ie 5.4)

Tax year 2

Does trader have period of account ending in tax year 2?

Tax year 3

- Tax 12m to period end
- (Normally CYB)

Yes

No

- Tax profits arising 6.4 ➝ 5.4 in tax year 2

How long is it?

12m
- Tax profits of period

<12m
- Tax profits of first 12m of business

>12m
- Tax 12m to period end

The cessation of trading

- Final tax year is tax year in which cessation date falls
- In final tax year tax all profits not taxed in earlier years less overlap

Overlap profits

Deduct from profits in final FY

1 Introduction

This chapter will concentrate on computing the figure to insert as **trading profit** in the income tax computation. These rules apply to unincorporated businesses only (ie individuals in business – sole traders and partners, **not** companies).

A sole trader/partnership may make up their accounts for any period they choose. As we have seen in earlier chapters, we use their accounting period as the basis for our adjustment of profit and capital allowances calculations.

However, income tax is calculated with reference to the **tax year** (also referred to as the **fiscal year** or **year of assessment**). The 2021/22 tax year runs 6 April 2021 to 5 April 2022.

1.1 Basis periods

A mechanism is needed to link the **taxable trading profits** (as adjusted for tax purposes and after the deduction of capital allowances) to a tax year. This mechanism is known as the **basis of assessment**, and the period whose profits are assessed in a tax year is called the **basis period**.

1.2 Current year basis

Open book reference

Income tax basis period rules

The basis of assessment for a **continuing business** is the **12-month period** of account **ending** in a tax year. The profits resulting from those accounts are taxed in that tax year. This is known as the **current year basis of assessment**. This rule is stated in the income tax basis period rules section of the reference material that you have access to within your assessment.

A sole trader who has been in business for several years and has prepared accounts for the year to 31 May each year will include **all** of the profits in the year ended 31 May 2020 in the tax return for 2020/21 because that is the tax year that the period of account ends in. Likewise, all of the profits from the year ended 31 May 2021 will be included in the tax return for 2021/22.

Activity 1: Current year basis (i)

A trader prepares accounts to 31 December each year.

Required

Which year's profits will be assessed in 2021/22?

[▼]

Picklist:

Period 6 April 2021 – 5 April 2022
Year ended 31 December 2020
Year ended 31 December 2021
Year ended 31 December 2022

Activity 2: Current year basis (ii)

Required

(a) **Which tax year would the profits of year ended 30 June 2021 be taxed in?**

[▼]

Picklist:

2020/21
2021/22

(b)   Which tax year would the profits of year ended 31 January 2021 be taxed in?

[▼]

Picklist:

2020/21
2021/22

2   The start of trading

Open book reference

Income tax basis period rules

On commencement of trade, the trader might not make up his first set of accounts for a 12-month period, therefore **special rules are needed to find the basis period in the first three tax years of a new business**. These rules always apply, even if the first set of accounts is for a 12-month period. Note that all these rules are summarised in the income tax basis period rules section of the reference material that you have access to within your assessment.

2.1   The first tax year

The tax year in which an unincorporated business starts is the first tax year in which the profits will be taxed.

The profits are taxed on an actual basis in the first year, ie the profits accruing from the start date until the next 5 April. So, if a trader starts to trade on 1 December 2021 and draws up accounts to 30 June 2022 making adjusted profits of £7,000, the first tax year is 2021/22 because that is the tax year in which they start their trade. In 2021/22, the basis period will be the date of commencement to the following 5 April, ie 1 December 2021 to 5 April 2022. Working to the nearest month, the profit made in that basis period is £7,000 × $\frac{4}{7}$ = £4,000.

Activity 3: The first tax year

Christian starts trading on 1 January 2020. In the y/e 31 December 2020 he makes profits of £24,000.

Required

What is the first tax year of the trade? (XXXX/XX format)

[   ]

What profits will be assessed in the first tax year?

£ [   ]

2.2   The second tax year

Finding the basis period for the second tax year may take more time, because there are four possibilities:

(a)   If the period of account that ends in the second tax year is 12 months, tax the whole 12 months.

(b)   If there is a period of account that ends in the second tax year, but it is less than 12 months, the basis period that must be used is the first 12 months of trading (ie increase the period to 12 months).

(c)   If there is a period of account that ends in the second tax year, but it is longer than 12 months, the basis period that must be used is the 12 months leading up to the end of that period of account (ie reduce the period to 12 months).

(d)   If there is no period of account that ends in the second tax year, because the first period of account is a very long one that does not end until a date in the third tax year, the basis period that must be used for the second tax year is the tax year itself (from 6 April to 5 April).

Opening year rules – second tax year

Length of accounting period ending in second tax year	Taxed in second tax year
• 12 months	CYB (ie 12m period ending in tax year)
• <12 months	First 12 months of profits
• >12 months	12m to normal accounting year end
• No accounting period	**Actual basis** (ie 6.4 – 5.4)

The following flowchart may help you.

Opening years – second tax year flowchart summary

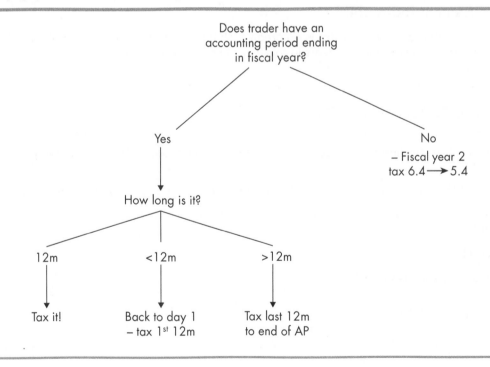

Activity 4: The second tax year (trader has 12-month accounting period)

Christian starts trading on 1 January 2020. In the y/e 31 December 2020 he makes profits of £24,000.

Required

What is the second tax year of the trade? (XXXX/XX format)

[   ]

What profits will be assessed in the second tax year?

[▼]

2.3 Overlap profits

You may have noticed in the previous example that some profits were taxed twice. This is a side effect of the opening year rules.

These profits are called **overlap profits**.

We will see shortly that overlap profits are deducted from profits in the trader's final tax year ensuring that, over the life of the business, all profits are only taxed once.

Overlap profits arise because HM Revenue & Customs (HMRC) would like all traders to have a 5 April year end.

If 5 April is selected as the year end, then no overlap profits can arise. This is a clear incentive for taxpayers to follow HMRC's wishes!

Assessment focus point

The calculation of overlap profits is an area which the Chief Assessor has identified as being a more challenging area for students in this task, so make sure you practise applying these rules to scenarios.

Activity 5: Overlap profits

Christian starts trading on 1 January 2020. In the y/e 31 December 2020 he makes profits of £24,000.

In his first tax year 2019/20, he is taxed on profits from 1 January 2020 to 5 April 2020 ie £6,000.

In his second tax year 2020/21, he is taxed on profits from 1 January 2020 to 31 December 2020 ie £24,000.

Required

His overlap period is (XX/XX/XX) [   ] **to** [   ].

His overlap profits are [£   ].

2.4 The third tax year

For the third tax year the basis period is the 12 months ending on the accounting date in the third tax year.

Further overlap profits may arise.

Activity 6: Opening year rules (short first period)

Linda starts trading on 1 January 2020. She decides on a 30 June year end and her results are:

	£
6m to 30/06/20	18,000
Y/e 30/06/21	48,000

Required

Complete the following table showing the results for the first three tax years of the business.

Solution

	Tax year (XXXX/XX)	Profits taxed		Amount taxed £
		From (XX/XX/XX)	To (XX/XX/XX)	
First tax year				
Second tax year				
Third tax year				
Overlap periods and profits				
First overlap period				
Second overlap period				
Total overlap				

Activity 7: Opening year rules (long first period ending in second tax year)

Peter begins trading on 1 July 2019. He decides on a December year end but draws up his first accounts to 31 December 2020.

He made £18,000 profits in the 18 months to 31 December 2020 and £30,000 in the 12 months to 31 December 2021.

Required

Complete the following table showing the results for the first three tax years of the business.

Solution

	Tax year (XXXX/XX)	Profits taxed		Amount taxed £
		From (XX/XX/XX)	To (XX/XX/XX)	
First tax year				

Second tax year				
Third tax year				
Overlap period and profits				

Activity 8: Opening year rules (long first period ending in third tax year)

Agnetha begins trading on 1 December 2019 and draws up her first accounts to 31 May 2021, her chosen year end. She makes £36,000 of profit in this period.

Required

Complete the following table showing the results for the first three tax years of the business.

Solution

	Tax year (XXXX/XX)	Profits taxed		Amount taxed £
		From (XX/XX/XX)	To (XX/XX/XX)	
First tax year				
Second tax year				
Third tax year				
Overlap period and profits				

3 The cessation of trading

Open book reference

Income tax basis period rules

The final year of assessment is the tax year that the date of cessation falls into. **The basis period for this final tax year normally runs from the end of the basis period for the previous tax year to the date of cessation.**

The previous (penultimate) year is a normal year, so we apply current year basis.

In the final year, we tax all the profits arising since those taxed in the penultimate year.

We are allowed to deduct overlap profits from the profits taxed in the final tax year. This ensures all profits are only taxed once over the life of the business.

These rules are covered within the income tax basis period rules section of the reference material that you have access to within your assessment.

Exceptionally, if a trade starts and ceases in the same tax year, the basis period for that year is the whole lifespan of the trade. If the final year is the second year, the basis period runs from 6 April at the start of the second year to the date of cessation.

Activity 9: Closing year rules (one period ending in final tax year)

Albert, who has been trading for some years making up his accounts to 31 December, ceases to trade on 30 April 2021 with profits as follows:

	Adjusted profits after capital allowances £
Year to 31/12/20	22,000
Four months to 30/04/21	12,000

Overlap profits at the start of the business were £4,000.

Required

Complete the following table showing the results for the final two tax years of the business.

Solution

	Tax year (XXXX/XX)	Profits taxed		Amount taxed £
		From (XX/XX/XX)	To (XX/XX/XX)	
Penultimate tax year				
Final tax year				

Activity 10: Closing year rules (two periods ending in final tax year)

Royce ceases trading on 31 March 2022. His recent results have been as follows:

	£
Y/e 31 December 2020	30,000
Y/e 31 December 2021	25,000
P/e 31 March 2022	4,000

Overlap profits on commencement were £12,000.

Required

Complete the following table showing the results for the final two tax years of the business.

Solution

| | Tax year (XXXX/XX) | Profits taxed | | Amount taxed £ |
		From (XX/XX/XX)	To (XX/XX/XX)	
Penultimate tax year				
Final tax year				

4 Choice of accounting date

The choice of accounting date may affect when tax is payable on trading profits. It may also create overlap profits and help or hinder tax planning.

A new trader should consider which accounting date would be best for tax purposes. There are a number of factors to consider from the point of view of taxation.

- If profits are expected to rise, a date early in the tax year (such as 30 April) will delay the time when rising accounting profits feed through into rising taxable profits. This is because, with an accounting date of 30 April, the taxable profits for each tax year are mainly the profits earned in the previous tax year. With an accounting date of 31 March, the taxable profits are almost entirely profits earned in the current tax year.

- An accounting date of 30 April gives the greatest time between earning the profits and paying the tax. For example, if a trader prepares accounts to 30 April 2021, this falls into the tax year 2021/22 with corresponding payments due. If the trader prepares accounts to 31 March 2021 (one month earlier), this falls into 2020/21 and the payments will be due one year earlier.

- Knowing profits well in advance of the end of the tax year makes tax planning easier.

- A 31 March/ 5 April year end is more straightforward and avoids overlap profits. In contrast, a 30 April year end gives 11 months overlap.

- The choice of accounting date affects the profits shown in each set of accounts, and this may affect the taxable profits (especially for heavily seasonal businesses).

> **Assessment focus point**
>
> Please refer to the reference material at the end of this Course Book to see which elements of this chapter will be available to you as a pop-up window in the live assessment.

- The profits of a 12-month period of account ending in a tax year are normally taxed in that tax year.

- In the first tax year, the basis period runs from the date the business starts to the following 5 April.

- There are three possibilities in the second tax year:

  - If a period of account of 12 months or more ends in the second tax year, the basis period for the second tax year is the 12 months to the end of that period of account.

  - If a period of account of less than 12 months ends in the second tax year, the basis period for the second tax year is the first 12 months from the start of trading.

  - If no period of account ends in the second tax year, the basis period for that year is 6 April to 5 April in the year.

- The basis period for the third tax year is the 12 months to the end of the period of account ending in that year.

- The basis period in the final tax year of a business runs from the end of the previous basis period to the date that the trade stops.

- When trade ceases, overlap profits are deducted from the final tax year's taxable profits.

- The choice of accounting date can impact an individual's tax position:

  - 30 April (ie early in tax year) delays time between profits being earned and taxed

  - Dates earlier in tax year also give more time for tax planning

  - 31 March/5 April avoids overlap profits whereas 30 April gives 11 months overlap

BPP
LEARNING
MEDIA

Keywords

- **Basis period:** The period whose profits are taxed in a tax year
- **Current year basis of assessment:** Taxes the 12-month period of account ending in that tax year
- **Overlap profits:** The profits that are taxed more than once when a business starts
- **Tax year, fiscal year** or **year of assessment:** The year from 6 April in one year to 5 April in the next year

Test your learning

1   Oliver starts to trade on 1 May 2020. He makes his first set of accounts up to 31 December 2020 and annually thereafter.

Fill in the following table setting out the basis periods for the first three tax years and the overlap period of profits.

Tax year	Basis period
Overlap profits	

2   **Identify whether the following statement is true or false.**

When the trade ceases, overlap profits are deducted from the final tax year's taxable profits.

	✓
True	
False	

3   Barlow stops trading on 31 December 2021, having been in business since January 2013. Previously he has always made accounts up to 31 May. Overlap profits on commencement were £10,000.

Results for the last few years (as adjusted for tax) are:

Period	Profits £
Period to 31.12.21	15,000
Year ended 31.5.21	25,000
Year ended 31.5.20	32,000
Year ended 31.5.19	18,000

Using the proforma layout provided, compute the taxable profits for the final three tax years of trading.

Tax year	Basis period	Taxable profits £

4   Amarjat started trading on 1 February 2021. He prepared his first accounts to 30 June 2022. Taxable profits for this 17 month period were £34,000.

Show the taxable profits for 2020/21, 2021/22 and 2022/23.

Tax year	Basis period	Taxable profits £

His overlap profits are:

£	

5   Susi started to trade on 1 December 2020. Her first accounts were prepared to 30 June 2021. Taxable profits for the first two periods of account were:

Period to 30 June 2021: £70,000

Year to 30 June 2022: £60,000

(a)   **Her taxable profits for 2020/21 are:**

£	

(b)   **Her taxable profits for 2021/22 are:**

£	

(c)   **Her taxable profits for 2022/23 are:**

£	

(d)   **Her overlap profits are:**

£	

6   **Identify whether the following statements are true or false.**

	True ✓	False ✓
If profits are expected to rise, a 31 March year end will delay the time when rising accounting profits feed through into rising taxable profits.		
A 31 March year end is more straightforward than a 30 April year end as it avoids overlap profits.		

Partnerships

Syllabus learning outcomes / objectives

1.4 Calculating taxable profits and losses of partners

Learners need to be able to:
- allocate profits between partners
- determine the basis period for continuing, new and departing partners.

Assessment context

In the assessment, you may be required to compute the split of partnership profits for new, continuing and leaving partners as well as the basis periods for the individual partners. The task involving analysing profits between partners is usually the best performing task within the asessement, so you must be able to demonstrate this skill.

Qualification context

You will have seen partnerships in your accounting studies, so the basic treatment will not be a surprise to you. The tax treatment of partnerships is unique to this unit.

Business context

Partners need to know how much tax they owe to the Government.

Chapter overview

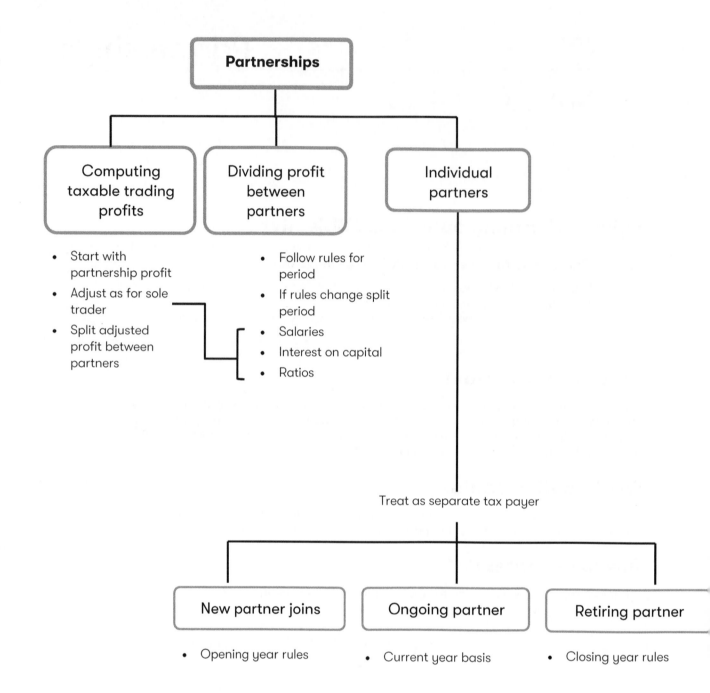

Partnerships

Computing taxable trading profits

- Start with partnership profit
- Adjust as for sole trader
- Split adjusted profit between partners

Dividing profit between partners

- Follow rules for period
- If rules change split period
- Salaries
- Interest on capital
- Ratios

Individual partners

Treat as separate tax payer

New partner joins

- Opening year rules

Ongoing partner

- Current year basis

Retiring partner

- Closing year rules

1 Introduction

In this chapter we look at the profits of a partnership and how these profits are split between the individual partners. We then go on to look at how the individual partners are taxed on their share of the profits.

2 Computing taxable trading profits of partnerships

A **partnership** is a group of self-employed people working together.

The partnership produces a statement of profit or loss for the whole business. Profits will be adjusted for tax purposes, and capital allowances will be calculated in exactly the same way as for a self-employed sole trader. This means that you must add back disallowable items. You must deduct specifically deductible items that have not been deducted in the accounts (for example, capital allowances) and also any income in the accounts that is not part of the taxable trading profit. Finally, add any amounts taxable as trading profits that have not been included in the accounts; for example, the market value of any goods taken for own use.

A particular point worth noting is that any partners' salaries or interest on capital deducted in the accounts must be added back when computing taxable trading profits of the partnership. These items are disallowable expenses because they are a form of drawings. They will be part of each partner's taxable trading profit as described below.

There is an additional stage here, though. The adjusted profits must be split between the partners.

Once profit has been split, each partner is treated as a sole trader and taxed separately.

3 Dividing taxable trading profits between partners

Once you have computed a partnership's taxable trading profit for a period of account, you must divide it between the partners concerned.

The partners may agree to share profits in any way they wish. The agreed division of profits will be set out in the partnership agreement and will always be stated for you in assessment tasks.

Method:

- First, allocate any salaries and interest on capital to the partners.
- Second, share the residue of profits between the partners in the agreed ratio.

Illustration 1: Dividing profit between the partners

Pearl and Ruby are in partnership. The partnership's taxable trading profits (as adjusted for tax purposes) for the year ended 31 March 2022 were £110,000. The partnership agreement provides for Pearl to be paid a salary of £20,000 per annum and for Ruby to be paid a salary of £30,000 per annum. Any remaining profits are divided between Pearl and Ruby in the ratio 2:1.

First allocate the partners' salaries and then divide the balance of the profit in accordance with the profit-sharing ratio:

	Total £	Pearl £	Ruby £
Salary	50,000	20,000	30,000
Profit (£110,000 – £30,000 – £20,000) 2:1	60,000	40,000	20,000
	110,000	60,000	50,000

Pearl has taxable profits of £60,000 and Ruby has taxable profits of £50,000 for the year ended 31 March 2022. These profits will be taxable in 2021/22.

Activity 1: Partnership profit allocation

Ron and Steve have been in partnership as farmers since 1 July 1999 sharing profits and losses as follows.

	Ron	Steve
Salary	5,000	Nil
Balance – profit-share ratio	3	2

During y/e 30 June 2021 the partnership made a trading profit of £60,000.

Required

Complete the table showing how the profits are allocated between the partners.

Solution

	Ron £	Steve £
Profit share		

Workings (not provided in the CBT)

	Ron £	Steve £	Total £

4 Change in profit-sharing agreement

Sometimes the profit-sharing agreement may change during a period of account.

Here we apportion the profit before and after the change. We then split the profits before the change using the old rules, and the profits after the change using the new rules.

Do not forget interest and salaries are annual figures, so will need to be time apportioned.

Illustration 2: Change in partnership agreement

Jenny and Chris are in partnership. Taxable trading profits of the partnership for the year ended 31 March 2022 are £60,000. Until 30 September 2021 profits are shared equally. From 1 October 2021 Jenny and Chris agree that the profits should be shared in the ratio 2:1.

Show how the taxable trading profits of the year to 31 March 2022 are divided between Jenny and Chris.

Your first step should be to apportion the profits to the periods before and after the change in the profit-sharing ratio:

1.4.21 – 30.9.21   6/12 × £60,000 = £30,000
1.10.21 – 31.3.22   6/12 × £60,000 = £30,000

Next, divide these profits between the partners:

	Total £	Jenny £	Chris £
1.4.21 – 30.9.21 (1:1)	30,000	15,000	15,000
1.10.21 – 31.3.22 (2:1)	30,000	20,000	10,000
	60,000	35,000	25,000

For the year to 31 March 2022, Jenny's taxable trading profits are £35,000 and Chris's taxable trading profits are £25,000.

Activity 2: Change in profit-sharing arrangements

During the next year, ended 30 June, the Ron and Steve partnership made profits of £90,000.

On 1 January the partners decided to change their profit-sharing arrangement.

The old arrangement had been:

	Ron	Steve
Salary	5,000	Nil
Balance – profit-share ratio	3	2

After the change both partners receive an equal share of all profits and no one receives a salary.

Required

Complete the table showing how the profits are allocated between the partners.

Solution

	Ron £	Steve £
Profit share		

Workings (not provided in the CBT)

5 The tax positions of individual partners

Once we have allocated profits between partners, we treat each partner as an individual sole trader.

We follow normal current year basis, ie we tax each partner's profits in the fiscal year in which their period ends.

Note. It is the actual accounting period end that is important when determining the tax year in which the profits are taxed. If we have split the period to allocate profit because of a change in profit-sharing arrangements, we usually ignore the date of the split when deciding the fiscal year in which the profits will be taxed.

6 Changes in partners

A partnership may continue but individual partners may choose to leave while new partners may join.

If partners have joined or left the partnership, they will have their own periods with different starting or finishing dates to ongoing partners.

It is important to identify the periods of each partner. We then apply the relevant tax rules:

- A new partner will be taxed using the opening year rules.
- An ongoing partner will be taxed using the current year basis.
- A retiring partner will be taxed using the closing year rules.

Illustration 3: Partner joining partnership

Francis and Caroline have been in partnership for many years, making up accounts to 31 December each year. Profits were shared equally until 1 June 2019, when Charles joined the partnership. From 1 June 2019 profits were shared in the ratio 2:2:1.

Profits adjusted for tax purposes are as follows.

Period	Taxable profit £
1.1.19 – 31.12.19	48,000
1.1.20 – 31.12.20	18,000
1.1.21 – 31.12.21	24,000

We need to calculate the taxable profits for each partner for 2019/20 to 2021/22.

We must first share the profits between the partners.

	Total £	Francis £	Caroline £	Charles £
Year ended 31.12.19				
1.1.19 – 31.5.19 (5/12)				
Profits 50:50	20,000	10,000	10,000	
1.6.19 – 31.12.19 (7/12)				
Profits 2:2:1	28,000	11,200	11,200	5,600
Total	48,000	21,200	21,200	5,600
Year ended 31.12.20				
Profits 2:2:1	18,000	7,200	7,200	3,600
Total for y/e 31.12.20	18,000	7,200	7,200	3,600

	Total £	Francis £	Caroline £	Charles £
Year ended 31.12.21				
Profits 2:2:1	24,000	9,600	9,600	4,800
Total for y/e 31.12.21	24,000	9,600	9,600	4,800

The next stage is to work out the basis periods and hence, the taxable profits for the partners in each tax year. The most important thing to remember at this stage is to **deal with each of the partners separately**.

Francis and Caroline are taxed on the current year basis of assessment throughout.

Year	Basis period	Francis £	Caroline £
2019/20	1.1.19 – 31.12.19	21,200	21,200
2020/21	1.1.20 – 31.12.20	7,200	7,200
2021/22	1.1.21 – 31.12.21	9,600	9,600

Charles joins the partnership on 1 June 2019, which falls in tax year 2019/20, so the opening year rules apply to him from 2019/20.

Year	Basis period	Working	Taxable profits £
2019/20	1.6.19 – 5.4.20	£5,600 + 3/12 × £3,600	6,500
2020/21	1.1.20 – 31.12.20		3,600
2021/22	1.1.21 – 31.12.21		4,800

Charles has overlap profits of £900 (£3,600 × 3/12) to carry forward and relieve in the tax year in which he leaves the partnership.

Illustration 4: Partner leaving a partnership

Dominic, Sebastian and India have traded in partnership, sharing profits equally for many years. On 1 May 2021 India left the partnership. Profits continue to be shared equally. Accounts have always been prepared to 30 September and recent results have been:

	Profit £
Y/e 30.9.19	36,000
Y/e 30.9.20	81,000
Y/e 30.9.21	60,000

Each of the partners had overlap profits of £10,000 on commencement of the business. We are asked to calculate the taxable trading profits of each partner for 2019/20 to 2021/22.

Firstly, allocate the profits of each period of account to the partners.

	Total £	Dominic £	Sebastian £	India £
Y/e 30.9.19	36,000	12,000	12,000	12,000
Y/e 30.9.20	81,000	27,000	27,000	27,000
Y/e 30.9.21				
1.10.20 – 30.4.21 (7/12)	35,000	11,667	11,667	11,666
1.5.21 – 30.9.21 (5/12)	25,000	12,500	12,500	–
	60,000	24,167	24,167	11,666

Dominic and Sebastian are taxed on the current year basis of assessment throughout:

	Dominic £	Sebastian £
2019/20 (y/e 30.9.19)	12,000	12,000
2020/21 (y/e 30.9.20)	27,000	27,000
2021/22 (y/e 30.9.21)	24,167	24,167

India is treated as ceasing to trade in 2021/22.

	£
2019/20 (y/e 30.9.19)	12,000
2020/21 (y/e 30.9.20)	27,000
2021/22 (p/e 30.4.21 less overlap profits)	
(£11,666 – £10,000)	1,666

Activity 3: Change in partnership personnel

M and G began a partnership on 1 June 2007, sharing profits and losses equally. On 1 December 2019, G retired and B joined them, the new arrangement being 2:1. Results have been as follows:

	£
Y/e 31.5.19	33,000
Y/e 31.5.20	51,000
Y/e 31.5.21	72,000

G's overlap profits were £5,000.

Required

Complete the following table showing the assessments on the partners for the tax years 2019/20 to 2021/22. If a partner has no taxable profit, show '0'. Identify B's overlap.

Solution

	M £	G £	B £
2019/20			
2020/21			
2021/22			
Overlap			

- A partnership is a group of self-employed individuals trading together.

- Calculate tax-adjusted profits for a partnership in the same way as you would calculate the tax-adjusted profits of a sole trader.

- Divide the tax-adjusted profits of a period of account between the partners in accordance with their profit-sharing arrangements during the period of account.

- If profit-sharing arrangements change during a period of account, time apportion profits to the periods before and after the change before allocating them to partners.

- Once you have found a partner's profit for a period of account you can consider which tax year that profit is taxed in. A continuing partner in a continuing business is taxed using the current year basis of assessment.

- The opening year rules apply to a partner joining the partnership. The closing year rules apply to a partner leaving the partnership.

Keywords

- **Partnership:** A group of self-employed individuals trading together

Test your learning

1   The adjusted profit of a partnership is divided between the partners in accordance with the profit-sharing agreement in existence during what period?

Tick ONE box.

	✓
The calendar year	
The tax year	
The period of account concerned	
The period agreed by the partners	

2   Dave and Joe are in partnership together and make a profit of £18,000 for the year to 31 December 2021. Up to 30 September 2021 they share profits and losses equally but thereafter, they share 3:2.

Dave's taxable profits for 2021/22 are:

£ ☐

and Joe's taxable profits for 2021/22 are:

£ ☐

3   Holly and Jasmine are in partnership sharing profits equally after paying a salary of £5,000 to Holly and a salary of £80,000 to Jasmine. Taxable profits for the year to 31 March 2022 were £200,000.

Using the proforma layout provided, show the taxable profits of each of the partners for the year.

	Total £	Holly £	Jasmine £
Salary			
Division of profits			

4   Barry and Steve have been in partnership for many years. Profits are shared three-quarters to Barry and one-quarter to Steve. For the year ended 31 March 2021, the partnership made a profit of £60,000 and for the year ended 31 March 2022, the profit was £80,000.

The profit taxable on Steve for 2021/22 is:

Tick ONE box.

	✓
£60,000	
£15,000	
£45,000	
£20,000	

5   Abdul and Ghita have been in partnership for many years. On 1 September 2021, Sase joins the partnership and profits are shared between the partners in the ratio 2:2:1 with Sase receiving the smallest profit share. For the year to 31 August 2022, the partnership makes a profit of £120,000.

The profits assessable on Sase in 2021/22 are:

£	

The profits assessable on Sase in 2022/23 are:

£	

The overlap profits arising for Sase are:

£	

6   William, Ann and John have been in partnership for many years, sharing profits equally. Accounts have always been prepared to 31 October each year. All partners had overlap profits of £5,000 on commencement. On 31 December 2021, William left the partnership. Profits continued to be shared equally. Recent results were:

	£
Y/e 31 October 2020	21,000
Y/e 31 October 2021	33,000
Y/e 31 October 2022	36,000

(a)   **Using the proforma layout provided, show how the profits of each period will be divided between the partners.**

	Total £	William £	Ann £	John £
Y/e 31.10.20				
Y/e 31.10.21				
Y/e 31.10.22				

(b)   **Using the proforma layout provided, show the taxable profits for each partner for 2020/21 to 2022/23.**

	William £	Ann £	John £

6

National insurance

Syllabus learning outcomes / objectives

1.5   Calculate the National Insurance Contributions (NICs) payable by self-
       employed taxpayers

       Learners need to understand:
       •   What income Class 2 and Class 4 NICs are payable on
       Learners need to be able to:
       •   Calculate Class 2 and Class 4 NICs

Assessment context

National insurance calculations are simple and straightforward and should earn you easy marks
in the assessment. The task covering National Insurance calculations has been identified by the
Chief Assessor as the best performing task in the assessment overall, so it is vital you can prepare
these calculations.

Qualification context

You will not see these rules in detail outside of this unit.

Business context

These taxes are a significant extra cost for self-employed people.

Chapter overview

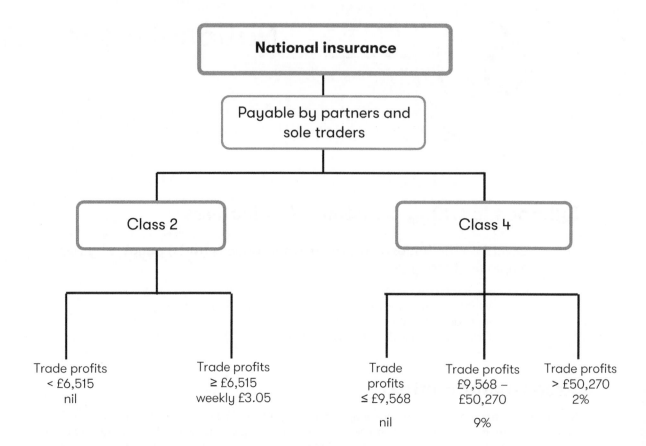

1 Introduction

Paying National Insurance Contributions (NICs) builds up an individual's entitlement to certain state benefits, such as pensions.

In this chapter we cover the NICs payable by self-employed individuals. We will briefly cover the NICs payable where an individual is employed later in this course book.

2 NICs payable by the self-employed

Self-employed people (ie partners and sole traders) must pay two types of NIC:

- Class 2 contributions
- Class 4 contributions

The information needed in order to calculate NIC is clearly stated in the national insurance (NI) section of the reference material you have access to in the assessment.

2.1 Class 2 contributions

National insurance

Open book reference

This is payable at a flat rate of £3.05 per week.

The amount of Class 2 contributions due are determined at the end of each tax year and are based on the number of weeks of self-employment in that year. This will then be collected through the self-assessment system, along with income tax and Class 4 contributions.

No contributions are due if trading profits for the year are less than the Small Profits Threshold of £6,515.

2.2 Class 4 contributions

National insurance

Open book reference

This is payable in addition to Class 2.

Class 4 contributions are based on the level of the individual's trading profits after loss relief for a tax year.

They are calculated as:

- 9% of 'profits' between the lower earnings limit (LEL) of £9,568 and the upper earnings limit (UEL) of £50,270

- 2% of 'profits' above the UEL of £50,270

Activity 1: National insurance contributions

Note. You should calculate the following to pounds and pence.

(a)   Mr Bull, a trader, has trading income of £14,000 for 2021/22.

   Required

   His Class 2 NI contributions for the year are:

   £ [   ]

   His Class 4 NI contributions at 9% are:

   £ [   ]

(b)   Mr Seye, a trader, has trading income of £78,000 in 2021/22.

   Required

   His Class 4 NI contributions at 9% are:

   £ [   ]

   His Class 4 NI contributions at 2% are:

   £ [   ]

Assessment focus point

Please refer to the reference material at the end of this Course Book to see which elements of this chapter will be available to you as a pop-up window in the live assessment.

BPP
LEARNING
MEDIA

Chapter summary

- Self-employed traders pay:
  - Class 2 contributions at a flat rate per week of £3.05 (in 2021/22), and
  - Class 4 contributions based on the level of their profits.
- Main rate Class 4 NICs are 9% of profits between the UEL and LEL.
- Additional Class 4 NICs are 2% of profits above the UEL.

BPP LEARNING MEDIA

Keywords

- **Class 2 contributions:** Flat rate contributions payable by the self-employed
- **Class 4 contributions:** Profit-related contributions payable by the self-employed

Test your learning

Compute the following total sole traders' liabilities to NICs for 2021/22.

Note. You should calculate the following to pounds and pence.

1 **Acker**

Taxable trading profits £5,050

£		.	

2 **Bailey**

Taxable trading profits £60,000

£		.	

3 **Cartwright**

Taxable trading profits £10,850

£		.	

Computing corporation tax

Syllabus learning outcomes / objectives

2.3   Calculate taxable profits and corporation tax payable

Learners need to be able to:

- Calculate the total profits from given trading income, property income, investment income, chargeable gains and qualifying charitable donations for periods

  - Longer than 12 months
  - Shorter than 12 months
  - Equal to 12 months

- Calculate corporation tax payable

Assessment context

In the assessment, you may be required you to calculate taxable total profits (TTP) and then go on to calculate corporation tax.

Qualification context

You will not see this topic outside of this assessment.

Business context

Companies need to know how much corporation tax they need to pay.

Chapter overview

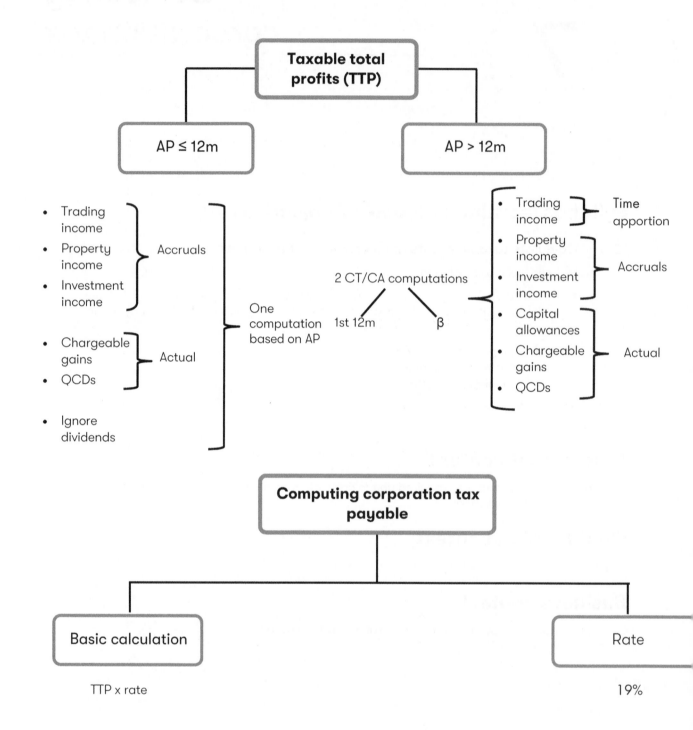

Taxable total profits (TTP)

AP ≤ 12m

- Trading income
- Property income
- Investment income

Accruals

- Chargeable gains
- QCDs

Actual

- Ignore dividends

One computation based on AP

AP > 12m

2 CT/CA computations

1st 12m   β

- Trading income — Time apportion
- Property income
- Investment income

Accruals

- Capital allowances
- Chargeable gains
- QCDs

Actual

Computing corporation tax payable

Basic calculation

TTP x rate

Rate

19%

1 Introduction

In this chapter, we will look at the different types of income earned by a company, how this income is included in the tax calculation and how to calculate corporation tax.

2 Taxable total profits (TTP)

Corporation tax is a tax payable by companies.

Taxable total profits (TTP) are the profits on which a company must pay corporation tax.

Period of account is the period for which the company prepares its accounts.

A company prepares a calculation of its taxable total profits by listing all its taxable profits and summing them together to get total profits. Qualifying charitable donations are then deducted to get TTP. See an example proforma in Illustration 1 below. Each category of income and deduction will be considered in more detail later in this Chapter.

The computation will usually be prepared for the company's period of account although there are special rules that apply where a company prepares a set of accounts for a period of more than 12 months (see later in this Chapter).

Illustration 1: Corporation tax computation for the X months to <date>

		£
Trading income		X
Investment income (NTL-R) (Interest income)		X
Property income		X
Chargeable gains		X
Total profits		X
Less qualifying charitable donations (QCDs)		(X)
Taxable total profits		X

2.1 Trading income

Trading income for a company is, broadly, computed in the same way that trading income for a sole trader is computed.

As a reminder, there are three important differences:

(a) Companies are entitled to an additional type of capital allowance referred to as a super-deduction. This detail was covered in the earlier capital allowance chapter.

(b) There are never any private use adjustments for a company when either adjusting the accounting profit or calculating capital allowances.

(c) Companies deal with a long period of account (accounts that have been made up for more than 12 months) in a different way to individuals or partnerships.

Note. Bad debts may be referred to as impairment losses in the financial statements of a company.

2.2 Investment income (NTL-R)

In a corporation tax computation, interest/investment income and expenses are often referred to as loan relationship income and expenses. The taxation treatment of the interest income/expense will depend on whether the loan relationship exists for trade/non-trade reasons.

Virtually **all interest receivable** by companies will be **non-trading loan relationship (NTL-R) income**. It is taxed as **investment income/NTL-R income** on the **accruals** basis. You may also see the income being referred to as a NTL-R credit. As the company will account for interest income on an accruals basis in its accounts, this interest income would be deducted in the adjustment to profits to remove it from the trade profit figure and would then be taxed as investment income.

Interest payable is deductible, but where it is deductible depends on the nature of the loan:

- If the loan is for a **trading purpose, the interest is deductible when computing the company's trading income.** Common examples of trading interest payable include interest on loans to buy plant and machinery or trading stock or bank overdraft interest. This tax treatment means that if the interest payable is showing as an expense in the statement of profit or loss, **no** adjustment is needed for tax purposes.

- If the loan is for a **non-trading purpose,** the interest is **deductible from investment income** (which is essentially all the company's interest income receivable) **to give a net 'investment income' figure to be used in computing taxable total profits.** Common examples of non-trading interest expense would be interest on loans used to buy investments such as shares or properties to rent out. The non-trading interest expense may be referred to as a NTL-R debit and it is the NTL-R credits and debits which are pooled to give the net 'investment income' figure in TTP. In some cases, there may be a net deficit of non-trading interest paid over non-trading interest received (or 'loss'), but the treatment of such a deficit (or loss) is not in your syllabus.

Assessment focus point

You will not be expected to calculate investment income in your Business Tax assessment. However, you need to be able to understand what income and expenses are included within this category.

2.3 Property income

A company with property business income must **pool the rents and expenses on all its properties, to give a single profit or loss**. Property business income is taxed on an **accruals basis** for companies.

Assessment focus point

You will not be expected to calculate property business income in your Business Tax assessment. However, you may be given a profit figure and be required to include it within the corporation tax computation, as appropriate.

2.4 Chargeable gains

Companies do not pay capital gains tax. Instead, their **net chargeable gains** (current period gains less current period and brought forward capital losses) **are brought into the computation of taxable total profits**.

We will look at gains in more detail later.

2.5 Qualifying charitable donations (QCDs)

Qualifying charitable donations are charitable gifts on which tax relief is given; however, they cannot be deducted as a trading expense. If a qualifying charitable donation has been deducted in computing the accounting profit, the amount deducted must be added back in computing **trading** profits (adjustment of profits), but the amount actually paid during the period can then be deducted from the total profits when computing taxable total profits.

2.6 Dividend income

Companies are not taxed on dividends they receive from other companies. If dividend income has been included in the net profit figure per the accounts, then this will need to be deducted in the adjustment to profit to ensure that the dividend income is not taxed.

2.7 Dividends paid

Companies may not deduct dividends paid from their taxable total profits. Given that dividends are not deductible in coming down to a net profit figure, you should not normally need to make any adjustment in the adjustment to profit for dividends paid.

Illustration 2: Adjustment of profits and calculation of TTP

ST Ltd draws up accounts for the year ended 31 March 2022 which show the following results:

	£	£
Gross profit on trading		180,000
Dividends received from other companies		7,900
Bank interest received		222
Profit on sale of investments		20,000
Less: Trade expenses (all allowable)	83,400	
Bank interest payable (overdraft)	200	
Debenture interest payable (gross)	3,200	
Qualifying charitable donation	100	
Depreciation charge	9,022	(95,922)
Profit before taxation		112,200

Notes.

1 The capital allowances for the accounting period total £5,500.

2 The debentures were issued on 1 August 2021 to raise working capital. The £3,200 charged in the accounts represents six months' interest (£2,400 paid and two months accrued).

3 The profit on the sale of investments resulted in a chargeable gain of £13,867.

The calculation of the company's taxable total profits is as follows:

	£	£
Profit for the year per accounts		112,200
Less: Dividends received	7,900	
Profit on investments	20,000	

	£	£
Interest received	222	
		(28,122)
		84,078
Add: Qualifying charitable donation	100	
Depreciation charge	9,022	
		9,122
		93,200
Less Capital allowances		(5,500)
Trading profits		87,700
Investment income (NTL-R income)		222
Chargeable gain		13,867
Total profits		101,789
Less Qualifying charitable donation		(100)
Taxable total profits		101,689

Note. The dividends received from other companies are not included within taxable total profits. Interest is deductible on the accruals basis.

Activity 1: Calculating taxable total profits

Abel Ltd, a UK trading company with no associated companies, produced the following results for the year ended 31 December 2021.

Income	£
Adjusted trading profits	2,440,000
Property income	150,000
Bank deposit interest accrued	40,000
Chargeable gains: 25 September 2021	350,000
28 December 2021	70,000
(There were capital losses of £80,000 brought forward at 1 January 2021)	
Loan interest paid (loan was used to buy investments)	10,000
Qualifying charitable payment	70,000
Dividends received	135,000

Required

Complete the following table calculating taxable total profits for the year ended 31 December 2021.

Solution

Corporation tax computation y/e 31 December 2021

	£
Trading profits	
Property income	
NTL-R income (Investment income)	
Chargeable gains	
Total profits	
Less qualifying charitable payments	
Taxable total profits	

3 Long periods of account

3.1 Accounting periods exceeding 12 months

A **period of account** is the period for which a company prepares its accounts.

An **accounting period** is the period for which corporation tax is charged.

A company's accounting period is usually the same as its period of account. However, **an accounting period cannot be longer than 12 months**. This means that **if a period of account exceeds 12 months, it must be divided into two accounting periods of**:

- The first 12 months
- The remaining balance of months

It is necessary to prepare separate computations of taxable total profits for each accounting period.

Splitting income and expenditure

Income and expenditure is split between the two computations using the following rules:

- Trading income (before deducting capital allowances) is apportioned on a time basis.

- Capital allowances and balancing charges are calculated separately for each accounting period. The annual investment allowance (AIA) and writing-down allowances (WDAs) will need to be apportioned for the short period.

- Property income is apportioned over the period the property is actually rented out, ie on an accruals basis.

- Investment income (NTL-R income) is apportioned on an accruals basis.

- Qualifying charitable donations are allocated to the accounting period in which they are paid.

- Chargeable gains by reference to the date the asset is sold.

Activity 2: Calculating taxable total profits – long period of account

B plc prepared accounts for a 16-month period to 31 December 2021. The results for the period include the following:

	£
Adjusted trading profit before capital allowances	3,600,000
Bank interest receivable (accrued evenly over the period)	32,000
Chargeable gain (sale of asset on 13.10.21)	40,000
Qualifying charitable donation paid (annually on 31.7)	20,000

The tax written-down value of plant and machinery qualifying for capital allowances at 1 September 2020 was £37,500. The only capital transaction during the 16-month period was the purchase of a new van for £5,289 on 15 November 2021.

Required

Complete the following table, calculating taxable total profit for the two accounting periods that comprise the long period of account.

Solution

	____ months to ____ £	____ months to ____ £
Adjusted trading profits		
Less capital allowances		
Trading profits		
NTL-R income (Investment income)		
Chargeable gain		
Total profits		
Less qualifying charitable donation		
TTP		

4 Computing the corporation tax liability

Open book reference

Corporation tax

Corporation tax rates are fixed for financial years. A **financial year** runs from 1 April to the following 31 March and is identified by the calendar year in which it begins.

For example, the year ended 31 March 2022 is the Financial Year 2021 (FY2021) as it begins on 1 April 2021. This should not be confused with a tax year for an individual, which runs from 6 April to the following 5 April.

The rate of corporation tax which applies from FY17 to FY21 is 19%.

Activity 3: Corporation tax payable

B plc has the following results for the year ended 31 March 2022:

	£
Trading profits	1,500,000
Chargeable gain	50,000
Qualifying charitable donations	30,000

Required

How much corporation tax is payable by B plc?

£ [   ]

Assessment focus point

In the live assessment you will be provided with reference material that can be accessed through pop-up windows. The content of this reference material has been reproduced at the back of this Course Book. Make sure you familiarise yourself with the content and practise referring to it as you work through this Course Book.

Chapter summary

- Adjustment of profit for companies is similar to that for individuals but companies are entitled to the super-deduction for capital allowances and there is no private use adjustment.

- To compute taxable total profits, aggregate all sources of income and chargeable gains. Deduct qualifying charitable donations.

- An accounting period cannot exceed 12 months in length.

- A long period of account must be split into two accounting periods: a period of 12 months and then a period covering the balance of the period of account.

- The taxable total profits will be charged to corporation tax at 19%

Keywords

- **Accounting period:** The period for which corporation tax is charged
- **Financial year:** Runs from 1 April to the following 31 March and is identified by the calendar year in which it begins
- **Period of account:** The period for which a company prepares its accounts
- **Qualifying charitable donations:** Charitable gifts on which tax relief is given
- **Taxable total profits:** The profits on which a company must pay corporation tax

Test your learning

1   Indicate whether the following statements are true or false.

	True ✓	False ✓
A company with a nine-month period of account will calculate capital allowances for nine months and deduct them from adjusted trading profits.		
A company with an 18-month period of account will calculate capital allowances for 18 months and deduct them from adjusted trading profits, and then prorate the answer between the appropriate accounting periods.		
A company with an 18-month period of account will calculate capital allowances for the first 12 months, then capital allowances for the remaining 6 months, and deduct them from the relevant prorated trading profits allocated to each accounting period.		
Dividends are not included in the taxable total profits. They are taxed separately.		

2   A company has accrued interest payable of £4,000 (gross) for the year ended 31 March 2022.

The interest is payable on a loan taken out to buy some machinery for use in the company's trade.

Identify how this will be treated in the corporation tax computation. Tick ONE box.

	✓
Added to trading income	
Added to net non-trading interest ie a NTL-R credit	
Deducted from trading income	
Deducted from net non-trading interest ie a NTLR debit	

3   On 30 June 2021, Edelweiss Ltd makes a donation to Help the Aged of £385. The donation is a qualifying charitable donation.

The amount of deduction available in respect of the charitable donation when calculating taxable total profits is:

£	

4   X Ltd had been making up accounts to 31 May for several years. Early in 2021, the directors decided to make accounts to 31 August 2021 (instead of 31 May 2021) and annually thereafter to 31 August.

Tick the box which correctly shows the two chargeable accounting periods for CT purposes for X Ltd.

	✓
1 June 2020 – 31 March 2021 and 1 April 2021 – 31 August 2021	
1 June 2020 – 31 May 2021 and 1 June 2021 – 31 August 2021	
1 June 2020 – 31 December 2020 and 1 January 2021 – 31 August 2021	
1 June 2020 – 31 August 2020 and 1 September 2020– 31 August 2021	

5   C Ltd prepares accounts for the 16 months to 30 April 2022. The results are as follows:

	£
Trading profits	320,000
Bank interest received (accrued evenly over period)	1,600
Chargeable gain (made 1 January 2022)	20,000
Qualifying charitable donation (paid 31 December 2021)	15,000

Using the proforma layout provided, calculate the taxable total profits for the accounting periods based on the above results. Input 0 if your answer is zero.

	_____ ended _____ £	_____ ended _____ £
Trading profits		
NTL-R income (Investment income)		
Chargeable gain		
Total profits		
Qualifying charitable donation		
Taxable total profits		

6   P Ltd had taxable total profits of £255,000 for its six-month accounting period to 31 March 2022.

Its corporation tax liability for the period will be:

£ _____

7   J Ltd had taxable total profits of £490,000 in the year ended 31 December 2021.

The corporation tax liability for the year is:

£	

8   **Decide whether the following statement is true or false.**

Financial Year 2021 (FY21) begins on 1 April 2021 and ends on 31 March 2022.

Tick ONE box.

	✓
True	
False	

8 Losses

Syllabus learning outcomes / objectives

6.1 Trading losses

Learners need to understand:

- options available to sole traders, partnerships and companies to utilise trading losses:
    - Opening years
    - Carry back
    - Current year
    - Carry forward
    - Terminal
- the best use of a trading loss for sole traders, partnerships and limited companies

Learners need to be able to:

- Calculate available loss relief using:
    - Carry back
    - Current year
    - Carry forward

Assessment context

Questions could focus on the rules for sole traders, partners or limited companies, so ensure you read the question carefully as the rules for companies are different to the rules for sole traders and partners.

Qualification context

You will not see these rules outside of this unit.

Business context

Using loss relief to generate a tax repayment is often a lifeline for struggling businesses.

Chapter overview

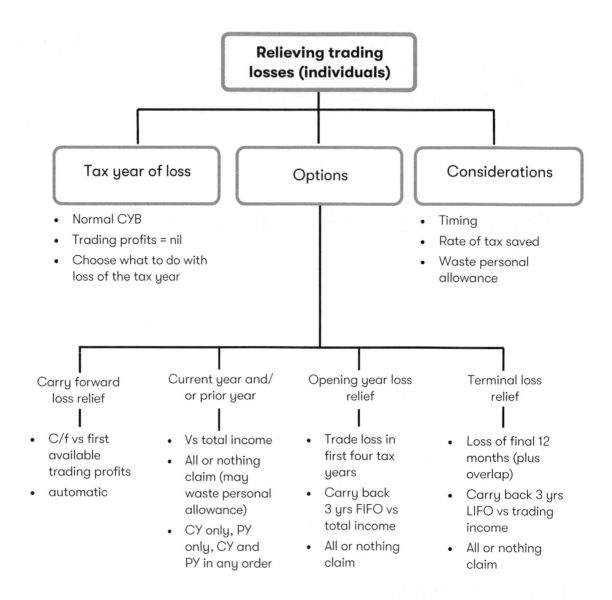

Relieving trading losses (individuals)

Tax year of loss

- Normal CYB
- Trading profits = nil
- Choose what to do with loss of the tax year

Options

Carry forward loss relief

- C/f vs first available trading profits
- automatic

Current year and/ or prior year

- Vs total income
- All or nothing claim (may waste personal allowance)
- CY only, PY only, CY and PY in any order

Opening year loss relief

- Trade loss in first four tax years
- Carry back 3 yrs FIFO vs total income
- All or nothing claim

Terminal loss relief

- Loss of final 12 months (plus overlap)
- Carry back 3 yrs LIFO vs trading income
- All or nothing claim

Considerations

- Timing
- Rate of tax saved
- Waste personal allowance

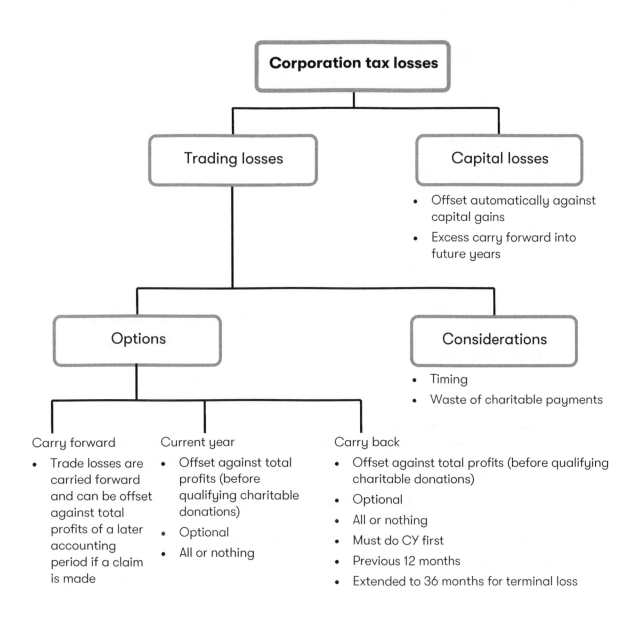

Corporation tax losses

Trading losses

Capital losses

- Offset automatically against capital gains
- Excess carry forward into future years

Options

Considerations

- Timing
- Waste of charitable payments

Carry forward

- Trade losses are carried forward and can be offset against total profits of a later accounting period if a claim is made

Current year

- Offset against total profits (before qualifying charitable donations)
- Optional
- All or nothing

Carry back

- Offset against total profits (before qualifying charitable donations)
- Optional
- All or nothing
- Must do CY first
- Previous 12 months
- Extended to 36 months for terminal loss

1 Introduction

Not all businesses make profits every year. In this chapter, we will see how a business can obtain tax relief for losses.

2 Trade losses

We have previously seen that the starting point for computing a business's trading results is to take the statement of profit or loss and adjust it for tax purposes. If this adjusted figure is negative, then there is a **trading loss**, rather than a taxable profit.

Note that the deduction of capital allowances can actually increase an adjusted loss, or even turn an adjusted profit into a trading loss.

If there is a trading loss, the **taxable trading figure in the relevant tax computation will be nil**; it is not the negative amount.

(a) If the trading loss is that of an individual (including partners), the loss will be allocated to a **tax year** using the basis period rules, and the **trading profit for that tax year will be nil**.

(b) If the trading loss is incurred by a limited company in an **accounting period**, the **trading profit for that accounting period will be nil**.

Note. Losses in a partnership are allocated to the partners in the same way as profits. Each partner will then decide on the best method of relief for their share of the loss.

 ### Illustration 1: How it works

If a trader makes a loss of £5,000 in the year to 31 December 2021, the **2021/22** taxable profits based on that period will be **£nil**.

There will be a trading loss in **2021/22** of £5,000 which can be relieved by using it to reduce the taxpayer's other taxable income.

The taxpayer has a choice as to how this loss is relieved, as follows:

* Carry forward of losses against future trading income
* Losses set against total income in the tax year of the loss (current year, CY)
* Losses set against total income of the previous tax year (prior year, PY)

There are also special loss relief rules which apply when a business is starting or ceasing to trade. These are known as opening year loss relief and terminal loss relief rules and are covered in more detail below.

Assessment focus point

There is a temporary extension to the loss carry back rules due to Covid 19, however, the AAT have confirmed that this is not examinable.

3 Trading loss relief options for individuals

3.1 Losses set against profits of the same trade

Open book reference

Trading losses

If no claim is made against total income (see below) or some of the loss is left after such a claim, then the balance must be relieved against profits of the same trade.

The loss is relieved against the first available future profits of the same trade.

Set-off is automatic and compulsory.

Any unrelieved loss may be carried forward indefinitely.

3.2 Losses set against total income

The loss is available for set-off against total income of:

- The tax year in which the loss-making accounting period ends (**year of the loss**); and/or
- The tax year immediately preceding the year of the loss.

A taxpayer does not have to deduct a loss under either method if they do not wish to do so. If they do wish to make either of these deductions, they would need to make a claim to do so.

If a claim is made, the maximum possible loss must be set off in that year (ie personal allowances cannot be saved). The taxpayer can choose which year to use the loss first eg current year and then preceding year or vice versa. Any loss left must be carried forward for use against first available profits of the same trade.

Claims to carry the loss forward must be made by 31 January, 22 months following the end of the tax year of the loss.

The pro forma below shows where the trade loss offsets appear in an income tax computation.

	Non-savings £
Trading income	X
Carry forward relief against profits of the same trade	(X)
Savings income	X
Rental income	X
Total income	X
Current year and/ or prior year relief against total income	(X)
Net income	X
Personal Allowance	(X)
Taxable income	X

Illustration 2: Loss relief

Ahmed, a sole trader, has the following taxable trading profits/(loss):

	£
Year to 30 September 2020 (and so taxed in 2020/21)	10,000
Year to 30 September 2021 (loss, trading profits = nil in 2021/22)	(49,000)
Year to 30 September 2022 (and so taxed in 2022/23)	20,000

His only other income is rental income of £15,000 a year.

The loss of £49,000 is a loss of **2021/22** and could be deducted from:

- **Total income of £25,000** (trading income of £10,000 + rental income of £15,000) in 2020/21

- **Total income** (rental income) of £15,000 in **2021/22**

If both of these claims are made, the loss remaining unrelieved of £9,000 is automatically deducted from the **taxable trading profits** of £20,000 arising in **2022/23**.

Claiming to relieve the loss against total income of the current year and the prior year is optional. If the sole trader chooses not to make a claim to deduct the loss from total income, the loss is carried forward to deduct from taxable trading profits in future years.

The disadvantage of deducting a loss from total income in the year of the loss and/or in the preceding year is that **personal allowances may be wasted**. You will recall that every individual has a personal allowance that they can set against their net income. Income of up to the personal allowance is effectively tax-free income, so there is no benefit once the net income is reduced to an amount lower than the personal allowance.

Activity 1: Income tax trading loss options

Edward runs a gift card shop and his recent actual and budgeted trading results are as follows.

Year ended	£
31.12.19	5,000
31.12.20	(8,000)
31.12.21	20,000

He also receives £12,000 rental income per annum.

Required

Show if the following statements are true or false by ticking the correct box for each.

Solution

	True ✓	False ✓
Edward may offset the loss against total income in 2019/20 and then in 2018/19.		
Edward may offset the loss against total income in 2021/22.		
Edward may offset the loss against trading income only in 2019/20.		
Edward may offset the loss against the rental income in 2020/21.		

Activity 2: Utilisation of income tax losses

Pike commenced trading on 1 October 2002, making up his accounts to 30 September 2003 and annually thereafter. His recent actual and budgeted results are as follows:

Year ended	£
30.9.20	2,000
30.9.21	(15,000)
30.9.22	8,000
30.9.23	4,000

He has received rental income as follows:

	£
2020/21	400
2021/22	1,000
2022/23	1,000
2023/24	1,000

(a) **Required**

Complete the following table showing Pike's total income for 2020/21 to 2023/24 assuming maximum and earliest claims against total income are made. Enter '0' in cells as appropriate.

Solution

	2020/21 £	2021/22 £	2022/23 £	2023/24 £
Trading income				
Loss carried forward				
Property income				
Total Income				
CY loss relief				
PY loss relief				
Net income				

(b) **Required**

Show if the following statement is true or false by ticking the correct box.

Solution

	True ✓	False ✓
Pike has used his loss in the most tax-efficient way possible		

3.3 Opening year loss relief

 Open book reference

There is a special loss relief option available if a trading loss is incurred in one of a sole trader or partnership's first four tax years.

In determining whether there is a tax loss, the opening year basis period rules are used as explained earlier in this coursebook. The use of the opening year basis period rules can mean that some profits can be taxed twice which are referred to as overlap profits. However, if a loss is incurred in an overlap period it can only be relieved once, in the earlier period. Loss relief must not be double counted.

If a loss is incurred in the first four tax years of trade it can be carried back three tax years on a first in, first out basis (FIFO) against the taxpayer's total income.

A claim for opening year loss relief applies to all three carry back years automatically provided that the loss is large enough. The taxpayer cannot choose to relieve the loss against just one or two of the tax years, or to relieve only part of the loss. This can mean that the personal allowance is wasted.

The advantage of opening year trade loss relief is that it enables losses to be carried back for three years and so gives relief earlier than the other loss reliefs.

For a 2021/22 loss, the claim must be made by 31 January 2024.

 Activity 3: Opening year loss relief

Jurgen Klose commenced trading on 1 July 2018. Results are as follows:

Year ended	£
30.6.19 Loss	(40,000)
30.6.20 Profit	24,000
30.6.21 Profit	30,000
30.6.22 Profit	36,000

Jurgen's total income prior to 2018/19 was £68,000 in each tax year and he has no other income.

(a) **Required**

Determine Jurgen's trading income assessments based on the above results, and to which year(s) Jurgen's trading loss is attributed under the opening year rules.

(b) **Required**

Explain what loss reliefs are available to Jurgen for his trading losses of 2018/19 and 2019/20. Advise Jurgen on the best use of his losses.

3.4 Terminal loss relief (TLR)

Carry forward relief is no longer available when a trade has ceased. A loss arising in the final tax year of assessment (after closing year rules are applied) may be relieved by loss relief against total income in the normal way.

However, trade loss relief against total income will often be insufficient on its own to deal with a loss incurred in the last months of trading. For this reason, there is a special relief, terminal trade loss relief, which allows a loss on cessation to be carried back for relief against taxable trading profits in previous years.

Terminal loss relief (TLR) allows relief against **trading** profits of the tax year of cessation and the three preceding years, on a last in, first out (LIFO) basis.

For a 2021/22 loss, a claim must be made within 4 years of the end of the last tax year of trading (ie by 5 April 2026).

Calculation of the terminal loss

The loss of the last period of account is increased by any overlap profits.

The loss available for relief under TLR is the actual loss in the last 12 months of trading, constructed as follows:

(a) **Final tax year**

	£
Unrelieved trading loss from 6 April to date of cessation (increased by overlap profits)	X

(b) **Penultimate tax year**

	£
Unrelieved trading loss (if any) arising from a date 12 months before cessation to 5 April	X̲
	X

If either (a) or (b) above yields a profit as opposed to a loss, the profit is regarded as zero for this purpose.

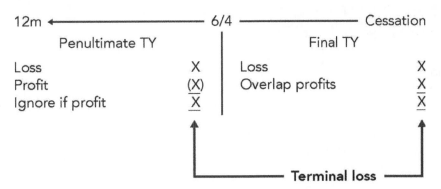

Activity 4: Terminal loss relief

Frieda commenced trading on 1 May 2012 making up accounts to 30 September each year. She ceased trading on 30 June 2021. The most recent results were:

Year ended	£
30.9.17	10,000
30.9.18	8,000
30.9.19	10,000
30.9.20	4,000
P/e 30.6.21	(27,000)

Frieda had overlap profits from commencement of trade of £3,000.

Required

(a) What is Frieda's maximum claim for terminal loss relief?

Solution

(a)	Unrelieved trading loss from 6 April to date of cessation (increased by overlap profits)		
(b)	Unrelieved trading loss (if any) arising from a date 12 months before cessation to 5 April		
	Terminal loss claim		

(b) Identify how much terminal loss relief can be utilised in the tax years 2017/18 and 2018/19

	£
2017/18	
2018/19	

4 Corporation tax losses

Open book reference

Trading losses

As we mentioned above, if the trading loss is incurred by a limited company in an **accounting period**, the trading profit for that accounting period will be nil.

You need to be aware of the following four methods by which a company may obtain relief for its trading losses:

- Carry forward
- Set off against current total profits (optional)
- Carry back against earlier profits (optional)
- Terminal loss relief (optional)

Assessment focus point

As for unincorporated businesses, there is a temporary extension to the loss carry back rules for companies due to Covid 19. However, the AAT has confirmed that this is not examinable.

You will also need to be aware of the impact that losses can have on qualifying charitable donations. This is included within the examples and tasks below.

We will look at each of the four methods of obtaining loss relief. These are similar to the rules for individuals but there are some significant differences. It is also important to note that companies do not have special opening year loss relief rules. The trading losses section of your reference data will be invaluable in helping you to remember the detail of each of the loss relief options and to help you remember the differences between how the reliefs work for unincorporated vs incorporated businesses.

4.1 Carry forward losses

4.1.1 Carry forward of trading losses

Trading losses are carried forward in a flexible manner. Unused trading losses are carried forward and a claim can be made to offset some or all of the loss against total profits of future accounting periods. There is no requirement to allocate the loss against the first available profits and the claim specifies the amount of loss to be offset.

Illustration 3: Carry forward loss relief

P Ltd has the following results for the three years to 31 March 2022:

	Year ended 31 March		
	2020 £	2021 £	2022 £
Trading profit/(loss)	(8,000)	3,000	6,000
NTL-R income	0	4,000	2,000

Carry forward loss relief would be relieved as follows, assuming that the company wants to use the carried forward losses as soon as possible and a claim is made:

	Year ended 31 March		
	2020 £	2021 £	2022 £
Trading profit	0	3,000	6,000
NTL-R income	–	4,000	2,000
Total profits	0	7,000	8,000
Less carry forward loss relief	–	(7,000)	(1,000)
Taxable total profits	0	0	7,000

Activity 5: Carry forward loss relief

Strontium Ltd has the following actual and budgeted results for the three years to 31 March 2022.

	Year ended 31 March		
	2020 £	2021 £	2022 £
Trading profit/(loss)	(20,000)	5,000	6,000
Property income	–	2,000	2,000

Required

Assuming Strontium Ltd carries the loss forward and claims to utilise as much loss as possible, the loss carried forward at 31 March 2022 is:

£	

4.2 Relief against total profits

4.2.1 Current year loss relief

Carrying the loss forward has a cash flow disadvantage for the company due to it only reducing future tax bills. The company may therefore prefer to consider using the loss to make a current year loss claim.

The trade loss may be relieved against total profits (including gains) before qualifying charitable donations in the period in which the loss arose.

The loss relief claim is 'all or nothing', so any qualifying charitable donations that become unrelieved are lost.

4.2.2 Carry back loss relief

Trading losses can be carried back against total profits (including gains) before qualifying charitable donations of the preceding 12 months.

The carry back claim may only be made **after** a current year claim (note that this is different to the rules for individuals).

This claim is also 'all or nothing' and any qualifying charitable donations which become unrelieved are lost.

Any loss remaining unrelieved after current period and **carry back loss relief** claims **must be carried forward** and offset according to the rules explained above.

A company is permitted to carry back the loss for 12 months. If the loss is carried back to an accounting period that partly falls outside the permitted carry back period, then the total income before qualifying charitable donations of this period must be time apportioned to determine how much of the profits may be relieved.

Activity 6: Current year and carry back relief

Kay Ltd has the following actual and budgeted results.

	Year ended 31 March		
	2020 £	2021 £	2022 £
Trading income	20,000	10,000	(100,000)
Capital gains	50,000	50,000	50,000

Required

Show if the following statements are true or false by ticking the correct box for each.

Solution

	True ✓	False ✓
Kay Ltd may claim to offset £60,000 of the loss against total profits in y/e 31.3.21.		
If Kay Ltd makes the maximum permissible claims, it will have £90,000 loss to carry forward at 31.3.22.		
Kay Ltd may claim to offset the loss against total profits in y/e 31.3.21 and then against total profits in y/e 31.3.22.		
Kay Ltd may claim to offset the loss against total profits in y/e 31.3.22 and carry the remaining loss forward to the y/e 31.3.23.		

Activity 7: Comprehensive example

Janet plc has the following actual and budgeted results.

	Y/e 30.9.19 £	P/e 31.3.20 £	Y/e 31.3.21 £	Y/e 31.3.22 £
Trading income	20,000	30,000	(155,000)	15,000
NTL-R income	10,000	10,000	10,000	10,000
Qualifying charitable payments	(5,000)	(5,000)	(5,000)	(5,000)

Required

Complete the following table, assuming the company will make the maximum permissible claims. Use the picklist for narrative entries. Insert '0' as appropriate.

Show all qualifying charitable donations, even if the company does not actually claim relief for them.

Solution

	Y/e 30.9.19 £	P/e 31.3.20 £	Y/e 31.3.21 £	Y/e 31.3.22 £
Trading profits	20,000	30,000	0	15,000
NTL-R income	10,000	10,000	10,000	10,000
Total profits				
▼				
▼				
▼				
▼				
Taxable total profits				

Picklist:

Current year relief
Losses carried forward
Prior year relief
Qualifying charitable donations

4.3 Terminal loss relief

When a company ceases trading, carry forward relief will no longer be available. As is the case for unincorporated businesses, an additional loss relief claim is available.

For a company, the carry back period is extended to 36 months for losses incurred in the 12 months prior to the cessation of trading. Losses can be carried back against total profits (before QCDs) of the preceding 36 months on a last in, first out (LIFO) basis, ie most recent period first.

As with the basic carry back relief, QCDs may be unrelieved.

Illustration 4: Terminal loss relief

Khiva Ltd ceased trading on 31 March 2022. It had the following results for its last five accounting periods:

	Y/e 31.3.18 £	Y/e 31.3.19 £	Y/e 31.3.20 £	Y/e 31.3.21 £	Y/e 31.3.22 £
Trading profit (loss)	3,000	9,000	16,000	12,000	(47,800)
NTL-R income	500	-	600	600	600
Chargeable gains	1,000	-	-	-	5,000
Qualifying charitable payments	(300)	-	(300)	(300)	-

Assuming that Khiva Ltd makes maximum possible claims to offset its trading loss it's TTP would be as follows:

Solution

	Y/e 31.3.18 £	Y/e 31.3.19 £	Y/e 31.3.20 £	Y/e 31.3.21 £	Y/e 31.3.22 £
Trading profits	3,000	9,000	16,000	12,000	-
NTL-R income	500	-	600	600	600
Chargeable gains	1,000	-	-	-	5,000
Total profits	4,500	9,000	16,600	12,600	5,600
Current year relief					(5,600)
Terminal loss relief		(9,000)	(16,600)	(12,600)	
Qualifying charitable donations	(300)		wasted	wasted	
Taxable total profits	4,200	0	0	0	0

Loss memorandum	£
Y/e 31.3.22	47,800
Current year claim	(5,600)
Terminal loss relief claim	
C/b to Y/e 31.3.21	(12,600)
C/b to Y/e 31.3.20	(16,600)
C/b to Y/e 31.3.19	(9,000)
Unrelieved trade loss	4,000

BPP
LEARNING
MEDIA

5 Capital losses for companies

5.1 Capital losses

These can only be set against capital gains. The order of relief here is:

1   First, against current period (company)/tax year (unincorporated business) gains

2   Second, any surplus losses are relieved against gains in future accounting periods/tax years

Note. Capital losses cannot be carried back to preceding years.

5.1.1 Companies

We have seen that capital gains form part of a company's taxable total profits (TTP) chargeable to corporation tax.

Any capital losses would be offset automatically against gains before considering how to allocate the trading loss.

5.1.2 Individuals

> ### Assessment focus point
>
> The AAT have confirmed that capital losses for individuals are not within the scope of the business tax syllabus.

6 Choosing loss relief

6.1 Individuals

As we have seen above, several alternative loss reliefs may be available for an individual, including:

- Carry forward of losses
- Losses set against total income in the tax year of the loss
- Losses set against total income of the previous tax year
- Opening year loss relief if the individual is in the first four tax years of their trade
- Terminal loss relief if the individual is ceasing to trade

In making a choice, consider:

(a) **The rate at which relief will be obtained.**

We saw in Chapter 1 that individuals can pay income tax at the starting rate, the basic rate, the higher rate and the additional rate.

The most beneficial method is to try to offset losses against any income being taxed at the highest rate.

(b) **How quickly relief will be obtained.** Relief is obtained earlier, by carrying back the loss. It is therefore usually beneficial to use opening year or terminal loss relief claims if they are available, or to set losses against income of the previous year and current year rather than to wait to carry forward loss relief.

(c) **The extent to which personal allowances might be wasted.**

6.2 Partnerships

Remember that for tax purposes a partnership is simply a group of sole traders. So, once any trade loss has been shared between the partners, each partner can use their share of the trade loss using whichever sole trade rules they would like. Each partner makes their own decision about what claims to make based on their own circumstances. If there is a partner joining/ leaving the partnership, then the special opening year/ terminal loss relief claims are available.

6.3 Companies

We have also seen that there are several alternative loss reliefs available for a company, including:

- Carry forward of losses
- Losses set against current period total profits
- Losses set against total profits from earlier years
- Terminal loss relief

In making a choice consider:

(a) **How quickly relief will be obtained:** loss relief against total profits using a current year and carry back claim (or indeed a terminal loss claim if available) is quicker than carry forward loss relief.

(b) **The extent to which relief for qualifying charitable donations might be wasted.**

Assessment focus point

Candidates often struggle with loss relief questions, so make sure you go over this chapter thoroughly before attempting further questions to ensure you are well prepared for the assessment. It is not enough just to read the questions and answers - you need to prepare the computations yourself to fully understand them.

- For an individual, a trading loss can be:

  - Carried forward to be deducted from the first available profits of the same trade

  - Deducted from total income in the tax year of the loss and/or in the preceding tax year

  - Carried back three years on a FIFO basis against total income if it's a loss incurred in the first four tax years

  - Carried back three years on a LIFO basis against trade profits for a terminal loss

- For a company, a trading loss can be:

  - Carried forward and set against future total profits if a claim is made

  - Deducted from total profits (before QCDs) in the accounting period of the loss

  - Deducted from total profits (before QCDs) in the 12 months preceding the period of the loss (after a current period offset)

  - Carried back 36 months on a LIFO basis against total profits if a terminal loss

- An individual can choose the order in which to claim for current year loss relief and prior year loss relief.

- For a company, a claim for current year loss relief must be made before a loss is carried back.

- Company capital losses can be set against current year gains and then carried forward to set against gains in the future.

- When selecting a loss relief, consider the rate at which relief is obtained, the timing of relief, and the effect on personal allowances or QCDs.

Keywords

- **Carry back loss relief:** Allows a company to set a trading loss against total profits (before deducting qualifying charitable donations) in the 12 months preceding the period of the loss (after it has made a claim against current year total profits first); or an individual to set a trading loss against total income in the tax year prior to the tax year of the loss (no need to make a current year claim first)

- **Carry forward loss relief:** Allows an individual to set a trading loss against the first available profits from the same trade in the future. For a company, the trade loss is carried forward and can be offset with a claim against future period's total profits

- **Current year loss relief:** Allows a company to set a trading loss against total profits before deducting qualifying charitable donations in the loss-making accounting period; and an individual to set a trading loss against total income in the tax year of the loss

- **Trading losses:** These arise when the accounting profit is adjusted for tax purposes, and this adjusted figure is negative

- **Opening years loss relief:** Allows a sole trader or partner to carry back a loss incurred in the first four years of trading against total income in the previous 3 tax years (FIFO)

- **Terminal loss relief:** Allows a sole trader/partner or company to carry back a loss incurred in the final 12 months of trade against income in the previous 3 years (LIFO). Set against trading profits only in the case of sole traders and partners, and against total profits (before QCDs) in the case of a company

Test your learning

1   Harold (a sole trader), who has been in business for many years, makes a trading loss of £20,000 in the year ended 31 January 2022.

In which year(s) may the loss be relieved against total income, assuming relief is claimed as soon as possible? Tick ONE box.

	✓
2021/22 only	
2022/23 and/or 2021/22	
2020/21 only	
2021/22 and/or 2020/21	

2   **Identify whether the following statement is true or false.**

For an individual, trading losses can only be carried forward for deduction in the six succeeding tax years.

	✓
True	
False	

3   **Where trade losses are carried forward by an individual, against what sort of income may they be relieved? Tick ONE box.**

	✓
Against non-savings income	
Against total income	
Against trading income arising in the same trade	
Against trading income arising in all trades carried on by the taxpayer	

4   Mallory (a sole trader), who has traded for many years, has the following recent tax-adjusted results:

Year ended 30 April 2020	Profit	£10,000
Year ended 30 April 2021	Loss	£(40,000)
Year ended 30 April 2022	Profit	£25,000

Mallory has other income of £9,000 each year.

Explain how the loss in the year to 30 April 2021 can be relieved.

5   **Martin**

Martin commenced in self-employment on 1 July 2020, preparing accounts to 5 April. His results for the first two periods of trading were as follows:

	£
Nine-month period ended 5 April 2021 – Trading loss	(24,200)
Year ended 5 April 2022 – Trading profit	9,800

For the tax years 2016/17 to 2018/19 Martin had the following income from employment:

	£
2016/17	44,100
2017/18	21,000
2018/19	57,000

Martin did not have any income during the period 6 April 2019 to 30 June 2020.

(a)   Allocate the trade loss to tax years.
(b)   Identify the loss relief claims that are available to Martin
(c)   Explain which of the available claims would be the most beneficial.

6   **Sylvie**

Sylvie has been in self-employment since 2009 but ceased trading on 31 December 2021. She has always prepared accounts to 31 December. Her results for the final five years of trading were as follows:

		£
Year ended 31 December 2017	– Trading profit	21,000
Year ended 31 December 2018	– Trading profit	13,800
Year ended 31 December 2019	– Trading profit	18,000
Year ended 31 December 2020	– Trading profit	3,500
Year ended 31 December 2021	– Trading loss	(24,300)

For each of the tax years 2017/18 to 2021/22 Sylvie has property business profits of £12,800.

Sylvie has unused overlap profits brought forward of £3,400.

(a)   Calculate Sylvie's trade loss for her final tax year
(b)   Identify the loss relief claims that are available to Sylvie; and
(c)   Explain which of the available claims would be the most beneficial

7   (a)   CR Ltd has the following results for the two years to 31 March 2022:

	Year ended 31 March	
	2021 £	2022 £
Trading profit (loss)	170,000	(320,000)
Interest	5,000	60,000
Chargeable gain (loss)	(20,000)	12,000
Qualifying charitable donation	5,000	5,000

Calculate the amount of trading loss remaining to be carried forward at 1 April 2023 assuming that all possible earlier loss relief claims against total profits are made.

£ [   ]

(b)   Calculate the amount of capital loss remaining to be carried forward at 1 April 2023.

£ [   ]

8   JB Ltd had the following results in the three accounting periods to 31 March 2022:

	Year ended 30 September 2020 £	Six months to 31 March 2021 £	Year ended 31 March 2022 £
Trading profit/(loss)	4,000	6,000	(10,000)
Qualifying charitable donation	1,000	3,000	1,500

Identify the amount, if any, of the trading loss incurred in the year ended 31 March 2022 that may be relieved against total profits in the year ended 30 September 2020. Tick ONE box.

	✓
£Nil	
£2,000	
£4,000	
£3,000	

9   State whether the following statements are true or false. Tick true or false for EACH row.

	True	False
A sole trader's trade loss will be carried forward to offset against the first available trade profits of the same trade if no other claim is made.		
A company's trade loss will be carried forward to offset against the first available trade profits of the same trade.		
A company's trade loss is carried forward and can be offset against total profits of future accounting periods.		
A sole trader's trade loss must be offset against current year's total income before being offset against the total income of the prior year.		

10   State whether the following statements are true or false. Tick true or false for EACH row.

	True	False
A sole trader incurring a trade loss in their second tax year can carry back their trade loss three tax years on a LIFO basis against total income		
A company can carry back a trade loss made in its first accounting period three years on a FIFO basis against its total profits		
Terminal loss relief is only available to unincorporated businesses		
For an unincorporated business, terminal loss relief is offset against trade profits only whereas for an incorporated business terminal loss relief is against total profits		

Self-assessment for individuals

9

Syllabus learning outcomes / objectives

4.1 The administrative requirements of UK tax law

Learners need to understand:

- tax return deadlines for sole traders and partnerships
- tax payment dates for sole traders and partners
- time limits for notifying chargeability to tax
- The enquiry window
- the time period within which amendments to a tax return can be made
- what records need to be maintained and for what time period

4.2 Penalties and interest for non-compliance

Learners need to understand:

- penalties for:
  - Late filing
  - Late payment
  - Failing to notify chargeability
  - Errors in tax returns
  - Not providing records in an enquiry
  - Not retaining records

Learners need to be able to:

- Calculate penalties and interest for non-compliance

Assessment context

There are a lot of very specific rules, dates and percentages in this chapter that could be tested in the assessment. Make sure you learn the detail and know when you can use the reference material.

Qualification context

You will not see the information in this chapter outside of this unit unless you are also studying *Personal Tax*.

Business context

It is vital for a tax adviser to ensure that their client's tax affairs are dealt with in a timely fashion and all information is properly submitted to HMRC. Serious financial penalties will arise if these deadlines are missed.

Chapter overview

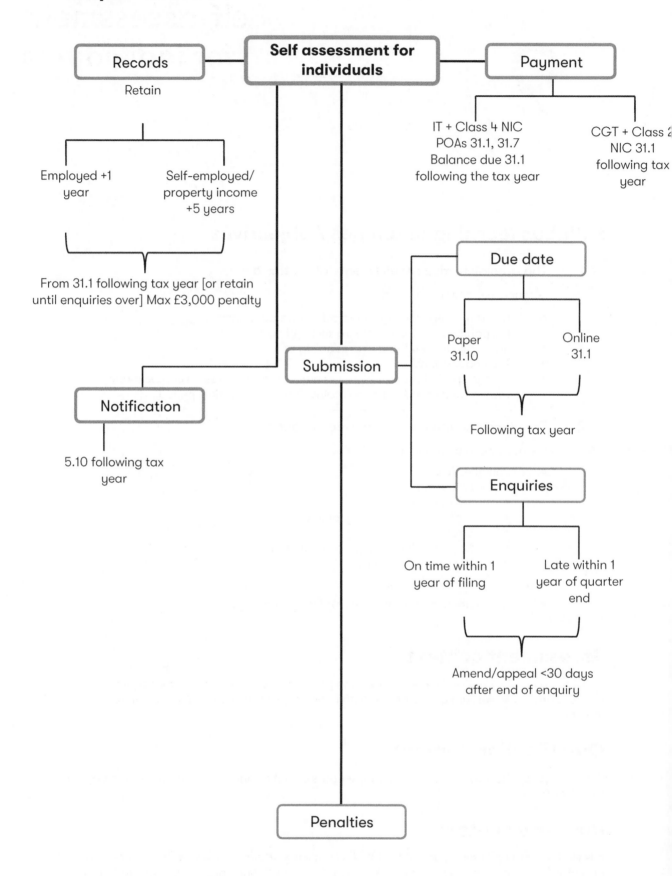

See next page

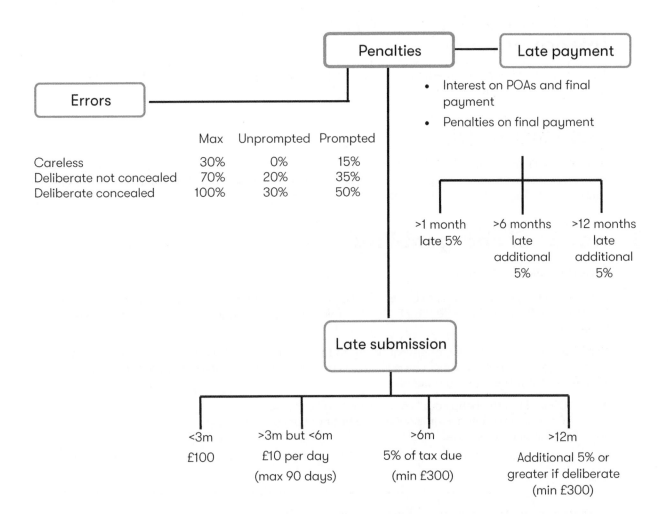

Penalties

Late payment

- Interest on POAs and final payment
- Penalties on final payment

	Max	Unprompted	Prompted
Careless	30%	0%	15%
Deliberate not concealed	70%	20%	35%
Deliberate concealed	100%	30%	50%

Errors

>1 month late 5%

>6 months late additional 5%

>12 months late additional 5%

Late submission

<3m
£100

>3m but <6m
£10 per day
(max 90 days)

>6m
5% of tax due
(min £300)

>12m
Additional 5% or greater if deliberate
(min £300)

1 Introduction

There are a number of strict deadlines that a taxpayer will need to meet. In this chapter, we look at those deadlines and the penalties that occur if those deadlines are not met.

2 The tax return

An individual's tax return comprises a tax form, together with supplementary pages for particular sources of income and capital gains if required. **We will look at self-assessment of income tax in this chapter.** Administration for companies is covered in the next chapter.

3 Notice of chargeability

Payment and administration

Open book reference

If you have income that needs to be reported on a self-assessment tax return, you have to notify HM Revenue & Customs (HMRC) by 5 October following the tax year in which the income was received.

Penalties for late notification of chargeability to tax are behaviour based and are calculated as a percentage of the potential lost revenue. This is the amount of tax outstanding as a result of the failure to notify. The maximum penalty is:

- 100% where the behaviour is deliberate and concealed
- 70% where the behaviour is deliberate but not concealed; and
- 30% in any other case.

Assessment focus point / Exam success skills

The AAT have confirmed that you should be aware that there are penalties for failing to notify chargeability to tax but that you will not be asked to calculate any amount of penalty. Details of these penalties is not given in the reference material available to you in your assessment.

---

4 Timetable for 2021/22

Payment and administration

Open book reference

31/10/2022	31/1/2023
Filing due date for paper returns	**Filing due date** for online returns
HMRC will calculate tax	Automatic electronic calculation of tax

Where a notice to make a return is issued after 31 July following the tax year, a period of three months is allowed for the filing of a paper return.

Where a notice to make a return is issued after 31 October following the tax year, a period of three months is allowed for the online filing of that return.

An individual may ask HMRC to do the calculation of tax due if a paper return is filed. Where an online return is filed, the tax computation is made automatically.

Illustration 1: Filing income tax returns

Advise the following clients of the latest filing date for their personal tax return for 2021/22 if notice to file the return is received on the following dates, and the return is:

(a)   Paper
(b)   Online

Notice to file tax return issued by HMRC:

Norma   on 6 April 2022
Melanie   on 10 August 2022
Olga   on 12 December 2022

The latest filing dates are:

	Paper	Online
Norma	31 October 2022	31 January 2023
Melanie	9 November 2022	31 January 2023
Olga	11 March 2023	11 March 2023

5 Retention of records

Open book reference

Payment and dministration

All records must be retained until the later of:

- One year following 31 January after the end of the tax year (eg 31 January 2024 for tax year 2021/22)

- Five years following 31 January after the end of the tax year (eg 31 January 2028 for tax year 2021/22) for taxpayers who are self-employed or have property income. Note. All records must be retained for this time, not just property and self-employment records.

- Time at which enquiries can no longer be opened

- Time at which enquiries are concluded

The maximum penalty for failure to keep records is £3,000.

6 Penalties for errors

Open book reference

If a taxpayer makes an error in their tax return, they can amend it within 12 months of the filing date. They can also make a claim for overpayment relief within four years of the end of the tax year.

A penalty may be imposed where a taxpayer makes an inaccurate return if they have:

(a) **Been careless** because they have not taken reasonable care in making the return or they discover the error later but do not take reasonable steps to inform HMRC

(b) **Made a deliberate error** but do not make arrangements to conceal it

(c) **Made a deliberate error and has attempted to conceal it**, eg by submitting false evidence in support of an inaccurate figure

If there is more than one error, HMRC may charge more than one penalty.

Penalties may be reduced if the errors are brought to HMRC's attention by the taxpayer.

This could be **unprompted**, where the taxpayer admits the error before HMRC has any knowledge of irregularity, or **prompted**, when the taxpayer suspects the error has been, or is about to be, discovered.

KEY TERM

> **Potential lost revenue (PLR)** is the tax that would have been lost if the error had gone undetected.

Open book reference

Penalties, which are given in the penalties for incorrect returns section of the reference data provided in your assessment, are as follows:

Type of error	Maximum penalty	Minimum penalty with unprompted disclosure	Minimum penalty with prompted disclosure
Genuine mistake	No penalty	No penalty	No penalty
Careless	30%	0%	15%
Deliberate but not concealed	70%	20%	35%
Deliberate and concealed	100%	30%	50%

The scale of the reduction will vary depending upon the help the taxpayer has given HMRC in respect of:

- Advising about the error, making full disclosure, and explaining how it was made
- Assisting HMRC to enable it to quantify the error
- Allowing access to records

A penalty for a careless error may be suspended by HMRC to allow the taxpayer to take action to ensure that the error does not occur again (eg where the error has arisen from failure to keep proper records).

HMRC will impose conditions which the taxpayer has to satisfy, eg establishing proper record-keeping systems.

The penalty will be cancelled if the conditions imposed by HMRC are complied with by the taxpayer within a period of up to two years.

A taxpayer may appeal against:

- The penalty being charged
- The amount of the penalty
- A decision by HMRC not to suspend a penalty
- Conditions set by HMRC in relation to the suspension of a penalty

Activity 1: Penalties

Kelly deliberately omitted an invoice from her trading income in her 2020/21 tax return but did not destroy the evidence. She later disclosed this error, before she had reason to believe HMRC might investigate the matter.

Required

Complete the following sentence:

Kelly's penalty can be reduced from [   ] % of the potential lost revenue (for a

deliberate, but not concealed error) to [   ] %,
with the unprompted disclosure of her error.

7 Penalties for late filing

Open book reference

The **filling due date** for a tax return is 31 October or 31 January in the following tax year, depending on whether paper or online returns are made. The penalties for filing a late tax return are:

Return outstanding	Penalty
⟶ 3 months	£100
3 ⟶ 6 months	Daily penalty of £10 per day (max 90 days)
6 ⟶ 12 months*	5% of the tax due (min £300)
12 months* ⟶	(a) 5% of the tax due if not deliberate (b) 70% of the tax due where withholding of information is deliberate and not concealed (c) 100% of the tax due where withholding of information is deliberate and concealed

*These tax-based penalties are subject to a minimum of £300

Penalties may be reduced for prompted and unprompted disclosures and cooperation with investigation.

These penalties are given in the payment and administration section of the reference material you will have access to in your assessment.

8 Due dates for 2021/22 self-assessed tax

8.1 Income tax

Open book reference

Payment and administration

A taxpayer must usually make **three payments of tax:**

Date	Payment
31 January in the tax year	First payment on account
31 July after the tax year	Second payment on account
31 January after the tax year	Final payment to settle any remaining liability

Each **payment on account (POA)** is equal to 50% of the tax payable under self-assessment (ie not deducted at source) for the previous year.

If HMRC is late in requesting a tax return, then the final payment date is extended to three months following the 'notice to deliver' date (provided the taxpayer has notified chargeability on time).

POAs may be reduced if the taxpayer expects this year's liability to be lower than last year's. Interest will be charged if POAs are reduced and the final tax is greater than expected.

POAs are not required if the income tax payable for the previous year is less than £1,000 or if more than 80% of last year's liability was deducted at source.

This data is provided to you in your assessment in the payment and administration section of your reference material.

Illustration 2: Payments on account

Jeremy's tax liability for 2020/21 totalled £12,000. None of the tax was deducted at source.

Each payment on account for 2021/22 would therefore be £6,000 (50% × £12,000)

8.2 Capital gains tax

Open book reference

Payment and administration

Capital gains tax is due on 31 January following the tax year. Capital gains tax is never paid by instalments (payments on account).

8.3 National insurance

Open book reference

Payment and administration

Class 4 National Insurance contributions (NICs) are paid along with the income tax due. Instalments and balancing payments are calculated in the same way.

Class 2 NICs are paid on 31 January following the tax year.

Activity 2: Payments on account and balancing payments

Vorus's tax for 2020/21 was as follows:

	£
Income tax liability	7,000
PAYE (tax deducted at source from employment income)	4,000
Capital gains tax	5,000

His tax for 2021/22 is as follows:

	£
Income tax liability	8,000
PAYE (tax deducted at source from employment income)	2,500
Capital gains tax	1,000

Required

How is his tax liability for 2021/22 settled?

Solution

	£

9 Penalties for late payment

Open book reference

Payment and administration

Penalties for late payment of tax will be imposed in respect of balancing payments of income tax.

A penalty is chargeable where tax is paid after the penalty date. **The penalty date is 30 days after the due date for tax.** Therefore, no penalty arises if the tax is paid within 30 days of the due date.

Paid	Penalty
⟶ 30 days	0%
30 days – 6 months	5% of unpaid tax at that date
6 months – 12 months	Further 5% of unpaid tax at that date (10%)
12 months ⟶	Further 5% of unpaid tax at that date (15%)

Penalties for late payment of tax **apply to balancing payments** of income tax only. They **do not apply to late payments on account**. The late payment penalties are set out for you in the payment and administration section of your reference data provided in your assessment.

10 Interest

Open book reference

Payment and administration

Interest is chargeable on **late payments on account and late balancing payments**. In both cases, interest runs from the **due date until the day before the actual date of payment**.

- POAs:
    - From 31 January during tax year
    - From 31 July following end of tax year

- Final payment:
    - From 31 January following end of tax year

If a taxpayer claims to reduce their payments on account and there is still a final payment to be made, interest is normally charged on the payments on account as if each of those payments had been the lower of:

(a) The reduced amount, plus 50% of the final income tax payable
(b) The amount which would have been payable had no claim for reduction been made

Assessment focus point

The AAT have stated that the principles of interest will be examinable but that the calculation of interest will not be required.

11 Repayment of tax and repayment interest

Overpaid tax is repaid unless a greater payment of tax is due in the following 30 days, in which case it is set off against that payment.

Repayment Interest is paid on overpayments of:

- Payments on account
- Final payments of tax
- Penalties

Interest runs from the later of the due date and the actual date of payment until the day before repayment is made.

12 Agent vs Principal

Where a taxpayer uses an agent, such as an accountant or tax adviser, to complete the tax return, it is the taxpayer's responsibility to ensure that the information disclosed in that return is correct. The taxpayer is referred to as the 'principal'.

The agent responsible for preparing the tax return must ensure confidentiality at all times. Only in limited circumstances may the agent disclose client information to third parties without the client's permission, for example if money laundering is suspected.

13 Compliance checks and enquiries

Payment and ministration

Open book reference

Usually, under self-assessment, HMRC will accept taxpayers' figures.

However, HMRC has the power to conduct a compliance check.

Some returns are selected for a compliance check at random, others for a particular reason – for example, if HMRC believes that there has been an underpayment of tax due to the taxpayer's failure to comply with tax legislation.

There are two types of compliance check:

- Pre-return check using information powers
- Enquiries into submitted returns

Examples of when a pre-return check may be carried out in practice include:

- To assist with clearances or ruling requests
- Where a previous check has identified poor record keeping
- To check that computer systems will produce the information needed to support a return
- To find out about planning or avoidance schemes
- Where fraud is suspected

HMRC must give notice of intention to conduct an enquiry not later than 12 months after submission of the return.

HMRC has only one opportunity to open a formal enquiry and a tax return cannot be subject to a formal enquiry more than once.

In the course of the enquiries, the taxpayer may be required to produce documents, accounts or other information. There is a penalty of £300 for failing to produce these documents, with an additional £60 penalty charged each day the failure continues. The taxpayer can appeal to the Tax Tribunal against this.

HMRC must issue a closure notice when the enquiries are complete, state the conclusions and amend the self-assessment accordingly. If the taxpayer is not satisfied with the amendment, they may, within 30 days, appeal to the Tax Tribunal.

If the enquiry is complex or where there is avoidance or a large amount of tax at risk, then HMRC may issue a partial closure notice. This is issued ahead of a final closure notice and allows the taxpayer certainty on discrete matters without having to wait for the full enquiry to be resolved.

Assessment focus point

Please refer to the reference material at the end of this Course Book to see which elements of this chapter will be available to you as a pop-up window in the live assessment.

- Taxpayers must notify HMRC by 5 October following the end of the tax year if a tax return is needed.

- A tax return must be filed by 31 January following a tax year, provided it is filed online. Paper returns must be filed by 31 October following the tax year.

- Taxpayers must keep records until the later of:

  (a) One year after 31 January following the tax year

  (b) Five years after 31 January following the tax year if in business or with property income

- A taxpayer can amend a tax return within 12 months of filing date or make a claim for overpayment relief within 4 years of the end of the tax year.

- A penalty may be imposed if the taxpayer makes an error in his tax return based on the potential lost revenue as a result of the error.

- A fixed penalty of £100 applies if a return is filed late; followed by a potential daily penalty of £10 if the return is filed between three and six months late.

- A tax-geared penalty will also apply if a return is filed more than 6 months late, with a further penalty if this is over 12 months late.

- Payments on account of income tax are required on 31 January in the tax year and on 31 July following the tax year.

- Balancing payments of income tax are due on 31 January following the tax year.

- Late payment penalties apply to balancing payments of income tax. They do not apply to late payments on account.

- Interest is chargeable on late payment of both payments on account and balancing payments.

- HMRC can enquire into a return within one year of receipt of the return. There is a penalty of £300 for failing to produce documents requested in an enquiry which increases by £60 per day that the failure continues.

- An accountant or tax adviser may act as the 'agent' for a client by preparing their tax return, but it remains the responsibility of the client, 'principal', to ensure the accuracy of the information submitted.

Keywords

- **Filing due date:** The date by which a return must be filed
- **Interest:** Charged on late payments on account and on late balancing payments
- **Payment on account:** An amount paid on account of income tax
- **Repayment interest:** Payable by HMRC on overpaid payments on account, balancing payments and penalties

Test your learning

1 The due filing date for an income tax return for 2021/22, assuming the taxpayer will submit the return online, is (insert date as XX/XX/XX):

[   ]

2 Select the correct answers to the four questions from the four picklists provided.

The 2021/22 payments on account will be calculated as

| 1 | ← |

of the income tax payable for

| 2 | ← |

and will be due on

| 3 | ← |

and

| 4 | ← |

Picklist 1:	Picklist 2:	Picklist 3:	Picklist 4:
25%	2019/20	31 January 2021	31 July 2022
50%	2020/21	1 January 2022	31 December 2022
100%	2021/22	31 January 2022	31 January 2023

3 A notice requiring a tax return for 2021/22 is issued in April 2022 and the return is filed online in May 2023. All income tax was paid in May 2023. No payments on account were due.

Explain what charges will be made on the taxpayer.

4 Susie filed her 2020/21 tax return online on 28 January 2022.

By what date must HMRC give notice that it is going to enquire into the return?

Tick ONE box.

	✓
31 January 2023	
31 March 2023	
6 April 2023	
28 January 2023	

5 Jamie paid income tax of £12,000 for 2020/21. In 2021/22, his tax payable was £16,000.

Jamie's 2021/22 payments on account will each be

| £ | |

and will be due on (insert date as XX/XX/XX)

[   ]

and

[   ]

Jamie's balancing payment will be

£	

and will be due on (insert date as XX/XX/XX)

6   Tim should have made two payments on account of his 2021/22 income tax payable of £5,000 each. He actually made both of these payments on 31 August 2022.

State the amount of any penalties for late payment.

£	

7   (a)   **By what date must a taxpayer generally submit a tax return for 2021/22 if it is filed as a paper return?**

	✓
30 September 2022	
31 October 2022	
31 December 2022	
31 January 2023	

        (b)   **On which dates are payment on accounts due for 2021/22?**

	✓
31 January 2023 and 31 July 2023	
31 January 2022 and 31 July 2022	
31 October 2022 and 31 January 2023	
31 July 2022 and 31 January 2023	

8   Lola accidentally fails to include an invoice of £17,000 on her 2021/22 tax return. She pays basic rate tax at 20%, and has not yet disclosed this error.

Identify the maximum penalty that could be imposed on her. Tick ONE box.

	✓
£5,100	
£3,400	
£1,020	
£2,380	

Self-assessment for companies

Syllabus learning outcomes / objectives

4.1   The administrative requirements of UK tax law

Learners need to understand:

- tax return filing deadlines for companies
- tax payment dates for companies
- time limits for notifying chargeability to tax
- the enquiry window
- the time period within which amendments to a tax return can be made
- what records need to be maintained and for what time period

4.2   Penalties and interest for non-compliance

Learners need to understand:

- penalties for

  - Late filing
  - Late payment
  - Failing to notify chargeability
  - Errors in tax returns
  - Not providing records in an enquiry
  - Not retaining records

Learners need to be able to:

- Calculate penalties and interest for non-compliance

Assessment context

The assessment may require you to explain various aspects of the taxation rules, specifically including payments, penalties, filing dates and payment dates.

Qualification context

You will not see these rules outside of this unit.

Business context

Serious financial consequences will arise if a company pays tax late or fails to file a tax return on time.

Chapter overview

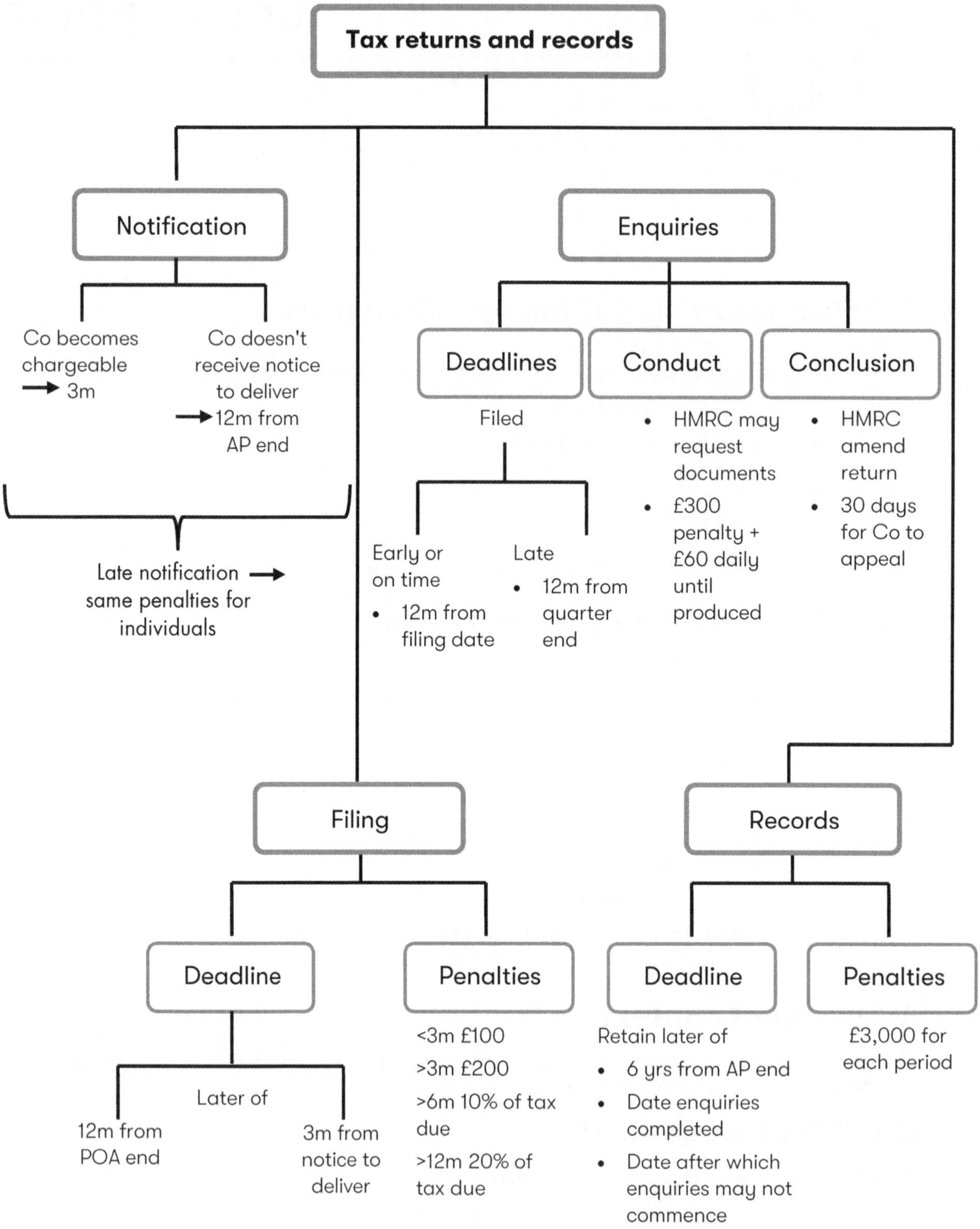

Tax returns and records
Notification
Co becomes chargeable → 3m
Co doesn't receive notice to deliver → 12m from AP end
Late notification → same penalties for individuals
Enquiries
Deadlines
Filed
Early or on time
• 12m from filing date
Late
• 12m from quarter end
Conduct
• HMRC may request documents
• £300 penalty + £60 daily until produced
Conclusion
• HMRC amend return
• 30 days for Co to appeal
Filing
Deadline
Later of
12m from POA end
3m from notice to deliver
Penalties
<3m £100
>3m £200
>6m 10% of tax due
>12m 20% of tax due
Records
Deadline
Retain later of
• 6 yrs from AP end
• Date enquiries completed
• Date after which enquiries may not commence
Penalties
£3,000 for each period

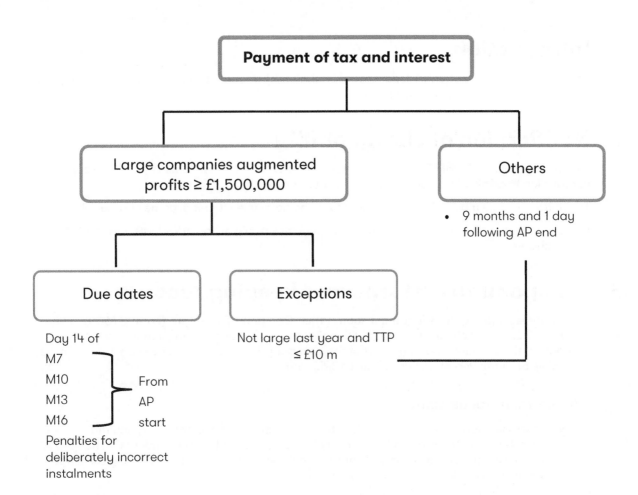

Payment of tax and interest

Large companies augmented profits ≥ £1,500,000

Others

- 9 months and 1 day following AP end

Due dates

Day 14 of

M7
M10   From
M13   AP
M16   start

Penalties for deliberately incorrect instalments

Exceptions

Not large last year and TTP ≤ £10 m

1 Introduction

We saw in the last chapter the deadlines and penalties that apply to individuals. In this chapter, we look at those that apply to companies.

2 Notification of chargeability

A company must notify HM Revenue & Customs (HMRC) when it first comes within the scope of corporation tax. This will usually be when it starts trading.

The notice must be made within three months of the date when it first became chargeable.

If notice of chargeability is not given the same penalties apply as for individuals covered in the earlier chapter.

3 Company tax returns and keeping records

All companies and organisations must submit their Company Tax Return (Form CT600) online, except in exceptional circumstances. Additionally, tax computations and (with very few exceptions) the accounts that form part of the Company Tax Return must be submitted in 'Inline eXtensible Business Reporting Language' (iXBRL) format.

Assessment focus point

If your assessment asks for a specific date to be determined from a calendar, you must remember that precision is essential. The Chief Assessor has noted that students do not always take sufficient care in this style of task. In addition, take care in identifying the length of time between two dates to identify a penalty due.

3.1 Filing date

Payment and administration

Open book reference

Complete accounts, computations and a tax return for each of the company's accounting periods is due on or before the **filing due date.** This is normally the **later of:**

(a)   **12 months after the end of the period of account concerned**
(b)   **3 months from the date on which the notice requiring the return was made**

An obligation to file a return arises only when the company receives a notice requiring a return.

Illustration 1: Filing date

Size Ltd prepares accounts for the 12 months to 30 September 2021. A notice requiring a CT600 return for the year ended 30 September 2021 was issued on 1 June 2022. The date by which Size Ltd must file its Company Tax Return for the year to 30 September 2021 is **30 September 2022, being the later of: 30 September 2022 (12 months from end of period of account) and 1 September 2022(3 months after notice to deliver).**

If a **period of account** is more than 12 months long, there will be **two accounting periods** based on the period of account. The first accounting period is 12 months long; the second is for the remainder of the period of account (PA).

A tax return must be filed for each accounting period. The tax returns for both accounting periods must be filed within 12 months of the end of the **period of account.**

Illustration 2: Long period of account

Octo Ltd prepares accounts for the 18 months to 30 June 2021.

The two accounting periods relating to this period of account are **year ended 31 December 2020 and six months to 30 June 2021**.

The date by which Octo Ltd must file its Company Tax Returns based on this period of account, assuming a notice requiring the returns was issued shortly after the end of the period of account, is **30 June 2022**.

3.2 Penalties

Open book reference

ayment and ministration

Companies are subject to the following late filing penalties:

Return outstanding	Penalty
<3 months late	£100
>3 months late	£200
>6 months late	10% of tax unpaid at 6m late date
>12 months late	20% of tax unpaid at 6m late date

3.3 Record keeping

Open book reference

ayment and ministration

Companies must keep records until the latest of:

(a) **Six years from the end of the accounting period**
(b) The date any enquiries (compliance checks) are completed
(c) The date after which enquiries may not be commenced

All business records and accounts, including contracts and receipts, must be kept.

Failure to keep records can lead to a penalty of up to £3,000 for each accounting period affected.

3.4 Penalties for errors

Open book reference

Penalties for incorrect returns

The rules that apply to individuals also apply to companies.

3.5 Compliance checks and enquiries

Open book reference

Payment and dministration

As with an individual, HMRC may conduct a compliance check into a company's tax return.

An enquiry is a compliance check into a return that has already been filed.

HMRC must give written notice of an enquiry within 12 months of the actual filing date.

Only one enquiry may be made in respect of any one return.

HMRC may request documents.

- There is a £300 penalty if the company does not provide them.
- HMRC may then charge £60 a day until these are produced.

An enquiry ends when HMRC gives notice that it has been completed.

- HMRC will amend the return.
- The company may appeal the amendments to the Tax Tribunal within 30 days.

In the same way that we saw for individuals, HMRC can issue a partial closure notice over certain matters where the enquiry is complex.

Illustration 3: Enquiries

Green Ltd prepares accounts for the 12 months to 30 April 2021. The Company Tax Return for the year was filed on 31 March 2022.

The date by which HMRC may commence an enquiry into the return based on these accounts is:

31 March 2023 (12 months from the actual filing date).

4 Payment of tax and interest

All tax must be paid electronically.

4.1 Non-large companies

Payment and administration

Open book reference

Corporation tax is due for payment nine months and one day after the end of the accounting period for a company with augmented profits (taxable total profits plus dividends) **of less than £1,500,000** for a 12-month accounting period.

Illustration 4: Corporation tax due date

K Ltd makes up accounts to 31 March 2022. Its profits do not exceed £1,500,000 and it has no dividend income. The corporation tax for the year to 31 March 2022 is £30,000.

The corporation tax is due on 1 January 2023.

4.2 Large companies

Payment and administration

Open book reference

Large companies, which have augmented profits of £1,500,000 or above (adjusted by the length of the period), are required to pay their estimated tax liability in four quarterly instalments, due on the 14th day of the 7th, 10th, 13th and 16th month after the start of the accounting period.

Illustration 5: Payment in instalments

A company which draws up accounts to 31 December 2021 will pay instalments as follows:

Instalment	Due date
1	14 July 2021
2	14 October 2021
3	14 January 2022
4	14 April 2022

Activity 1: Payment of corporation tax

A plc has taxable total profits (TTP) of £2.1m in the year to 31 March 2022

Required

Show how the corporation tax in respect of the year to 31 March 2022 will be paid.

Solution

	£

You will note that tax must be paid before the end of the accounting period on profits that have not yet been earned.

(a) At each quarter end, the directors will have to estimate how much the total tax bill will be for the year.

(b) They then calculate the proportion of this tax due to date (eg by the time of the second instalment $\frac{2}{4}$, ie $\frac{1}{2}$ of the tax is due).

(c) They will then pay over the difference compared to what they have paid to date.

4.3 Interest to HMRC

Open book reference

Payment and administration

Interest arises on late-paid instalments (from the due date to the actual payment date).

4.4 Interest from HMRC

Interest on overpaid instalments will run from the date that the tax was originally paid to the repayment date (note that interest on overpaid tax cannot run any earlier than from the due date of the first instalment).

Interest on tax paid late is a deductible expense and interest on overpaid tax is taxable. This will be added to, or subtracted from, interest income.

4.5 Exceptions

Open book reference

Corporation tax – payment and administration

If a company is a large company for an accounting period, it will not have to pay corporation tax by instalments for that period if:

(a) **Its augmented profits do not exceed £10 million**; and

(b) **It was not a large company in the previous year.**

4.6 Incorrect instalments

Penalties will be applied if the company deliberately underpays its instalments.

HMRC may require the company to justify why it paid the instalments it did. HMRC may request working papers. A fixed penalty, followed by a daily penalty, may be imposed until the information is supplied.

4.7 Long period of account

A long period of account gives rise to two accounting periods. Each accounting period will have its own due date(s).

Illustration 6: Long period of account

Z Ltd, which is not a large company, has a 15-month period to 30 September 2021.

Z Ltd will have two chargeable accounting periods:

* 12 months to 30 June 2021
* 3 months to 30 September 2021

Z Ltd will therefore have two payment dates:

* 1 April 2022
* 1 July 2022

Assessment focus point

Much of this information is included in the reference material which is available to you as a pop-up window in the live assessment.

Chapter summary

- A company must usually file its CT600 online return within 12 months of the end of the period of account concerned.

- Fixed penalties arise if the return is up to six months late. If the return is over six months late, there may be a tax-geared penalty.

- Companies must normally keep records until six years after the end of the accounting period concerned.

- HMRC can enquire into a return. Notice of an enquiry must usually be given within 12 months of the actual filing date.

- Large companies must pay their CT liability in four instalments, starting in the seventh month of the accounting period. The final instalment is due in the fourth month following the end of the accounting period.

- Other companies must pay their corporation tax liability nine months and one day after the end of an accounting period.

Keywords

- **Filing due date:** The date by which a tax return must be filed
- **Large companies:** Companies with augmented profits that exceed £1,500,000 for a 12-month accounting period

Test your learning

1   A company has been preparing accounts to 30 June for many years. It submitted its CT600 return for the year to 30 June 2020 on 1 June 2021.

    By what date must HMRC give notice that it is going to commence an enquiry into the return?

2   A company filed its CT600 return for the year to 31 December 2020 on 28 February 2022.

    What is the maximum penalty in respect of the late filing of the return for the year to 31 December 2020?

£	

3   Girton Ltd has taxable profits of £150,000 in the year ended 31 December 2021.

    When will its first payment of corporation tax be due?

	✓
14 July 2021	
1 October 2022	
31 December 2022	
1 January 2023	

4   Eaton Ltd has augmented profits of £2,400,000 for both its years ended 31 December 2020 and 31 December 2021.

    The final payment of the corporation tax liability for the year ended 31 December 2021 will be due on:

	✓
14 July 2021	
14 April 2022	
1 October 2022	
31 December 2022	

5   M Ltd, a large company, has an estimated corporation tax liability of £240,000 in respect of its accounting year to 31 March 2022.

    What will be the amount of each of the company's quarterly instalments?

£	

Chargeable gains for companies

Syllabus learning outcomes / objectives

3.1   Calculate chargeable gains and allowable losses on the sale of capital assets by limited companies

Learners need to be able to calculate:

- chargeable gains and allowable losses
- rollover relief
- indexation allowance

Assessment context

The assessment will test the basics of chargeable gains made by companies which are covered in this chapter.

Qualification context

You will not see the information in this chapter outside of this unit.

Business context

Companies sell assets for a variety of reasons. It is important to realise when a charge to tax arises, how much that tax charge will be and whether any relief is available to mitigate the tax due.

Chapter overview

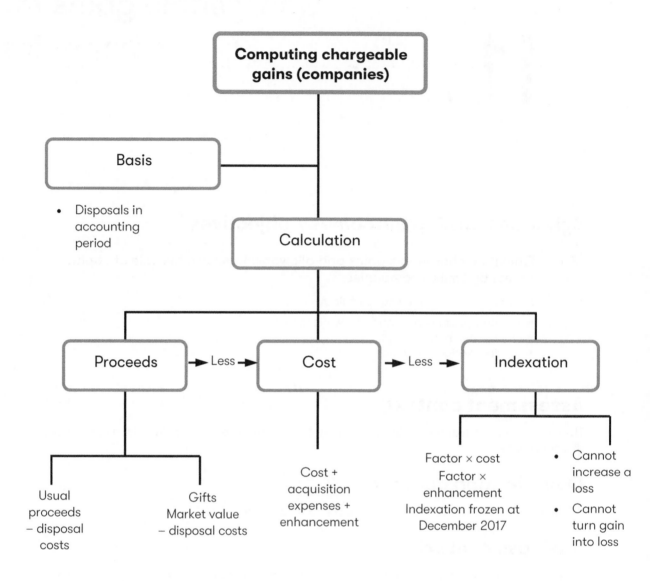

- Disposals in accounting period

BPP
LEARNING
MEDIA

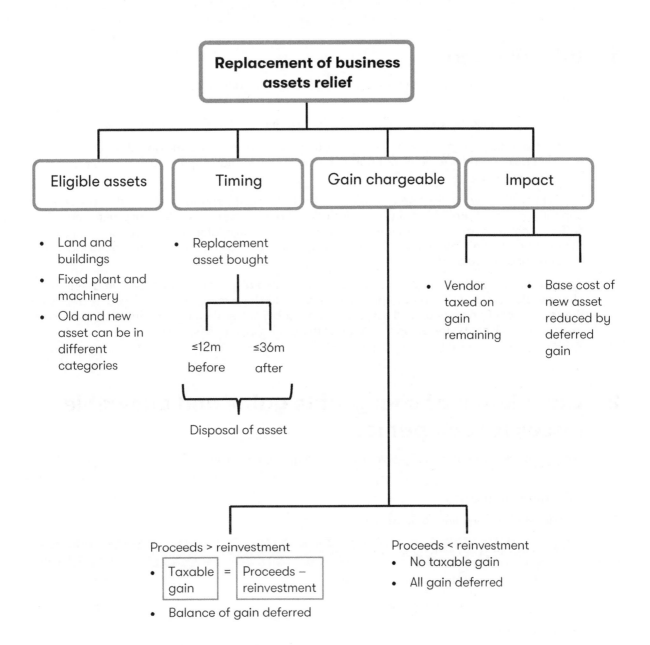

Replacement of business assets relief

Eligible assets
- Land and buildings
- Fixed plant and machinery
- Old and new asset can be in different categories

Timing
- Replacement asset bought

  ≤12m before   ≤36m after

  Disposal of asset

Gain chargeable

Proceeds > reinvestment
- Taxable gain = Proceeds − reinvestment
- Balance of gain deferred

Proceeds < reinvestment
- No taxable gain
- All gain deferred

Impact
- Vendor taxed on gain remaining
- Base cost of new asset reduced by deferred gain

1 Introduction

Income is a regular receipt that is expected to recur. A gain arises from a one-off disposal of a capital item.

Individuals pay **income tax** on income and **capital gains tax** (CGT) on capital gains.

Companies only pay one type of tax, corporation tax, on all their income and chargeable gains. For companies we refer to gains as chargeable gains rather than capital gains (which we use for an individual).

In this chapter we will look at how to calculate the gain a company will make on the sale of a capital item. The chargeable gain will be included in a company's taxable total profits and will suffer corporation tax as we saw earlier in the coursebook. In a later chapter we will consider how the rules are different for an individual disposing of a capital asset and how the capital gains tax thereon will be calculated.

For a disposal to be taxable, there must be a **chargeable disposal** of a **chargeable asset** by a **chargeable person**. A chargeable person is an individual or a company, a chargeable disposal is the sale or gift of an asset and all assets are chargeable unless they are specifically classified as exempt. You will not be tested on the detail of these rules in your assessment.

2 Calculation of chargeable gains and allowable losses for companies

The gain on disposal of a chargeable asset is calculated as follows:

Formula to learn

Basic chargeable gains computation

	£
Disposal consideration (or market value)	X
Less incidental costs of disposal	(X)
Net proceeds	X
Less allowable costs (including acquisition costs)	(X)
Less enhancement expenditure	(X)
Unindexed gain	X
Less indexation on cost	(X)
Less indexation on enhancement expenditure	(X)
Indexed gain/ chargeable gain	X

We now look at each of the items in the above proforma in turn.

2.1 Disposal consideration

Usually, this is proceeds received. Note though, that a disposal is deemed to take place at market value (MV) when the disposal is:

- A gift
- A sale at undervalue (for example, a sale to a group company for less than MV)

2.2 Costs

The following costs are deducted in the above proforma:

(a) **Incidental costs of disposal**

These are the costs of selling an asset. They may include advertising costs, estate agents' fees, legal costs and valuation fees. These costs should be deducted separately from any other allowable costs.

(b) **Allowable costs**

These include:

(i)   The original purchase price of the asset
(ii)   Costs incurred in purchasing the asset (estate agents' fees, legal fees, etc)

(c) **Enhancement expenditure**

Enhancement expenditure is capital expenditure which enhances the value of the asset and is reflected in the state or nature of the asset at the time of disposal.

 Illustration 1: Calculation of unindexed gain

Tulip Ltd bought a factory for £25,000. It paid legal costs of £600 on the purchase.

Tulip Ltd spent £8,000 building an extension to the factory.

Tulip Ltd sold the factory for £60,000. It paid estate agents' fees of £1,200 and legal costs of £750.

Tulip Ltd's unindexed gain on sale is:

£	24,450

	£
Disposal consideration	60,000
Less: incidental costs of disposal (1,200 + 750)	(1,950)
Net proceeds	58,050
Less: allowable costs (25,000 + 600)	(25,600)
Less: enhancement expenditure	(8,000)
Unindexed gain	24,450

 Activity 1: Unindexed gain calculation

Rose plc bought an asset for £15,000 in February 1986. It incurred legal fees of £500. Rose plc sold the asset for £38,500 incurring expenses of £1,500. While it owned the asset, it improved it at a cost of £3,000.

Required

Complete the table showing Rose plc's unindexed gain.

Solution

	£
Proceeds	
Less selling expenses	

	£
Net proceeds	
Less cost	
Less legal fees on purchase	
Less enhancement	
Unindexed gain	

2.3 Indexation allowance

Indexation allowance (IA) is given as a deduction to remove the effects of inflation from a gain.

It is calculated with reference to the movement of the retail price index (RPI) over the period of ownership. However, it was frozen in December 2017 and so indexation can only ever be given for ownership up to December 2017.

The allowance is applied to the cost.

If the asset has subsequently been enhanced, IA must be applied separately to the enhancement as there will be different levels of inflation on the differing time periods.

You will be given the IA factor to use in your assessment.

 Illustration 2: Indexation allowance

K Ltd bought an asset on 19 August 2000 for £10,000. Enhancement expenditure of £1,000 was incurred on 12 June 2007. The asset was sold for £41,500 on 20 February 2022. The disposal costs were £1,500.

Calculate the chargeable gain arising on the sale of the asset. Indexation factors: August 2000 to December 2017 = 0.631; June 2007 to December 2017 = 0.342.

	£
Disposal consideration	41,500
Less incidental costs of disposal	(1,500)
Net proceeds	40,000
Less purchase price	(10,000)
Less enhancement expenditure	(1,000)
Unindexed gain	29,000
Less indexation on purchase price	
£10,000 × 0.631	(6,310)
Less indexation on enhancement expenditure	
£1,000 × 0.342	(342)
Chargeable gain	22,348

Activity 2: Chargeable gain calculation

Dunstable Ltd

	£
Asset purchased February 1986	15,000
Legal fees on purchase	500
Sale July 2021	58,500
Selling expenses July 2021	1,500
Enhancement expenditure October 1995	3,000
IA February 1986 – December 2017	1.879
IA October 1995 – December 2017	0.856

Required

Complete the table showing Dunstable Ltd's gain.

Solution

	£
Proceeds	
Less selling expenses	
Net proceeds	
Less cost	
Less legal fees on purchase	
Less enhancement	
Unindexed gain	
Less indexation on cost	
Less indexation on enhancement expenditure	
Chargeable gain	

The indexation allowance cannot create or increase an allowable loss. If there is a gain before the indexation allowance, the allowance can reduce that gain to zero, but no further. If there is a loss before the indexation allowance, there is no indexation allowance.

Activity 3: Indexation

JEK Ltd bought an asset for £50,000. Indexation is 0.761.

Required

What is the chargeable gain/(loss) if it was sold for:

(a)   £20,000?   £ [   ]

(b)   £70,000?   £ [   ]

(c)   £150,000?   £ [   ]

Workings (not provided in the CBT)

2.4   Capital losses

If a company sells an asset and realises a capital loss, this loss must only be offset against any current period chargeable gains. If there are no/ insufficient current period gains to offset the capital loss then any unused capital loss will be carried forward to be offset against the company's first available chargeable gains.

3   Replacement of business asset (rollover) relief

3.1   The relief

 Open book reference

Chargeable gains – reliefs

Rollover relief allows some/ all of the chargeable gain made on the sale of certain assets to be deferred where a business reinvests in another asset during a certain time period.

Rollover relief is available to **both individuals and companies**. However, in the business tax assessment it will only be examined in the context of a company.

An indexed gain may be 'rolled over' where it arises **on the disposal of a business asset** (the 'old' asset) **if another business asset** (the 'new' asset) **is acquired.**

The following conditions must be met:

(a)   The old asset and the new asset must **both be used in a trade.**
(b)   The old asset and the new asset must **both be qualifying assets.**

The 'new' asset can be one asset or more than one asset and the new asset can be for use in a different trade to the old asset.

 BPP LEARNING MEDIA

Deferral is usually obtained by deducting the indexed gain on the old asset from the cost of the new asset to give a revised base cost. On a future disposal of the new asset, indexation allowance will be given on the revised base cost.

3.2 Qualifying assets

Both the old and new assets must fall into one of the following categories:

- Land and buildings used for the purpose of the trade
- Fixed plant and machinery

3.3 Timing

Reinvestment of the proceeds of the old asset must take place in a period beginning **one year before**; and ending **three years after**, the date of the disposal.

 Illustration 3: Rollover relief – all proceeds reinvested

A freehold factory was purchased by Halo Ltd on 13 May 2002 for £60,000 and sold for £110,000 on 18 September 2021. A replacement factory was purchased on 6 December 2021 for £120,000. Rollover relief was claimed on the sale of the first factory. IA from May 2002 - December 2017 is 0.578.

(a)   Gain on sale September 2021

	£
Disposal proceeds	110,000
Less cost	(60,000)
Less IA 0.578 × £60,000	(34,680)
Gain (all proceeds reinvested therefore defer full gain)	15,320

(b)   Revised base cost of asset purchased in December 2021

Original cost	120,000
Less rolled over gain	(15,320)
Revised base cost (this will be used to calculate gain on subsequent sale of new asset)	104,680

3.4 Taxed now

For all the gain to be deferred, all the proceeds of the old asset must be reinvested in the new asset. Any proceeds not reinvested in a qualifying asset are deducted from the gain to be rolled over.

If the amount of proceeds not reinvested exceeds the gain, no amount of the gain can therefore be rolled over. This is the same as saying the amount chargeable is the lower of the gain and the amount not reinvested.

 Illustration 4: Rollover relief – not all proceeds reinvested

Fence Ltd realised an indexed gain of £300,000 on the disposal of an office block used in its business. The office block was sold for £700,000. A new office block was bought for £600,000 in the following month.

The proceeds not reinvested are £100,000 so this amount of the gain is immediately chargeable. The remaining gain of £200,000 can be rolled over and set against the base cost of the new office block. This means the base cost of the new office block is £(600,000 − 200,000) = £400,000.

Activity 4: Rollover relief

Henry Ltd sells fixed plant for £200,000. It cost £150,000, indexation allowance is 10%. Six months later, Henry Ltd buys a building for £190,000.

Both assets are used in the trade.

Required

The gain taxed on Henry Ltd now is

£ [   ] .

The base cost of the building is

£ [   ] .

Workings (not provided in the CBT)

Assessment focus point

In the live assessment you will be provided with reference material that can be accessed through pop-up windows. The content of this reference material has been reproduced at the back of this Course Book.

Chapter summary

- A chargeable gain arises when there is a chargeable disposal of a chargeable asset by a chargeable person.

- Enhancement expenditure can be deducted in computing a chargeable gain if it is reflected in the state and nature of the asset at the time of disposal.

- Indexation allowance gives relief for the inflation element of a gain for a company. It was frozen in December 2017.

- Rollover relief can be used by a company to defer a gain when a qualifying business asset is replaced with another qualifying business asset.

- Qualifying business assets for rollover relief include land and buildings and fixed plant and machinery. Both the old and the new assets must be used for the purposes of a trade.

- If sale proceeds are not fully reinvested, an amount of the indexed gain equal to the proceeds not reinvested is immediately chargeable. The remainder of the gain may be rolled over.

- The rolled-over gain reduces the cost of the new asset to give a revised base cost. On a future disposal of the new asset indexation will be calculated based on the revised base cost.

- The new asset must be acquired in the period commencing one year before, and ending three years after, the disposal of the old asset.

Keywords

- **Enhancement expenditure:** Capital expenditure that enhances the value of the asset and is reflected in the state or nature of the asset at the time of disposal

Test your learning

1   Fill in the blanks with words of explanation.

Indexation allowance runs from the date [　　　　　　] to [　　　　　　] .

2   J plc bought a plot of land in July 2006 for £80,000. It spent £10,000 on drainage in April 2009 and sold the land for £200,000 in August 2021. The indexation factor from July 2006 to December 2017 is 0.401 and from April 2009 to December 2017 it is 0.315.

Using the proforma layout provided, compute the gain on sale.

	£
Proceeds of sale	
Less cost	
Less enhancement expenditure	
Less indexation allowance on cost	
Less indexation allowance on enhancement	
Chargeable gain	

3   K Ltd sold a factory on 10 November 2021. It purchased the following assets:

Date of purchase	Asset
21 September 2020	Office block
15 February 2022	Freehold factory
4 June 2023	Forklift truck
8 December 2024	Freehold warehouse

All of the above assets are used for the purpose of the trade of K Ltd.

Against which purchase may K Ltd claim rollover relief in respect of the gain arising on disposal of the factory?

	✓
Office block	
Freehold factory	
Forklift truck	
Freehold warehouse	

4   T Ltd bought land for £100,000 in March 2008. In March 2021, this land was sold for £400,000 and replacement land was bought for £380,000. Indexation from March 2008 to December 2017 is 0.311. The replacement land was sold in May 2022 for £500,000. Both pieces of land were used in T Ltd's trade, which is still continuing.

What is the chargeable gain arising in May 2022? Assume all available reliefs were claimed.

£ [　　　　　　]

5 Fill in the blank boxes.

A company sells freehold land and buildings.

If relief for replacement of business assets is to be claimed, reinvestment of the proceeds must take place in a period beginning

| | months before and ending

| | months after the date of disposal.

6 H Ltd sells a warehouse for £400,000. The warehouse cost £220,000 and the indexation allowance available is £40,000. The company acquires another warehouse 10 months later for £375,000 and claims rollover relief.

The chargeable gain after rollover relief is:

£ | |

12

Share disposals

Syllabus learning outcomes / objectives

3.2   Calculate chargeable gains and allowable losses for limited companies on share disposals

Learners need to be able to:

- Apply matching rules for companies
- Account for:
    - Bonus issues
    - Rights issues
    - Indexation allowance

Assessment context

This task is likely to be assessed by free data entry of all workings and will be human marked.

Qualification context

You will not see these rules anywhere else in your qualification. Similar rules for share disposals by individuals are covered in the personal tax unit.

Business context

A tax practitioner needs to be able to calculate chargeable gain on the disposal of shares for their clients.

Chapter overview

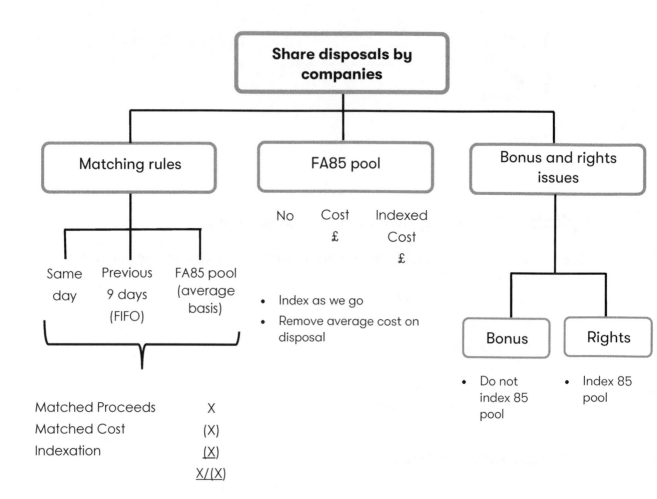

1 Introduction

Imagine Company A owns some shares in Company B, which have been purchased over a period of time at fluctuating costs. When some of these B shares are sold it is hard to identify precisely which shares are being disposed of, and therefore what their cost was. In this chapter we look at the rules which help us identify which shares are being sold, in order to provide a cost for the chargeable gain calculation.

2 Matching rules for companies

The matching rules set out the order in which companies are deemed to dispose of shares for tax purposes.

Shares being sold should be matched with purchases in the following order:

1   Acquisitions on the same day
2   Acquisitions in the previous nine days – FIFO basis
3   Shares from the FA 1985 pool

Assessment focus point

Application of the matching rules for companies is the area the Chief Assessor has noted as being where student performance is weakest.

Illustration 1: Application of the matching rules for companies

Z Ltd acquired the following shares in L plc:

9 November 2007	10,000 shares
15 December 2009	20,000 shares
11 July 2021	5,000 shares
15 July 2021	5,000 shares

Z Ltd disposed of 20,000 of the shares on 15 July 2021.

We match the 20,000 shares sold to acquisitions as follows.

(a)   Acquisition on same day: 5,000 shares acquired 15 July 2021.

(b)   Acquisitions in previous 9 days: 5,000 shares acquired 11 July 2021.

(c)   FA 1985 share pool: 10,000 shares out of 30,000 shares in FA 1985 share pool (9 November 2007 and 15 December 2009).

A disposal computation is produced for each matching rule.

3 The FA1985 pool

While shares bought in the previous 9 days are tracked separately under the matching rules, earlier purchases of shares are pooled together into what is known as the FA 1985 share pool.

The FA1985 share pool comprises of shares acquired by a company on or after 1 April 1985.

We must keep track of:

(a)   The number of shares in the pool
(b)   The original cost of the shares in the pool
(c)   The indexed cost of the shares in the pool (original cost plus indexation)

Once the matching rules have been applied a separate gain calculation is prepared for each 'match.'

Basic computation

	£	£
For each batch of matched shares:		
Proportion of proceeds	X	
Less cost (W1 if from share pool)	(X)	
		X

(W1) Share pool

Contains 3 columns

	No of shares	Cost £	Indexed cost £
Shares bought/sold	X	X	X

You must record each **operative event** in the FA 1985 pool. An operative event is a disposal or acquisition of shares that decreases or increases the amount of expenditure within the pool. However, prior to recording an operative event, an indexation allowance (sometimes described as an indexed rise) must be computed up to the date of the operative event you are looking at. You must look at each operative event in chronological order.

As explained earlier, the indexation allowance was frozen in December 2017. Therefore, for any share acquisitions after this date, add in the number of shares and cost, but do not add in any indexed rise.

The following illustration demonstrates the FA85 share pool.

Illustration 2: FA85 pool

In April 1985 J Ltd bought 20,000 shares in Low plc with a cost of £16,329. Now assume that J Ltd acquired 4,000 more shares in Low plc on 1 January 1990 at a cost of £6,000.

Show the value of the FA 1985 pool on 1 January 1990 following the acquisition. The indexation factor April 1985 – January 1990 = 0.261.

	No of shares	Cost £	Indexed cost £
1 April 1985	20,000	16,329	16,329
Index to January 1990			
0.261 × £16,329			4,262
			20,591
January 1990 acquisition	4,000	6,000	6,000
	24,000	22,329	26,591

If there are several operative events, the procedure described must be performed several times over. In the case of a disposal, following the calculation of the indexed rise, the cost and the indexed cost attributable to the shares disposed of are deducted from the cost and the indexed cost columns within the FA 1985 pool. This is computed on a pro-rata basis if only part of the holding is being sold.

Illustration 3: FA85 pool – a disposal from the pool

Following on from the above example, suppose that J Ltd now disposes of 12,000 shares in Low plc on 9 January 2022 for £26,000.

Show the value of the FA 1985 pool on 10 January 2022 following the disposal. Compute the gain on the disposal. The indexation factor for the period of January 1990 – December 2017 = 1.327.

(W1)

	No of shares	Cost £	Indexed cost £
Value at January 1990	24,000	22,329	26,591
Indexed rise to December 2017			
(1.327 × £26,591)			35,286
	24,000	22,329	61,877
Disposal			
(cost or indexed cost × $\frac{12,000}{24,000}$)	(12,000)	(11,165)	(30,939)
Pool c/f	12,000	11,164	30,938

The gain on the disposal is calculated as follows:

	£
Sale proceeds	26,000
Less cost (W1)	(11,165)
	14,835
Less indexation (£30,939 – £11,165)	(19,774)
Gain	Nil

Note that the indexation for the shares sold is the difference between the indexed cost and the cost, and that the indexation cannot create or increase a loss.

Activity 1: Matching rules for companies

ABC Ltd bought 1,000 shares in XYZ Ltd for £2,750 in August 1996 and another 1,000 for £3,250 in December 1998. On 4 July 2021, it bought 500 shares for £2,511 and on 10 July 2021, it bought 1,000 shares for £4,822.

ABC Ltd sold 2,500 shares on 10 July 2021 for £12,500.

Indexed rises: August 1996 to December 1998   =   0.008

December 1998 to December 2017   =   0.692

Required

Compute the gain on the disposal of these shares. Clearly show the balance to be carried forward.

Solution

		£	£

		£	£

4   Bonus and rights issues

Bonus issues are free shares given to existing shareholders in proportion to their existing shareholding. For example, a shareholder may own 2,000 shares. The company makes 1 share for every 2 shares held bonus issue (known as a 1 for 2 bonus issue). The shareholder will then have an extra 1,000 shares, giving them 3,000 shares overall.

Bonus shares are treated as having been acquired at the date of the original acquisition of the underlying shares giving rise to the bonus issue. Since the original shares are usually in the FA85 share pool this means that the bonus shares will typically be added to the pool.

Indexation is not required when bonus shares are received, as there is no additional cost.

If a bonus issue occurs where there is a match to some shares acquired in the previous 9 days then the new shares will attach pro rata to the number of shares in each match and will be added to each gains calculation with nil cost.

In a rights issue, a shareholder is offered the right to buy additional shares by the company in proportion to the shares already held.

The difference between a bonus and a rights issue is that, in a rights issue, the new shares are paid for. This results in an adjustment to the original cost.

BPP
LEARNING
MEDIA

For matching purposes, the new shares are always treated as if acquired on the same day as the shareholder's original shareholding. So, as we saw above, if all the original shares are in the FA85 share pool then the right issue shares will go into the FA85 pool.

Indexation will be required if there is a rights issue prior to December 2017, as the shares are acquired at a cost. The FA 1985 pool will need to be indexed to the date of the rights issue as this is classed as an 'operative event'.

If the rights issue occurs after December 2017, indexation will have been frozen. In this situation, the shares will be added into the FA85 pool but with no indexation.

Activity 2: Bonus and rights issues for companies

Wotan Ltd sold 800 shares in Krimpton Ltd on 5 September 2021 for £10,000. The holding had been built up as follows:

- 500 acquired for £1,000 on 1 May 1985
- 1 for 2 rights issue for £5 per share on 5 August 1987
- 1 for 1 bonus issue on 15 September 1989
- 1 for 3 rights issue for £6 per share on 10 March 2019

Indexation factors are as follows:

May 1985 → August 1987	0.072
August 1987 → September 1989	0.142
September 1989 → December 2017	1.385
August 1987 → December 2017	1.724

Required

Calculate the chargeable gain in September 2021.

Solution

		£	£

		£	£

Assessment focus point

Please refer to the reference material at the end of this Course Book to see which elements of this chapter will be available to you as a pop-up window in the live assessment.

Chapter summary

- The matching rules for companies are:

    - Same-day acquisitions
    - Previous 9 days' acquisitions on a FIFO basis
    - Shares in the FA 1985 share pool

- In the FA 1985 share pool, we must keep track of the number of shares, the cost of the shares and the indexed cost.

- Operative events increase or decrease the amount of expenditure within the FA 1985 pool.

- Bonus issue and rights issue shares are acquired in proportion to the shareholder's existing holding.

- The difference between a bonus and a rights issue is that in a rights issue, shares are paid for.

- For a company, a rights issue is treated as an operative event, whereas a bonus issue is not.

Keywords

- **Bonus shares:** Shares that are issued free to shareholders, based on original holdings
- **Operative events:** Disposals/acquisitions of shares that decrease/increase the amount of expenditure within the FA 1985 pool
- **Rights issues:** Similar to bonus issues except that in a rights issue, shares must be paid for

Test your learning

1 **Tick to show whether the following statement is true or false.**

In both a bonus issue and a rights issue, there is an adjustment to the original cost of the shares.

	✓
True	
False	

2 **What are the share matching rules for disposals by companies?**

3 Q Ltd bought 10,000 shares in R plc in May 2003 at a cost of £90,000. There was a 1 for 4 rights issue in June 2009 at the cost of £12 per share and Q Ltd took up all of its rights entitlement.

Q Ltd sold 10,000 shares in R plc for £150,000 in January 2022.

The indexed rise between May 2003 and June 2009 is 0.176; and between June 2009 and December 2017, is 0.303.

(a) **Using the proforma layout provided, show the share pool.**

	No of shares	Cost £	Indexed cost £

(b) **Using the proforma layout provided, compute the gain on sale.**

	£

13

Business disposals

Syllabus learning outcomes / objectives

5.1   Business disposals

Learners need to understand:

- the income tax and capital gains tax implications of disposing of an unincorporated business

- The capital gains tax reliefs (gift relief, business asset disposal relief) available on disposal of:

  - An unincorporated business
  - Shares in a personal company

Learners need to be able to:

- Calculate capital gains on disposal of:

  - Trade and assets

  - Shares in a personal company

  - Capital gains tax reliefs available on disposal of:

    - Trade and assets
    - Shares in a personal company

  - Post-tax proceeds following a business disposal

Assessment context

One of the tasks in your assessment will test business disposals.

Qualification context

You will not see these rules outside of this unit.

Business context

Individuals disposing of their business interests are very common in practice and this chapter will give you an understanding of some of the tax considerations.

Chapter overview

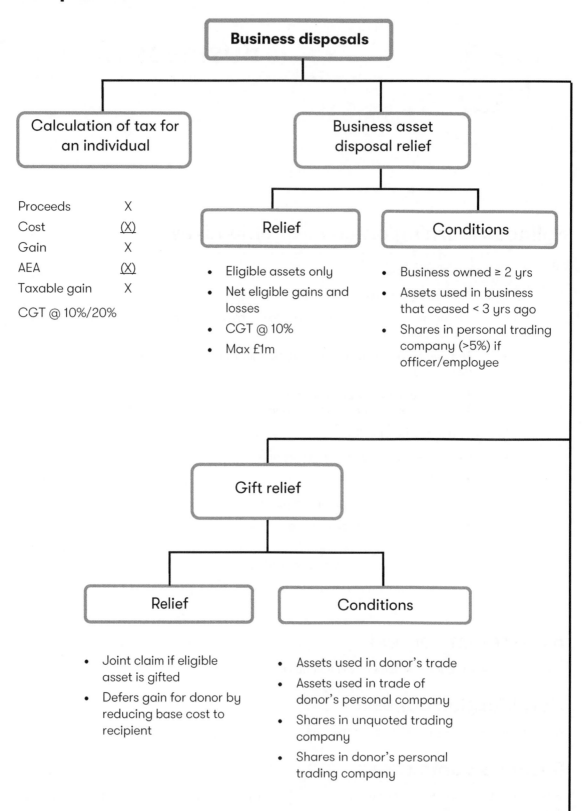

Business disposals

Calculation of tax for an individual

Proceeds	X
Cost	(X)
Gain	X
AEA	(X)
Taxable gain	X
CGT @ 10%/20%	

Business asset disposal relief

Relief
- Eligible assets only
- Net eligible gains and losses
- CGT @ 10%
- Max £1m

Conditions
- Business owned ≥ 2 yrs
- Assets used in business that ceased < 3 yrs ago
- Shares in personal trading company (>5%) if officer/employee

Gift relief

Relief
- Joint claim if eligible asset is gifted
- Defers gain for donor by reducing base cost to recipient

Conditions
- Assets used in donor's trade
- Assets used in trade of donor's personal company
- Shares in unquoted trading company
- Shares in donor's personal trading company

```
                                                    ┌──────────────────────────────────────┐
                ┌──────────────────────┐            │                                      │
   ┌────────────┴──────────────┐         ┌───────────┴───────────────┐
   │   Disposal of an          │         │   Disposal of an           │
   │   unincorporated business │         │   unincorporated business  │
   └───────────────────────────┘         └────────────────────────────┘
```

- Consider sale of each group of assets:
  - GW & L&B – chargeable gain
  - P&M – no capital loss, balancing adjustments for CAs
  - NCAs – trade profit adjustment
- Closing year basis period rules for income tax
- Terminal loss relief available if trading loss
- Class 2 and 4 NICs cease
- Consider BADR and gift relief on chargeable gains
- Post-tax proceeds
  - Proceeds   X
  - Less IT   (X)
  - Less CGT   <u>(X)</u>
                X

1 Introduction

This chapter looks at the tax implications of individuals disposing of their businesses. This could be a business that they have run as a sole trader or partnership, or it could be a business that they have set up as a company. Their choice of business structure will change the way they are taxed on the business disposal. This chapter will explain how each type of disposal works for tax purposes.

With disposals of either type of business, the individual will be disposing of chargeable asset(s) and, as such, will be making chargeable/capital gains. The chargeable/capital gains are calculated in a similar way to the company calculations we have already seen, except that individuals do not receive indexation allowance. Once the chargeable/capital gains are calculated, the individual will pay capital gains tax on them, rather than corporation tax as we saw for companies.

This chapter starts by outlining how capital gains tax is calculated for an individual and considers some reliefs which may be available in the context of a business disposal. We will then take that knowledge and use it to look specifically at the disposal of a sole trade/partnership business and the disposal of shares in a company which will be the main focus of the task in your assessment.

2 Calculation of capital gains tax for an individual

2.1 The capital gains calculation

A chargeable/capital gain for an individual is calculated in the same way as we saw earlier for a company except that an individual is not entitled to relief for inflation through indexation allowance. You will see the gains being referred to simply as gains or chargeable or capital gains could be used.

Disposal consideration (or market value)	X
Less incidental costs of disposal	(X)
Net proceeds	X
Less allowable cost (including acquisition cost)	(X)
Less enhancement expenditure	(X)
Capital gain/(capital loss)	X/(X)

The rules for determining each of the figures in the gain calculation are the same as we saw earlier in the coursebook.

 ### Illustration 1: Calculation of capital gain

Jack bought a holiday cottage for £25,000. He paid legal costs of £600 on the purchase.

Jack spent £8,000 building an extension to the cottage.

Jack sold the cottage for £60,000. He paid estate agents' fees of £1,200 and legal costs of £750.

Jack's gain on sale is:

£	24,450

	£
Disposal consideration	60,000
Less: incidental costs of disposal (1,200 + 750)	(1,950)
Net proceeds	58,050
Less: allowable costs (25,000 + 600)	(25,600)
Less: enhancement expenditure	(8,000)
Capital gain	24,450

2.2 Computing taxable gains in a tax year

An individual pays capital gains tax on any **taxable gains** arising in a **tax year** (6 April to 5 April).

All the capital gains made in the tax year are added together, any current year capital loss is deducted, and then the annual exempt amount (see below) is deducted to arrive at taxable gains, to which CGT will be applied.

2.3 Annual exempt amount

 Open book reference

> **Annual exempt amount (AEA)/annual exemption** is the amount of gain that will be tax free. For 2021/22, this is £12,300.

This may also be referred to as an **annual exemption** in your assessment. It is deducted from gains in the tax year which means that for 2021/22, the first £12,300 of chargeable/capital gains are tax free for an individual.

Formula to learn

Year-end computation

	£
Gains	X
Current year capital losses	(X)
Annual exempt amount	(12,300)
Taxable gains	X

Note. Unused annual exempt amounts cannot be carried forward.

2.4 Computing capital gains tax payable

Open book reference

Capital gains tax

An individual's taxable gains are chargeable to CGT at the rate of 10% or 20% depending on **their taxable income** in the tax year.

If the individual is a basic rate taxpayer, then CGT is payable at 10% on an amount of taxable gains up to the amount of their **unused** basic rate band; and at 20% on the excess.

If the individual is a higher or additional rate taxpayer, then CGT is payable at 20% on all their taxable gains. Note that the basic rate band covers taxable income and gains up to £37,700 (in 2021/22).

Illustration 2: Calculating capital gains tax

(a) In 2021/22, Sally has taxable income (ie the amount after the deduction of the personal allowance) of £10,000 and taxable gains (ie after the deduction of the annual exempt amount) of £20,000.

Sally's CGT liability is:

£20,000 × 10%   £2,000

The taxable income uses £10,000 of the basic rate band, leaving £27,700 of the basic rate band unused, therefore all of the taxable gain is taxed at 10%.

(b) In 2021/22 Hector has taxable income of £60,000 (ie he is a higher rate taxpayer), and made taxable gains of £10,000.

Hector's CGT liability is:

£10,000 × 20%   £2,000

All of Hector's basic rate band has been taken up by the taxable income, therefore the taxable gain is taxed at 20%.

(c) Isabel has taxable income of £30,200 in 2021/22 as well as taxable gains of £25,000.

Isabel has (£37,700 − £30,200) = £7,500 of her basic rate band unused. Isabel's CGT liability is:

	£
7,500 × 10%	750
£17,500 × 20%	3,500
£25,000	4,250

Activity 1: Computing capital gains tax payable

Mr Dunstable had a chargeable gain of £18,800 in 2021/22 and taxable income of £34,200.

Required

What is Mr Dunstable's capital gains tax payable?

£ [   ] .

Workings (not provided in the CBT)

	£

3 Business asset disposal relief

3.1 The relief

Open book reference

Chargeable gains – reliefs

Individuals can claim business asset disposal relief to reduce the rate of capital gains tax (CGT) on a material disposal of business assets.

Gains on assets qualifying for **business asset disposal relief (BADR)** are **taxed at 10%** regardless of the level of a person's taxable income. If there are several assets being disposed of which qualify for BADR the eligible gains and losses are netted together and the net gains eligible for BADR are taxed at 10%.

If a taxpayer has both gains that are eligible for business asset disposal relief and gains that are ineligible, they should offset the annual exempt amount against the ineligible gains first.

Although gains eligible for the relief are taxed at 10%, they are deemed to be taxed before ineligible gains when deciding whether any of the basic rate band remains available.

Assessment focus point / Exam success skills

The AAT have confirmed that they will not examine any planning aspects in relation to capital losses nor any brought forward capital losses. They may, however, expect you to understand that if a capital loss arises on a disposal of a business asset that this will be netted against any business gains before applying the 10% business asset disposal relief rate. You could also be expected to understand that the annual exempt amount would be offset against ineligible gains prior to gains eligible for BADR.

BPP LEARNING MEDIA

Illustration 3: BADR, annual exempt amount and basic rate band

Steve makes gains eligible for business asset disposal relief (BADR) of £15,000, and gains not eligible for business asset disposal relief of £40,000. He has taxable income of £25,000.

The CGT payable is:

	£	£
Gains eligible for BADR	15,000	
Gains not eligible for BADR		40,000
Annual exemption		(12,300)
Taxable gains	15,000	27,700
Tax:		
£15,000 × 10% (gains eligible for BADR)		1,500
£24,000 × 20%		4,800
CGT due:		6,300

Note. Basic rate band after income tax = £37,700 - £25,000 = £12,700. The £15,000 of gains eligible for BADR use this remaining basic rate band meaning that the ineligible gains will be taxed at 20%.

Activity 2: Business asset disposal relief – calculation of capital gains tax

Poins disposes of his business on 21 August 2021, realising a gain of £10,000 which qualifies for business asset disposal relief. He has other gains in the year of £50,300 which do not qualify for business asset disposal relief.

Poins has taxable income of £22,570.

Required

Capital gains tax payable at 10% due to BADR is £ [   ].

Capital gains tax payable at 10% to utilise the remaining basic rate

band is £ [   ].

Capital gains tax payable at 20% is £ [   ].

Workings (not provided in the CBT)

	Eligible gains £	Other gains £

	Eligible gains £	Other gains £

3.2 Conditions

Business asset disposal relief applies when there has been a material disposal of business assets, such as a:

- disposal of the whole/part of an unincorporated business
- disposal of assets used in an unincorporated business that has ceased trading; or
- disposal of certain shares/ securities.

These are explained in further detail below.

3.2.1 Disposal of an unincorporated business

The disposal of the whole or part of a business (as a going concern) which has been owned by the individual throughout the period of two years ending with the date of the disposal.

A business includes one carried on as a partnership of which the individual is a partner.

The business must be a trade, profession or vocation conducted on a commercial basis with a view to the realisation of profits.

Relief is only available on relevant business assets. These are assets used for the purposes of the business and cannot include shares and securities or assets held by the business as investments. Gains and losses on relevant business assets are netted off.

3.2.2 Disposal of assets used in an unincorporated business that has ceased trading

The disposal of assets used in the business prior to the cessation of the business, provided that:

- The business was owned for two years prior to the cessation
- The assets were sold within three years of the cessation

3.2.3 Disposal of shares

The disposal of shares or securities will qualify for business asset disposal relief where:

- The company is the individual's personal company (ie owns at least 5% of the shares and can exercise 5% of the votes);

- The company is a trading company; and

- The individual is an officer or employee of the company.

For business asset disposal relief to be available the conditions above must have been met:

- For two years before the date of disposal; or

- For two years up to the date at which the company ceases to trade. The shares must then be sold within three years of this date.

Activity 3: Disposals eligible for business asset disposal relief

The following assets are disposed of in 2021/22 by various individuals.

Identify which, if any, are eligible disposals for business asset disposal relief. Tick the relevant box.

Solution

	✓
A partner's share of a business in which the individual has been a partner since August 2014	
A freehold factory which the individual uses in his business and has owned for ten years	
Unquoted shares (≥5%) held by the individual in a personal trading company in which he is employed and which he has owned for the previous three years.	
Quoted shares (≥5%) held by the individual in a personal trading company in which he is employed and which he has owned for the previous three years.	

3.3 Lifetime limit

There is a lifetime limit of £1 million of gains on which business asset disposal relief can be claimed. Once gains up to this amount have been covered by business asset disposal relief any later gains will be ineligible.

Activity 4: Business asset disposal relief – calculating gains eligible for relief

Hal has run his business for many years. In January 2022, he sells it, realising the following gains and (losses).

Equity	£
Goodwill	500,000
Factory	300,000
Office block	(100,000)
Shares	80,000

All the assets were used in his business except the shares.

He has never previously claimed business asset disposal relief.

Required

(a)   **The total net taxable gain eligible for business asset disposal relief is**

£ [　　　　　　] .

The total net taxable gain not eligible for business asset disposal relief is

£ [　　　　　　] .

Workings (not provided in the CBT)

	£	£

(b)   If the gain on the factory was £9,800,000, then the total net taxable gain eligible for business asset disposal relief is

£ [　　　　　　] .

The total net taxable gain not eligible for business asset disposal relief is

£ [　　　　　　] .

Workings (not provided in the CBT)

	£	£

	£	£

3.4 Claim

The relief must be claimed within one year following the 31 January after the tax year of disposal. Relief for 2021/22 must, therefore, be claimed by 31 January 2024.

4 Gift relief

4.1 The relief

Open book reference

Chargeable gains – reliefs

Individuals can claim **gift relief** to defer a gain arising **on the gift of a business asset**.

The gift is deemed to be made at market value (MV).

The transferee is deemed to acquire the asset for its market value, less the deferred gain.

Illustration 4: Gift relief

John bought a business asset in 2010 for £20,000. On 1 May 2021, John gave the asset to Marie-Louise. They agree to claim gift relief so that John doesn't have to pay capital gains tax as a result of the gift. The market value of the asset on the date of the gift was £90,000.

John is deemed to dispose of the asset for its market value of £90,000, so the gain arising on the gift is:

	£
Deemed disposal proceeds	90,000
Less cost	(20,000)
Gain	70,000

The gain of £70,000 is deferred by setting it against the value of £90,000, at which Marie-Louise is deemed to acquire the gift. Therefore, Marie-Louise is deemed to acquire the gift for £20,000 (£90,000 – £70,000) and this will be used as the base cost for future disposals.

4.2 Conditions

The disposal must be made to a UK individual.

Qualifying assets for gift relief purposes include:

(a) Assets used in a trade carried on:

    (i) By the donor; or
    (ii) By the donor's personal company

(b) Shares in:

    (i) An unquoted trading company; or

(ii)   The donor's personal trading company

A 'personal company' is one in which not less than 5% of the voting rights are controlled by the donor.

4.3 Impact of claim

The donor's gain in relation to the gifted asset is reduced to nil.

The gain is rolled over into (deducted from) the base cost of the asset now owned by the recipient.

The gift relief claim to defer the gain must be made jointly by the donor and the recipient.

Activity 5: Gift relief

Bill gave a workshop used in his trade to his son, Ludovic. Its market value was £25,000.

Bill had purchased the workshop for £7,000.

A valid gift relief claim is made.

Required

The gift relief claim must be signed by [▼] .

Picklist:

Bill and Ludovic
Bill only
Ludovic only

Bill's chargeable gain on disposal is

£ [   ] .

Ludovic's base cost is

£ [   ] .

Workings (not provided in the CBT)

Activity 6: With and without gift relief

Julie bought 10,000 shares in an unquoted trading company for £50,000 in July 2008. Julie gave her shares to Jack in May 2021 when they were worth £85,000. Jack sold the shares for £95,000 in December 2021.

Required

(a)   If gift relief is not claimed, Julie's chargeable gain is

£ [   ]

and Jack's chargeable gain is

£ [   ] .

(b)   If gift relief is claimed, Julie's chargeable gain is

£ [   ]

and Jack's chargeable gain is

£ [   ] .

Workings (not provided in the CBT)

5 Disposal of an unincorporated business

5.1 The disposal

When a sole trader disposes of their sole trade business, we need to consider each category of assets which have been disposed of and the tax consequences for each. It is important not to consider this as a disposal of 'one' asset being the business as a whole.

In determining the tax position, each category of assets will be valued at their market value. The business will often be worth more than the sum of the individual assets and this excess value is attributed to goodwill, which is a chargeable asset for capital gains purposes.

The tax on each category of assets is outlined below:

Goodwill	Deemed sold at MV.
	If internally generated goodwill, the base cost will be £nil. Otherwise, a base cost would be stated clearly in the scenario.
	Gives rise to a chargeable (or capital) gain.
Land and Buildings	Chargeable (or capital) gain/ (loss)
Plant and Machinery	If sold at a profit, any gain will usually not be taxable.
	If sold at a loss (which is more usual), no capital loss will be available as the business will have claimed capital allowances on the assets.
	As the trader will be ceasing to trade, for capital allowance purposes the MV of plant and machinery will be deducted and then balancing adjustments will arise.
Net current assets	These are not chargeable assets for capital gains purposes. Instead, an adjustment will be made to the trading profit based on the MV of the net current assets.
	If the asset's MV exceeds their cost this will increase trading profit.
	If the asset's MV is less than their cost this will reduce trading profit.

Activity 7: Disposal of an unincorporated business 1

Piotr is selling his sole trade business. His assets at the date of sale are detailed below.

Required

For each of the assets detailed below, state the impact of the sale for tax purposes by dragging appropriate response into the 'impact' column.

Asset	Market value £	Original cost £	TWDV £	Impact
Factory	120,000	100,000		
Warehouse	90,000	100,000		

Asset	Market value £	Original cost £	TWDV £	Impact
Plant & machinery	20,000	60,000	5,000	
Goodwill	26,000	0		
Inventory	5,000	6,000		

Drag and drop options:

Chargeable gain
Capital loss
Increase in trading profit
Decrease in trading profit

5.2 Income tax consequences

For income tax purposes, the sole trader will have ceased to trade. This means that the closing year basis period rules will be used to determine the final tax year's trading profits. They will be taxed on any profits not yet taxed less overlap.

In addition, the cessation of trade will trigger balancing adjustments for capital allowances.

The sale of net current assets will give an adjustment to trading profits based on the difference between the MV of the assets and their cost. If MV > cost, there will be an increase in trade profits and if MV < cost, there will be a decrease in trade profits.

If a trading loss is incurred, it can be offset against current year and/or prior year total income or a terminal loss relief claim is available to carry back the trade loss three years on a LIFO basis against trade profits only.

5.3 National insurance consequences

Class 2 NIC contributions will stop at the date the sole trader ceases to trade.

Class 4 NIC contributions for the year will be calculated based on the trade profit for the tax year determined by the closing year basis period rules. The thresholds are not time apportioned if the trade ceases part way through the year.

5.4 Capital gains tax consequences

The sale of goodwill and land and buildings will give rise to chargeable (or capital) gains/ allowable losses.

Provided the sole trader has been trading for more than two years prior to the sale, the disposal will qualify for business asset disposal relief. If the trader ceases to trade prior to selling the business, the assets must have been held for two years prior to the cessation of trade and the business must be sold within three years. Remember that if any of the assets are not used in the individual's trade, for example if a rental property or shares are owned, those gains will not be eligible for business asset disposal relief.

If the business is gifted, any assets used in the donor's trade will be eligible for a joint gift relief claim. This will defer the gain made by the donor by reducing the base cost of the assets to the recipient.

Activity 8: Disposal of an unincorporated business 2

Mr A disposes of his sole trade business on 31 October 2021. The business was set up in 2015.

Mr B wishes to retire and so ceases to trade on 31 October 2021. He had set up his business in 2000.

Mrs C disposes of her trading business on 31 October 2021. She had set the business up 1 January 2019. The assets of the business include a rental property.

Identify whether each of the following statements are true or false.

Statement	True ✓	False ✓
As Mr A has been trading two years prior to the sale of his business, business asset disposal relief will be available on his gain.		
In order for Mr B to be able to claim business asset disposal relief he would need to sell his business by 31 October 2023.		
In order for Mr B to be able to claim business asset disposal relief he would need to sell his business by 31 October 2024, and he would need to be employed by the business.		
Mrs C will be able to claim business asset disposal relief on her gains.		

5.5 Post-tax proceeds from the sale of an unincorporated business

When a business owner considers selling their business they will want to know how much cash they will realise from a sale. This involves determining the post-tax proceeds from the sale of an unincorporated business.

Post-tax proceeds are calculated as follows:

	£
Proceeds	X
Less IT/NICs on adjustments to profits (given in question)	(X)
Less capital gains tax on gains @ 10%/ 20%	(X)
Post-tax proceeds	X

Activity 9: Disposal of an unincorporated business 3

Bella is a higher rate taxpayer for income tax purposes. On 31 December 2021 she sells her sole trade business which she set up in 2010. She sells her business for £295,000 with her assets as stated below:

Asset	Market value £	Original cost £	TWDV £
Factory	200,000	150,000	
Plant & machinery	50,000	60,000	5,000
Goodwill	30,000	0	

Asset	Market value £	Original cost £	TWDV £
Inventory	15,000	20,000	

The income tax and NIC impact of the sale of the plant and machinery and inventory increases Bella's tax due by £16,800.

Required

Calculate Bella's post-tax proceeds from the sale of her business.

£	

6 Disposal of an incorporated business

6.1 The disposal

If an individual set up in business using a company rather than an unincorporated business, then in order to dispose of that business the individual must sell their shares. In contrast to the sale of the sole trade business, this is the disposal of only one asset - the shares in the company. The company itself will continue to trade with no major tax consequences - the only thing happening to the company is that it has a different owner (shareholder).

For the individual, we will need to consider capital gains tax on the sale of their shares.

6.2 Capital gains tax consequences

The individual will make a chargeable (or capital) gain on the sale of their shares equal to the difference between proceeds and cost.

If the individual owns at least 5% of the shares, is an officer or employee of the company and it is a trading company then, provided the shares have been owned for two years prior to disposal, the gain will be eligible for business asset disposal relief. If the company has ceased trading prior to being sold, the conditions to qualify must have been met for two years prior to the trade ceasing and then the shares must be sold within three years of the cessation of trade.

If the shares are gifted, then gift relief will be available if either the shares are in an unquoted trading company or they are shares in the donor's personal trading company.

6.3 Post-tax proceeds from a sale of shares

The post-tax proceeds from a sale of shares are calculated as follows:

	£
Proceeds	X
Less capital gains tax on gain @ 10%/ 20%	(X)
Post-tax proceeds	X

Activity 10: Disposal of an incorporated business

Anton sold his shares in Dancing Ltd on 1 March 2022 for £350,000. He is the sole shareholder and director of Dancing Ltd, a trading company, and had bought his shares for £15,000 in 2000. Anton has no other disposals during 2021/22 and is a higher rate taxpayer.

Required

Calculate Anton's taxable gain from the sale of his shares.

£ [   ]

Calculate the tax that will be charged on Anton's taxable gains assuming all beneficial claims are made.

£ [   ]

Calculate Anton's post-tax proceeds from the sale of his shares.

£ [   ]

Assessment focus point
In the live assessment you will be provided with the reference material which has been reproduced at the end of this Course Book. Please review this material to see which elements of this chapter will be available to you as a pop-up window in the live assessment.

- Individuals calculate gains in a similar way as companies except that individuals are not entitled to indexation allowance. Individuals are, however, entitled to an annual exempt amount.

- The net gains of an individual are brought together, and the annual exempt amount is deducted to calculate the individual's taxable gains.

- Capital gains tax will be due on the taxable gains at 10% for any gains falling in any remaining basis rate band after income tax and at 20% for gains falling in the higher/ additional rate bands.

- Business asset disposal relief reduces the rate of CGT on gains made by an individual on certain business disposals, to 10%.

- There is a lifetime limit of £1 million for business asset disposal relief.

- Business asset disposal relief applies to disposals of an unincorporated business (or part of a business), disposals of business assets on cessation, and shares in a trading company that is the individual's personal company and of which they are an officer or employee.

- Gift relief can be used by an individual to defer a gain on the gift of business assets.

- The recipient acquires the gift at its market value, less the amount of the deferred gain.

- Qualifying assets for gift relief include assets used in a trade by the donor or his personal company, unquoted shares in a trading company and shares in a personal trading company.

- On the sale of an unincorporated business, we must consider the tax on each category of assets sold separately:

  - Land and buildings and Goodwill will give rise to chargeable (or capital) gains/capital losses

  - Plant & machinery results in no chargeable gains consequences but there will be a balancing adjustment for capital allowance purposes

  - Net current assets have an impact to trading profits

- The individual will use closing year basis period rules to calculate their income tax in the final tax year of trading and will cease paying Class 2 and 4 NIC.

- Post-tax proceeds are calculated by taking proceeds less the income tax and NICs due on the trading profit adjustments less the capital gains tax due on any chargeable gains.

- On the sale of an incorporated business there is one disposal of shares giving rise to a chargeable (or capital) gain on which capital gains tax will be due.

- Post-tax proceeds are calculated as proceeds less the capital gains tax due on the gain.

Keywords

- **Annual exempt amount:** The amount of gains on which no CGT is payable
- **Chargeable (or capital) gains:** The gains made before the deduction of the annual exempt amount
- **Taxable gains:** The gains made after the deduction of the annual exempt amount
- **Business asset disposal relief:** Reduces the effective rate of tax on the disposal of certain business assets from 20% (if they would be taxed at the higher rate) to 10%
- **Gift relief:** Can defer a gain on a gift of business assets by an individual
- **Post-tax proceeds:** The proceeds received on a disposal after any tax due thereon has been deducted

Test your learning

1   Yvette buys an investment property for £325,000. She sells the property on 12 December 2021 for £560,000.

Her chargeable gain on sale is:

£ [ ]

2   Martha is a higher rate taxpayer who made chargeable gains (before the annual exempt amount) of £24,200 in October 2021.

Martha's CGT liability for 2021/22 is:

£ [ ]

3   Ian sold his business as a going concern to John in May 2021. The gains on sale were £1,400,000. Ian had not previously made any claims for business asset disposal relief and made no other disposals in 2021/22. Ian is a higher rate taxpayer.

Ian's CGT liability for 2021/22 is:

£ [ ]

4   Jemma sold her shareholding in J Ltd in January 2022. She had acquired the shares in August 2007 for £10,000. The proceeds of sale were £80,000. The disposal qualified for business asset disposal relief.

Jemma's CGT on the disposal, assuming she has already used the annual exempt amount for 2021/22, is:

£ [ ]

5   **Decide whether the following statement is true or false.**

If Sara gives some jewellery to her daughter Emily, gift relief can be claimed.

	✓
True	
False	

6   Tommy gave Sinbad a factory in June 2021 that had been used in his trade. The factory cost £50,000 in October 2007 and was worth £200,000 at the date of the gift. Sinbad sold the factory for £350,000 in May 2022. Ignore the annual exempt amount.

If gift relief is claimed, the gain on the gift by Tommy is:

£ [ ]

and the gain on the sale by Sinbad is:

£ [ ]

7   Sunil sold his shareholding in W Ltd in February 2022. He had subscribed for the shares in June 2016 for £20,000. The proceeds of sale were £50,000. W Ltd is an unquoted trading company and Sunil is the sole shareholder and an employee of the company. Sunil is a higher rate taxpayer.

Sunil's CGT liability for 2021/22 is:

£ [ ]

His post-tax proceeds on disposal of his shares are:

£ [ ]

8   State which of the following statements **regarding disposals of unincorporated businesses** are true or false:

Statement	True ✓	False ✓
On the disposal of a sole trade business we compare proceeds to cost to calculate the chargeable gain/ allowable loss.		
If inventory costing £10,000 is sold for £12,000 it will give a chargeable gain of £2,000.		
A capital loss arises where plant and machinery is sold for less than cost.		
A gain equal to the market value of goodwill will arise on disposal of an unincorporated business.		
If a business with assets worth £100,000 is sold for £120,000 this will generate £20,000 of goodwill.		

Tax planning for businesses

Syllabus learning outcomes / objectives

6.2 Badges of trade

Learners need to understand:

- How to identify if clients are trading through the application of the badges of trade

6.3 Tax planning for businesses

Learners need to know:

- The tax rates which apply:
  - To sole traders
  - To companies
  - On extraction of profits from companies

Learners need to understand:

- Implications of different business structures on tax planning

- Impact on tax when using different methods of extracting profits, including salary and dividends

- Tax planning opportunities to ensure taxable income is optimally allocated between spouses/ civil partners

Assessment context

One of the tasks in your assessment will include some of the tax planning ideas covered within this chapter.

Qualification context

You will not see the information in this chapter outside of this unit unless you are also studying Personal Tax.

Business context

The tax included within this chapter is very useful if you are advising a client who is thinking about setting up a business. People often don't realise that different business structures have very different tax consequences. Of course, if you, or a friend, ever plan on setting up your own business then this knowledge would be useful then too!

Chapter overview

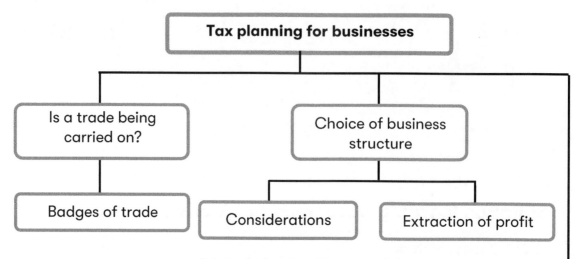

Tax planning for businesses

Is a trade being carried on?

Badges of trade

- Subject matter
- Ownership
- Frequency of transactions
- Improvement expenditure
- Reason for sale
- Profit motive
- Existence of similar transactions
- Source of finance
- Method of acquisition

Choice of business structure

Considerations

Sole trader/ partnership

- More private, fewer regulations
- Pays income tax, Class 2 & 4 NICs
- Two payments on account, 31 July, 31 January
- Taxed before any profits extracted

Company

- Separate legal entity, more rules and regulations
- Pays corporation tax, Class 1 NICs on any employee salaries
- Due 9 months and 1 day after end of accounting period
- Profit extraction has tax consequences

Extraction of profit

Salary

- Salary and class 1 employer's NIC due thereon are tax deductible for the company
- Individual pays income tax and employee's NIC on salary

Dividend

- Not tax deductible for company and no NICs
- Individual pays income tax at lower rates and no NICs

Spouse or civil partner planning

Income tax planning

- Ensure use of both personal allowances
- Ensure further income is received by spouse paying lower rates of tax

Capital gains tax planning

- Assets pass at nil gain nil loss
- Ensure both annual exempt amounts utilised
- Further gains to be taxed on spouse paying lower rate of tax
- Ability to claim reliefs

1 Introduction

In this chapter we look at tax planning for businesses.

We will start by looking at the rules which are used in determining whether an individual is trading or not. These rules are known as the badges of trade and were introduced in the earlier computing trading income chapter.

We will move on to look at one of the most basic decisions that needs to be made when setting up in business - choice of business structure. As well as practical and legal considerations, the tax consequences of different structures are different. We will consider the choice of setting up the business as an unincorporated business (i.e. as a sole trader or partnership) or as an incorporated business (i.e. a company).

Next, we need to consider how we extract profits from the new business and what tax consequences this may have.

Finally, we will consider some spouse/ civil partner tax planning ideas.

2 Is a trade being carried on?

It is important to know whether profits of an individual or company should be assessed as trading income.

For example, a person who buys and sells stamps may be trading as a stamp dealer. Alternatively, stamp collecting may be a hobby of that person. In this case, he is probably not trading.

If a trade is not being carried on, any profit arising from selling items could be exempt from tax or chargeable to capital gains tax. If a trade is being carried on then the individual will be liable to income tax and national insurance contributions based on their trading profits.

To make this decision we use some tests known as the 'badges of trade' to determine whether an individual is trading or not.

2.1 Badges of trade

The following tests are used by the courts when distinguishing trading from investment or capital transactions and have evolved over the years as a result of the outcome of many court cases arguing trade versus investment:

2.1.1 Subject matter

Some items are commonly held as an **investment**, for example, works of art and antiques. A subsequent disposal may produce a gain of a capital nature rather than a trading profit. However, where the subject matter of a transaction is such that it would not normally be held as an investment (for example, 1,000,000 rolls of toilet paper), it is presumed that any profit on resale is a trading profit.

2.1.2 Ownership

Consider the length of ownership of the asset. The purchase of items followed by sale soon afterwards indicates trading. Conversely, if items are held for a long time before sale there is less likely to be a trade.

2.1.3 Frequency of transactions

A series of similar transactions indicates trading. Conversely, a single transaction is unlikely to be considered as a trade.

2.1.4 Improvement expenditure

If work is done to make an asset more marketable, or steps are taken to find purchasers, there is likely to be a trade. For example, when a group of accountants bought, blended and recasked a quantity of brandy, they were held to be taxable on a trading profit when the brandy was later sold. Advertisement of the goods for sale is also a factor which makes It more likely there is a trade.

2.1.5 Reason for sale

Where objective criteria clearly indicate that a trade is being carried on, the taxpayer's intentions are irrelevant. If, however, a transaction (objectively) has a dual purpose, you should consider the taxpayer's intentions. For example, the taxpayer could buy a property, restore it and sell it. You need to consider whether it was purchased purely for resale, which would indicate trade, or did the taxpayer buy it with the intention of making it their home and then changed their mind – not trade.

2.1.6 Motive for profit

If an item is bought with the intention of selling it at a profit, a trade is likely to exist.

2.1.7 Existence of similar trading transactions or interests

The existence of similar trading transactions or interests would suggest that a trade exist. If an accountant sold a car it would be unlikely to constitute a trade as there is no direct link between their existing interests and the sale. However, if a car mechanic sold a car there is a direct link between their existing trade and the sale. It would be likely that the sale of the car would be a trading transaction.

2.1.8 The source of finance

If an asset is acquired using short term finance, a trade is likely to exist. This is particularly the case where it will be necessary to dispose of the asset to repay the funds.

2.1.9 Method of acquisition

If goods are acquired unintentionally, for example, by gift or inheritance, their later sale is unlikely to constitute trading.

3 Choice of business structure

3.1 Introduction

When starting a business, an individual must decide whether to set up as unincorporated business (i.e. a sole trader or partnership) or as an incorporated business (i.e. a company). This choice has very different practical, legal and tax considerations.

3.2 Considerations

The table below sets out the key differences in an individual's choice of business structure:

	Sole trader/ Partnership	Company
Liability	The individual and the business are the same entity. The individual is personally liable for the liabilities of the business.	The company is a separate legal entity from the owners, with the individual owning shares in the company. The individual's assets are protected by limited liability.
Accounts, Regulations and Privacy	An unincorporated business has fewer rules and regulations with which to comply and does not need to file accounts at Companies House. This gives more privacy.	A company is subject to more rules and regulations including the Companies Act. There is a requirement to file accounts at Companies House, so results are public.

	Sole trader/ Partnership	Company
Tax on profits	Trading profits (adjusted for tax) subject to income tax at non-savings rates (20/40/45%) dependent on levels of taxable income. The personal allowance may be available. Classes 2 and 4 NICs will also be due. Class 2 NIC £3.05 per week Class 4 NIC 9% on trading profits between £9,568 and £50,270 and 2% above.	The company pays corporation tax on trading profits (adjusted for tax) at 19%. Class 1 NICs will be due on cash earnings of any employees and are deductible for the company. The company suffers Class 1 employer NIC at 13.8% on earnings over £8,840. A £4,000 employment allowance is available to offset the first £4,000 of employer's NIC due (although this is not available to companies with a single director and no other employees). The employee will pay Class 1 employee's NIC at 12% on cash earnings between £9,568 and £50,270 and 2% above.
Tax payments	Two payments on account 31 January 2022 and 31 July 2022.	Probably a small company, therefore tax is due nine months and one day after end of the accounting period.
Extraction of profits	The sole trader extracts profits as drawings or owner's "salary". Income tax is paid on trade profits before any drawings or owner's salary is deducted so how the profits are extracted, or how much, has no tax consequences.	Profits need to be extracted from the company to the individual, usually by way of either director's salary or dividends (or a combination). The different tax consequences are covered in the next section.

Activity 1: Sole trader versus company

Select whether the following statements are true or false:

Statement	True ✓	False ✓
A sole trader business is a separate legal entity from its owner.		
Profits can be extracted from a sole trade business with no tax consequences.		
Sole traders pay income tax on their trade profits at 20%		
Companies pay their tax in two payments on account.		
A sole trader will pay Class 2 and Class 4 NICs.		
A company pays Class 1 employee's NIC on any cash earnings in excess of £8,840 at 13.8%.		

3.3 Extraction of profit

The profits of an unincorporated business before deduction of any drawings or owners' salaries are taxed to income tax on the sole trader or partner. They can therefore extract profit by way of drawings or owner's salary and with no tax consequences.

In contrast, if the business is set up as a company, the owner will be a separate entity to the company, and they will need to consider how to extract their profits from the company. The most common methods of profit extraction are for the owner to take a salary or dividend. These have very different tax consequences for both the individual and the company which are summarised below:

Method	Company	Individual
Salary	Class 1 employer's NIC will be due on any cash salary in excess of £8,840 at 13.8%. The company has a £4,000 employment allowance which can be deducted from the first employer's NIC due(although this is not available to companies with a single director and no other employees). The salary and the Class 1 employer's NIC are deductible from trading profits thus reducing TTP and saving corporation tax.	Income tax will be due on any salary in excess of the personal allowance at 20%, 40% or 45% dependent on the individual's other income. Class 1 employee's NIC will be due at 12% on any cash salary in excess of £9,568 up to £50,270. If the cash salary exceeds £50,270 there is 2% NIC on the excess.
Dividends	Not tax deductible for the company. No NICs.	Income tax will be due on any dividends in excess of the personal allowance at 7.5%, 32.5% or 38.1% dependent on the individual's other income. No NICs.

Illustration 1: Extraction of profit 1

Inga is the sole shareholder and director of Labrador Ltd. The company doesn't have any other employees. During the year ended 31 December 2022, Labrador Ltd makes tax adjusted trading profits of £20,000 and has no other income or gains.

Inga has other employment income of £18,000 and dividend income of £2,000 making her a basic rate taxpayer.

Calculate the maximum dividend that Inga can take this year and the post-tax cash that she would receive.

	£
Labrador Ltd's TTP	20,000
Less corporation tax @ 19%	(3,800)
Profits available to distribute as a dividend = dividend	16,200
As a basic rate taxpayer, Inga will suffer 7.5% income tax on this dividend with no NIC. (7.5% × £16,200)	(1,215)
After-tax dividend kept by Inga	14,985

If Inga instead chose to extract all of her profits as a salary, calculate how much post-tax cash she would receive.

	£
Labrador Ltd's TTP	20,000
Employer's NIC will be due at 13.8% on any salary that Inga chooses to take from the company. So, the TTP figures represents 113.8% of the salary. Employer's NIC on salary to withdraw (13.8/113.8 × £20,000) (Note)	(2,425)
Salary for Inga to withdraw (100/113.8 × £20,000)	17,575
This salary will be taxed on Inga, a basic rate taxpayer, at a rate of 20% income tax and 12% employee's NICs. Thus 32% tax will be suffered (32% × £17,575)	(5,624)
After tax salary kept by Inga	11,951

Note. As Inga is the sole director and employee of the company, there is no employment allowance available.

Activity 2: Extraction of profit 2

Dash is the sole shareholder of Pringle Ltd. During the year ended 31 December 2022, Pringle Ltd makes tax adjusted trading profits of £75,000 and has no other income or gains.

Dash has other employment income of £60,000 and dividend income of £6,000 making her a higher rate taxpayer.

If Dash extracts the maximum possible dividend, how much income will she receive after tax.

	£

If Dash instead chose to extract all of her profits as a salary, calculate how much post-tax cash she would receive.

	£

4 Spouse or civil partner tax planning

4.1 Income tax planning

Where a couple are married or in a civil partnership, they are treated separately for tax purposes. Each will pay income tax based on their own income with their own personal allowance.

However, income generating assets, such as shares or rental property, can usually be passed between themselves with no tax consequences (referred to as nil gain nil loss transfers) allowing the couple to reduce their combined income tax by:

- Ensuring both partners are fully utilising their personal allowance
- Moving income generating assets from a partner paying higher or additional rate tax to a partner paying basic rate tax.

4.2 Capital gains tax planning

Passing capital assets between spouses/ civil partners also allows for capital gains tax planning. Where assets are to be sold realising chargeable gains, ownership should be arranged in such a way that allows each spouse to fully utilise their own annual exempt amount and then for any further gains to be realised by the spouse paying the lower rate of capital gains tax. Consideration could also be given as to whether only one spouse might be able to claim business asset disposal relief.

Activity 3: Spouse /civil partner tax planning

William and Isla have been married for many years and have two young children. William works full time on a salary of £70,000 and earns dividends of £5,000 each year and is thus a higher rate taxpayer. Isla is expecting their third child and will not have any income for the next tax year.

The couple are considering investing in shares and thus earning dividend income.

Advise the couple as to who should buy the shares in order to minimise their overall tax bill.

Solution

Assessment focus point

Please refer to the reference material at the end of this Course Book to see which elements of this chapter will be available to you as a pop-up window in the live assessment.

- The badges of trade give guidance as to whether or not a trade is being carried on.

- A new business can be set up as a sole trade/ partnership or a company

  - There is no legal distinction between the owner and an unincorporated business

  - A company is a separate legal entity from its shareholders

  - Unincorporated business have to comply with fewer rules and regulations than companies

  - Sole traders/partners pay income tax and classes 2 & 4 NICs on trade profits whereas companies pay corporation tax

  - Sole traders/partners pay their tax in two payments on account whereas a company usually pays corporation tax 9 months and 1 day after the end of its accounting period

  - A sole trader can extract their profit with no tax consequences. For a company extraction of profit has tax consequences

- Extraction of profit from a company

  - A salary creates class 1 employer's NIC for the company. The salary and employer's NIC are tax deductible reducing the company's corporation tax

  - The individual pays income tax and employee's NIC on the salary

  - Dividends are not tax deductible for the company and there are no NICs for wither the company or the shareholder

  - The individual pays income tax only on the dividend income

- Married couples/ civil partners should plan to use both individuals' personal allowances (for income tax) and annual exempt amounts (for capital gains tax). Any income/ gains should then arise on the individual paying tax at the lowest rate. Assets can pass between spouses/ civil partners at nil gain nil loss.

BPP
LEARNING
MEDIA

Keywords

- **Badges of trade:** Indicate whether or not a trade is being carried on

- **Business structure:** How the business is set up. Can be an unincorporated business such as a sole trader or partnership or incorporated such as a company

- **Extraction of profit:** How the owner of a business removes profit from it

Test your learning

1   Tick to show whether each statement about sole traders and companies is true or false.

Statement	True ✓	False ✓
A company must comply with fewer rules and regulations than a sole trader.		
A sole trader can extract profits from the business with no direct tax consequence.		
Class 1 employee's NIC is paid at 13.8% on any cash salary paid to an employee.		
A company pays its tax in two payments on account (31 July and 31 January).		

2   Tick to show whether each statement about extraction of profits from a company is true or false.

Statement	True ✓	False ✓
There are fewer NICs due when profits are extracted by way of dividend rather than salary.		
A dividend payment will reduce the company's corporation tax liability.		
When a company pays a salary, the salary and the employer's NIC thereon is tax deductible for the company.		
Where profits are extracted as a dividend the individual will pay income tax at 20%/40%/45%		
A basic rate taxpayer will suffer a combined total of 32% tax on any salary they receive.		
A higher rate taxpayer will suffer a combined total of 52% tax on any salary they receive.		

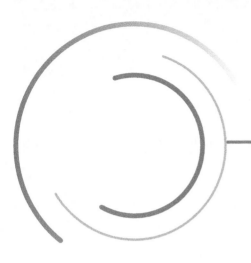

Activity answers

CHAPTER 1 Tax framework

Activity 1: Tax avoidance and tax evasion

The correct answer is: Action 1 only

Action 1 is tax evasion as it involves misleading HMRC to delay a legitimate tax charge.

Action 2 is tax planning.

Activity 2: Taxable income

£	5,930

	Non-savings income £
Trading income	16,000
Property income	2,500
Dividends	
Net income	18,500
Less personal allowance	(12,570)
Taxable income	5,930

Activity 3: Calculation of income tax liability

£	886

	Non-savings income £
Employment income	17,000
Total income	17,000
PA	(12,570)
Taxable income	4,430
Non-savings income	
4,430 × 20%	886
Tax liability	886

CHAPTER 2 Computing trading income

Activity 1: Adjustment of profits (i)

	£
Profit for the year in accounts	38,000
Add entertaining expenses	2,000
Add depreciation	4,000
	44,000
Less capital allowances	(3,500)
Taxable trading profit	40,500

Activity 2: Capital versus revenue

	Revenue ✓	Capital ✓
Paying employee wages	✓	
Paying rent for premises	✓	
Buying machinery		✓
Buying a van		✓
Building an extension to shop		✓
Paying for repairs to car	✓	

Activity 3: Calculation of add back

Amount to add back	✓
£17,450	
£16,000	
£18,450	✓
£11,450	

The fine will not be deductible and will therefore need to be added back as will the cost of the specialist tax consultancy work. The redundancy payments are allowable because they were incurred wholly and exclusively for the purposes of the trade. The payment of a salary to the proprietor of a business is not deductible because it is just a method of extracting a profit from the business and that profit is taxable in the normal way as part of the taxable trading profits. 15% of leasing costs of car with CO_2 emissions exceeding 50g/km are disallowable. Add back 1,000 + 2000 + 15,000 + 15% x 3,000 = £18,450.

Activity 4: Entertainment and gifts

Expenditure	£	Add back ✓
Staff tennis outing for 30 employees	1,800	
2,000 tee shirts with firm's logo given to race runners	4,500	
Advertising and sponsorship of an athletic event	2,000	
Entertaining customers	7,300	✓
Staff Christmas party (30 employees)	2,400	

Activity 5: Adjustment of profits (ii)

Adjustment to profit	£	£
Net profit per the accounts		30,900
Add back		
Depreciation	5,000	
Entertaining	100	
Staff wages	5,000	
Council tax	1,000	
Total added back		11,100
Deduct		
Bank interest		(4,000)
Adjusted profits before capital allowances		38,000

CHAPTER 3 Capital allowances

Activity 1: Annual investment allowance

Delson can claim an annual investment allowance of | £ | 750,000 | .

Workings (on-screen free text area provided in the CBT as part of larger question)

Nine-month period.

Max entitlement is therefore $\frac{9}{12}$ × £1,000,000 = £750,000

Assets eligible are:

		£
15 January 2022	Manufacturing equipment	650,000
16 January 2022	Computer equipment	60,000
7 May 2022	Office furniture	30,000
13 May 2022	Delivery vans	20,000
		760,000

As the eligible assets are greater than the limit, Delson may only claim £750,000.

Note. The balance of expenditure, and the car, will be eligible for other allowances.

Activity 2: Writing-down allowances in the general pool

	AIA	General pool	Total allowances
TWDV b/f		10,000	
Additions			
Car		18,000	
Van	29,000		
Manufacturing plant (Total = £1,030,000)	971,000	59,000	
AIA (see note)	(1,000,000)		1,000,000
Disposals		(2,000)	
		85,000	
WDA @ 18%		(15,300)	15,300
			1,015,300
TWDV c/f		69,700	

Activity 3: Short period of account

	AIA	General pool	Total allowances
TWDV b/f		12,000	
P/e 31.12.21			
Disposal			
7.7 van		(2,000)	
AIA additions			
15.4 Plant (total £1,046,750)	750,000	296,750	
AIA $1,000,000 \times \frac{9}{12}$	(750,000)		750,000
Non-AIA addition			
13.4 car		7,000	
		313,750	
WDA @ 18% $\times \frac{9}{12}$		(42,356)	42,356
TWDV c/f		271,394	
			792,356

Activity 4: Cessation of a business

(a) If Baxter sells his plant for £15,500 then he will have a | balancing charge | of

£ | 1,500 | .

Workings (on-screen free text area provided in the CBT as part of larger question)

	General pool	Allowances
TWDV b/f	12,000	
Additions	2,000	
Disposals	(15,500)	
	(1,500)	
Balancing charge	1,500	(1,500)
TWDV c/f	–	

(b)   If Baxter sells his plant for £11,500 then he will have a | balancing allowance | of

£ | 2,500 .

Workings (on-screen free text area provided in the CBT as part of larger question)

	General pool	Allowances
TWDV b/f	12,000	
Additions	2,000	
Disposals	(11,500)	
	2,500	
Balancing allowance	(2,500)	2,500
TWDV c/f	–	

Activity 5: Special rate pool

	General pool	Special rate	Total allowances
Y/e 31.3.22			
TWDV b/f	25,000	10,000	
Additions	17,000	8,000	
	42,000	18,000	
WDA 18%/6%	(7,560)	(1,080)	8,640
TWDV c/f	34,440	16,920	

Activity 6: Private-use assets

(a)   Sweeney's capital allowances

	General pool	Private-use asset	Total allowances
TWDV b/f	16,000	20,000	
WDA @ 18%	(2,880)		2,880
WDA @ 6%		(1,200)	960
			3,840
TWDV c/f	13,120	18,800	

Note. As there is no restriction for the private use of an employee, and it has emissions of ≤ 50g, Doris's car would be in the main pool. Only 80% of the allowances on Sweeney's car are claimed on his private use car.

Sweeney's car has CO_2 emissions in excess of 50g/km so it is written down at the special rate rather than the main rate.

(b) What capital allowances would Sweeney claim if the business ceased in this period and both cars were sold for £15,000 each?

Sweeney would have a | balancing allowance | of | £ | 5,000 | .

Workings (on-screen free text area provided in the CBT as part of larger question)

	£
Sweeney's car	
Balancing allowance (20,000 – 15,000) × 80% =	4,000
Main pool (Doris's car)	
Balancing allowance (16,000 – 15,000) =	1,000
	5,000

Note. There is no restriction for the private use of an employee.

Activity 7: Enhanced capital allowances for companies

The capital allowances claim that Backwell Ltd can make for the period ended 30 June 2021 is:

	AIA	FYA	Super deduction	General pool	Special rate pool	Private use asset	Total allowances
TWDV brought forward at 1 January 2021				81,000			
Plant	41,000						
Salesman's car				11,000			
Finance director's car					50,000		
Machinery			36,000				
AIA	(41,000)						41,000
Super-deduction			(36,000)				46,800
Disposals				(30,000)			
				62,000	50,000		
WDA 18%/ 6%				(11,160)	(3,000)		14,160
C/fwd/ total				50,840	47,000		101,960

Activity 8: Calculation of capital allowances

The capital allowances claim that Oscar can make for the period ended 30 June 2022 is calculated as follows:

	AIA	FYA	General pool	Total allowances
18 m/e 30 June 2022				
B/f			481,000	
Disposal 1.6.22			(30,000)	
AIA acquisition				
10.7.21 Plant	1,410,000			
12.9.21 Plant	550,000			
AIA (see note)	(1,500,000)			1,500,000
	460,000			
Transfer balance to pool	(460,000)		460,000	
FYA acquisition				
10.8.21 Car		11,000		
FYA @ 100%		(11,000)		11,000
			911,000	
WDA @ 18% × 18/12			(245,970)	245,970
C/f			665,030	
Allowances				1,756,970

Notes.

1. The AIA limit and WDA are scaled up for the 18-month period, whereas the FYA is never scaled up or down. The limit is (£1,000,000 × 18/12). The total AIA is therefore £1,500,000.

2. This working would not be the same had it related to a company, as the 18-month period would be split into two accounting periods (a 12-month period and a 6-month period). In addition, the two purchases of plant would have been eligible for the super-deduction in preference to the AIA. We look at accounting periods for companies later in the Course Book.

Activity 9: SBAs

£2,000,000 × 3% × 6/12 = £30,000

The cost of acquisition excludes acquisition fees. The SBA must be time-apportioned in the year of acquisition.

Statement 1 is incorrect as the seller may claim a time-apportioned SBA in the year of disposal.

Statement 2 is correct, as Rose Ltd would have claimed (3 × 3% × £2,000,000) = £180,000 of SBAs at the date of disposal, which are added to the proceeds in its chargeable gain computation.

Statement 3 is incorrect, as SBAs are based on the original qualifying cost of £2 million.

Statement 4 is correct, as the building was brought into qualifying use by Petal plc on 1 July 2024, and therefore the WDA must be multiplied by 9/12.

CHAPTER 4 Taxing unincorporated businesses

Activity 1: Current year basis (i)

Correct option is year ended 31 December 2021.

Workings (not provided in the CBT)

Tax the profits arising in the accounting period ending in fiscal year 2021/22 ie the accounting period that ends between 6 April 2021 and 5 April 2022.

Activity 2: Current year basis (ii)

(a)   Correct option is tax year 2021/22

      Workings (not provided in the CBT)

      Period ended 30 June 2021 ends between 6 April 2021 and 5 April 2022, ie tax year 2021/22.

(b)   Correct option is tax year 2020/21

      Workings (not provided in the CBT)

      Period ended 31 January 2021 ends between 6 April 2020 and 5 April 2021, ie tax year 2020/21.

Activity 3: The first tax year

What is the first tax year of the trade? (XXXX/XX format)

2019/20

What profits will be assessed in the first fiscal year?

£	6,000

Workings (not provided in the CBT)

2019/20
Actual basis 01/01/20 to 05/04/20
$\frac{3}{12} \times 24,000 = £6,000$

Activity 4: The second tax year (trader has 12 month accounting period)

What is the second tax year of the trade? (XXXX/XX format)

2020/21

What profits will be assessed in the second tax year?

£	24,000

Workings (not provided in the CBT)

Trade begins in tax year 2019/20 so this is the first year.
The second year is therefore 2020/21
12m period ending in 2020/21 $\Rightarrow$ basis period = 12 months to the end of AP
ie. y/e 31.12.20 = £24,000

Activity 5: Overlap profits

His overlap period is (XX/XX/XX) | 01/01/20 | to | 05/04/20 |

His overlap profits are £ | 6,000

Activity 6: Opening year rules (short first period)

	Profits taxed			
	Fiscal year (XXXX/XX)	From (XX/XX/XX)	To (XX/XX/XX)	Amount taxed £
First fiscal year	2019/20	01/01/20	05/04/20	9,000
Second fiscal year	2020/21	01/01/20	31/12/20	42,000
Third fiscal year	2021/22	01/07/20	30/06/21	48,000
Overlap periods and profits				
First overlap period		01/01/20	05/04/20	9,000
Second overlap period		01/07/20	31/12/20	24,000
Total overlap				33,000

Workings (not provided in the CBT)

	£
2019/20 **Actual** 01/01/20 to 05/04/20	
$\frac{3}{6} \times 18,000 = £9,000$	
2020/21	
6m period ending in 2020/21 $\Rightarrow$ tax first 12 months of profits	
6m to 30/06/20	18,000
6m to 31/12/20 ($\frac{6}{12} \times 48,000$)	24,000
	42,000
2021/22 – CYB 12m period ending 30/06/21	48,000
Overlap 01/01/20 to 05/04/20	
$\frac{3}{6} \times 18,000$	9,000
Plus 01/07/20 to 31/12/20	
$\frac{6}{12} \times 48,000$	24,000
Total	33,000

Activity 7: Opening year rules (long first period ending in second tax year)

	Profits taxed			
	Tax year (XXXX/XX)	From (XX/XX/XX)	To (XX/XX/XX)	Amount taxed £
First tax year	2019/20	01/07/19	05/04/20	9,000
Second tax year	2020/21	01/01/20	31/12/20	12,000
Third tax year	2021/22	01/01/21	31/12/21	30,000
Overlap period and profits		01/01/20	05/04/20	3,000

Workings (not provided in the CBT)

2019/20
Actual 01/07/19 to 05/04/20
$\frac{9}{18} \times 18{,}000 = £9{,}000$
2020/21
18m period ending in 2020/21 $\Rightarrow$ tax 12m to accounting year end $\Rightarrow$ 01/01/20 to 31/12/20
$\frac{12}{18} \times 18{,}000 = £12{,}000$
2021/22
Y/e 31/12/21 £30,000
Overlap 01/01/20 to 05/04/20
$\frac{3}{18} \times 18{,}000 = £3{,}000$

Activity 8: Opening year rules (long first period ending in third tax year)

	Profits taxed			
	Tax year (XXXX/XX)	From (XX/XX/XX)	To (XX/XX/XX)	Amount taxed £
First tax year	2019/20	01/12/19	05/04/20	8,000
Second tax year	2020/21	06/04/20	05/04/21	24,000
Third tax year	2021/22	01/06/20	31/05/21	24,000
Overlap period and profits		01/06/20	05/04/21	20,000

Workings (not provided in the CBT)

2019/20
Actual 01/12/19 to 05/04/20
$\frac{4}{18} \times 36{,}000$ = £8,000
2020/21
– no accounting period ending in 2020/21 $\Rightarrow$ **Actual** 06/04/20 to 05/04/21
$\frac{12}{18} \times 36{,}000$ = £24,000
2021/22
12m to y/e $\Rightarrow$ 12m to 31/05/21
$\frac{12}{18} \times 36{,}000$ = £24,000
Overlap 01/06/20 to 05/04/21
$\frac{10}{18} \times 36{,}000$ = £20,000

Activity 9: Closing year rules (one period ending in final tax year)

	Profits taxed			
	Tax year (XXXX/XX)	From (XX/XX/XX)	To (XX/XX/XX)	Amount taxed £
Penultimate tax year	2020/21	01/01/2020	31/12/2020	22,000
Final tax year	2021/22	01/01/2021	30/04/2021	8,000

Workings (not provided in the CBT)

Business finishes 30/04/21 so final year is 2021/22	
2020/21 CYB (y/e 31/12/20)	22,000
2021/22 4 months: 01/01/21 – 30/04/21	12,000
Less overlap profits	(4,000)
	8,000

Activity 10: Closing year rules (two periods ending in final tax year)

	Profits taxed			
	Tax year (XXXX/XX)	From (XX/XX/XX)	To (XX/XX/XX)	Amount taxed £
Penultimate tax year	2020/21	01/01/2020	31/12/2020	30,000
Final tax year	2021/22	01/01/2021	31/03/2022	17,000

Workings (not provided in the CBT)

Business finishes on 31 March 2022 ie in fiscal year 2021/22. This is his final year.

2020/21	y/e 31 December 2020	30,000
2021/22	y/e 31 December 2021	25,000
	p/e 31 March 2022	4,000
		29,000
	Less overlap profits	(12,000)
		17,000

CHAPTER 5 Partnerships

Activity 1: Partnership profit allocation

	Ron £	Steve £
Profit share	38,000	22,000

Workings (not provided in the CBT)

	Ron £	Steve £	Total £
Year ended 30 June			
Salary	5,000	–	5,000
Balance (3:2)	33,000	22,000	55,000 (bal)
Assessments	38,000	22,000	60,000

Activity 2: Change in profit-sharing arrangements

	Ron £	Steve £
Profit share	50,500	39,500

Workings (not provided in the CBT)

	Ron £	Steve £	Total £
Year ended 30 June			
1 July – 31 December			
Salary $\frac{6}{12} \times 5,000$	2,500		2,500
Balance (3:2)	25,500	17,000	42,500
$\frac{6}{12} \times 90,000$			45,000
1 January – 30 June			
$\frac{6}{12} \times 90,000$			
Split 1:1	22,500	22,500	45,000
	50,500	39,500	90,000

Activity 3: Change in partnership personnel

	M £	G £	B £
2019/20	16,500	24,250	5,667
2020/21	29,750	0	20,500
2021/22	48,000	0	24,000
Overlap			17,667

Workings (not provided in the CBT)

Sharing of profits

	Total £	M £	G £	B £
Y/e 31.5.19, ie £33,000				
(1:1)	33,000	16,500	16,500	–
Y/e 31.5.20, ie £51,000				
Up to 1.12.19 (1:1) $51,000 \times \frac{6}{12}$	25,500	12,750	12,750	–
From 1.12.19 (2:1 each) $51,000 \times \frac{6}{12}$	25,500	17,000		8,500
	51,000	29,750	12,750	8,500
Y/e 31.5.21, ie £72,000				
(2:1)	72,000	48,000		24,000

New partner (B): Trading profits

	£
Started trading 1.12.19	
6 months to 31.5.20	8,500
Year ended 31.5.21	24,000

New partner (B): Trading assessments

	£
2019/20 actual 1.12.19 – 5.4.20 $8,500 \times \frac{4}{6}$	5,667
2020/21 (first 12 months), ie 1.12.19 – 30.11.20 $8,500 + \frac{6}{12} \times 24,000$	20,500
2021/22 (y/e 31.5.21)	24,000

New partner (B): Overlap

	£
1.12.19 – 5.4.20	5,667
1.6.20 – 30.11.20 ($\frac{6}{12} \times 24,000$)	12,000
	17,667

Retiring partner (G): Trading assessments

	£
Retires on 1.12.19, ie 2019/20	
2019/20 (y/e 31.5.19)	16,500
2019/20 (p/e 1.12.19)	12,750
Less overlap	(5,000)
Total 2019/20	24,250

Continuing partner (M): Trading assessments

	£
2019/20 (y/e 31.5.19)	£16,500
2020/21 (y/e 31.5.20)	£29,750
2021/22 (y/e 31.5.21)	£48,000

CHAPTER 6 National insurance

Activity 1: National insurance contributions

(a)   Mr Bull

His Class 2 NI contributions for the year are:

£ | 158.60

His Class 4 NI contributions at 9% are:

£ | 398.88

Workings (not provided in the CBT)

Class 2	52 × £3.05	£158.60
Class 4	(£14,000 – £9,568) × 9%	£398.88

(b)   Mr Seye

His Class 4 NI contributions at 9% are:

£ | 3,663.18

His Class 4 NI contributions at 2% are:

£ | 554.60

Workings (not provided in the CBT)

Class 4 at 9%	(£50,270 – £9,568) × 9%	£3,663.18
Class 4 at 2%	(£78,000 – £50,270) × 2%	£554.60

CHAPTER 7 Computing corporation tax

Activity 1: Calculating taxable total profits

Corporation tax computation y/e 31 December 2021

	£
Trading profits	2,440,000
Property income	150,000
NTL-R income (Investment income) (40,000 - 10,000)	30,000
Chargeable gains (350,000 + 70,000 – 80,000)	340,000
Total profits	2,960,000
Less qualifying charitable payment	(70,000)
Taxable total profits	2,890,000

Note. The dividends received are not taxable.

Activity 2: Calculating taxable total profits – long period of account

Long period of account

	12 months to 31.8.21 £	4 months to 31.12.21 £
Adjusted trading profits (12:4)	2,700,000	900,000
Less capital allowances (W1)	(6,750)	(8,721)
Trading profits	2,693,250	891,279
NTL-R income (Investment income) (12:4)	24,000	8,000
Chargeable gain	–	40,000
Total profits	2,717,250	939,279
Less qualifying charitable donation	(20,000)	–
TTP	2,697,250	939,279

Workings (not provided in CBT)

	Super-deduction	General pool	Allowances
1.9.20 to 31.8.21 (12m)			
TWDV @ 1.9.20		37,500	
WDA (18%)		(6,750)	6,750
		30,750	
1.9.21 to 31.12.21 (4m)			
Addition	5,289		
Super-deduction (130%)	(5,289)		6,876
WDA (18%) × $\frac{4}{12}$		(1,845)	1,845
		28,905	
			8,721

Activity 3: Corporation tax payable

£	288,800

Workings (not provided in CBT)

	£
Trading profits	1,500,000
Chargeable gain	50,000
Qualifying charitable donations	(30,000)
Taxable total profits	1,520,000
Corporation tax due £1,520,000 × 19%	£288,800

CHAPTER 8 Losses

Activity 1: Income tax trading loss options

Show if the following statements are true or false by ticking the correct box for each.

	True ✓	False ✓
Edward may offset the loss against total income in 2019/20 and then in 2018/19.		✓
Edward may offset the loss against total income in 2021/22.		✓
Edward may offset the loss against trading income only in 2019/20.		✓
Edward may offset the loss against the rental income in 2020/21.	✓	

Notes.

1   The loss has been made in tax year 2020/21. It can, therefore, be used in 2020/21 and/or 2019/20, so the first option is false.

2   If Edward lets the loss carry forward to 2021/22, then it offsets automatically against trading income only, so the second option is false.

3   If Edward chooses to carry the loss back to 2019/20, it will offset against total income, not just trading income, so the third option is false.

4   If Edward makes a claim for 2020/21, it will offset against his total income. The only income he has is rental income so the fourth option is true.

Activity 2: Utilisation of income tax losses

(a)   Complete the following table showing Pike's total income for 2020/22 to 2023/24, assuming maximum and earliest claims against total income are made. Enter '0' in cells as appropriate.

	2020/21 £	2021/22 £	2022/23 £	2023/24 £
Trading income	2,000	0	8,000	4,000
Loss carried forward	0	0	(8,000)	(3,600)
	0	0	0	400
Property income	400	1,000	1,000	1,000
Total Income	2,400	1,000	1,000	1,400
CY loss relief	0	(1,000)	0	0
PY loss relief	(2,400)	0	0	0
Net income	0	0	1,000	1,400

Workings (not provided in the CBT)

	Trading loss
Loss made in 2021/22	15,000
Carry back against total income in 2020/21	(2,400)
Use against total income in current year 2021/22	(1,000)
Carry forward against trading income in year 2022/23	(8,000)
Carry forward against trading income in year 2023/24 (balancing figure)	(3,600)
	0

(b) Show if the following statement is true or false by ticking the correct box.

	True ✓	False ✓
Pike has used his loss in the most tax-efficient way possible		✓

Explanation

Pike's income is below the personal allowance in all years, so it is a waste to carry back the loss or use it in the year of the loss.

It is wasteful to use it in the future years as well but Pike has no control over this. The carry forward is automatic.

Note. The question told you to use the loss as soon as possible, so prior year relief should be claimed before current year.

Activity 3: Opening year loss relief

(a)

Trading assessments		£
2018/19	Actual (1.7.18 - 5.4.19)	Nil
2019/20	12m to end of accounting period (y/e 30.6.19)	Nil
2020/21	CYB (y/e 30.6.20)	24,000
2021/22	CYB (y/e 30.6.21)	30,000
2022/23	CYB (y/e 30.6.22)	36,000

The trading losses are attributed as follows:

Trading assessments		£
2018/19	9/12 × (£40,000)	(30,000)
2019/20	12m to end of accounting period	(40,000)
	Less used in 2018/19	30,000
		(10,000)

(b)   **2018/19 loss of £30,000:**

Relief available against total income of 2018/19 (£nil) and/or 2017/18 (£68,000) under normal loss relief against total income.

Relief against total income of 2015/16, 2016/17 and 2017/18 (£68,000 pa) in that order under early trade loss relief – the loss would be offset fully against 2015/16 income.

Carry forward relief against the first available trading profits of the same trade – £24,000 would be relieved in 2020/21 and the remainder in 2021/22.

2019/20 loss of £10,000:

Relief available against total income of 2019/20 (£nil) and/or 2018/19 (£nil) under normal loss relief against total income.

Relief against total income of 2016/17, 2017/18 and 2018/19 (£68,000 pa) in that order under early trade loss relief – the loss would be offset fully against 2016/17 income.

Carry forward relief against the first available trading profits of the same trade - depending on the relief used for the 2018/19 loss, relief would be obtained against 2020/21 or 2021/22 income.

Advice

Early years loss relief is the most beneficial claim for both losses - relief is obtained at the earliest point, generating repayments, and furthermore Jurgen was a higher rate taxpayer in the years prior to starting his trade and so relief for his losses will be mainly obtained at 40%.

Activity 4: Terminal loss relief

(a)   Frieda's terminal loss:

(a)	Unrelieved trading loss from 6 April to date of cessation (increased by overlap profits)		
	6.4.21 - 30.6.21 = 3/9 × (£27,000)	(9,000)	
	Overlap profits	(3,000)	
			(12,000)
(b)	Unrelieved trading loss (if any) arising from a date 12 months before cessation to 5 April		
	1.10.20 - 5.4.21 = 6/9 × (£27,000)	(18,000)	
	1.7.20 - 30.9.20 = 3/12 × £4,000	1,000	
			(17,000)
	Terminal loss claim		(29,000)

b)   2017/18   £nil

2018/19   £8,000

Since there is no assessment for 2021/22 the £29,000 will be carried back and set against the assessments for:

	£
Terminal loss	29,000
2020/21	(4,000)
2019/20	(10,000)
2018/19	(8,000)
Unrelieved terminal loss	7,000

This amount cannot be carried back any further (ie to 2017/18) and is lost.

Activity 5: Carry forward loss relief

The loss carried forward at 31 March 2022 is

£	5,000

Workings (not provided in the CBT)

	Year ended 31 March		
	2020 £	2021 £	2022 £
Trading profit	–	5,000	6,000
Property income	–	2,000	2,000
Total profits	–	7,000	8,000
Less trade loss carried forward		(7,000)	(8,000)
TTP	–	–	–

Loss memorandum			£
Y/e 31 March 2020			20,000
Loss relief y/e 31 March 2021			(7,000)
			13,000
Loss relief y/e 31 March 2022			(8,000)
c/f			5,000

Activity 6: Current year and carry back relief

	True ✓	False ✓
Kay Ltd may claim to offset £60,000 of the loss against total profits in y/e 31.3.21.		✓
If Kay Ltd makes the maximum permissible claims, it will have £90,000 loss to carry forward at 31.3.22.		✓
Kay Ltd may claim to offset the loss against total profits in y/e 31.3.21 and then against total profits in y/e 31.3.22.		✓
Kay Ltd may claim to offset the loss against total profits in y/e 31.3.22 and carry the remaining loss forward to the y/e 31.3.23.	✓	

Workings (not provided in CBT)

The loss arises in year ended 31 March 2022, so this is the current year.

We cannot carry back to the prior year of 31 March 2021 unless we have made a current year claim in y/e 31.3.22 first, so the first statement is false because only £50,000 of the loss would remain after a current year claim.

If the company makes the maximum permissible claims, it will offset in the current year of 31.3.22, then carry back to y/e 31.3.21, setting losses against total profits including gains (see below). It will have insufficient losses to reduce the y/e 31.3.21 income to nil so there will be no losses to carry forward. The second statement is, therefore, false.

If we wish to offset in y/e 31.3.21 and y/e 31.3.22, we must offset y/e 31.3.22 before y/e 31.3.21, so the third statement is false.

We can choose to offset the loss in y/e 31.3.22 only, so the fourth statement is true. Once we have offset in y/e 31.3.22, we could choose to make a further claim to offset in y/e 31.3.21 or to carry it forward into future accounting periods.

	Year ended 31 March		
	2020 £	2021 £	2022 £
Trading income	20,000	10,000	–
Capital gains	50,000	50,000	50,000
Total profits	70,000	60,000	50,000
Loss relief	–	(ii) (50,000)	(i) (50,000)
TTP	70,000	10,000	–

Workings (not provided in CBT)

Loss memorandum	£
Y/e 31.3.22	100,000
Less relief y/e 31.3.22(optional claim)	(50,000)(i)
Less relief y/e 31.3.21(additional optional claim after y/e 31.3.22 claim)	(50,000)(ii)
	Nil

Activity 7: Comprehensive example

	Y/e 30.9.19 £	P/e 31.3.20 £	Y/e 31.3.21 £	Y/e 31.3.22 £
Trading profits	20,000	30,000	0	15,000
NTL-R income	10,000	10,000	10,000	10,000
Total profits	30,000	40,000	10,000	25,000
Current year relief	0	0	(10,000)(i)	0
Prior year relief	(15,000)(iii)	(40,000)(ii)	0	0
Losses carried forward	0	0	0	(25,000)
	15,000	0	0	0
Qualifying charitable donations	(5,000)	(5,000)	(5,000)	(5,000)
Taxable total profits	10,000	0	0	0

Picklist:

Current year relief
Losses carried forward
Prior year relief
Qualifying charitable donations

Workings (not provided in CBT)

Loss memo   £

Y/e 31.3.21   155,000

Current – y/e 31.3.21   (i)   (10,000)

Carry back – 6m P/E 31.3.20   (ii)   (40,000)

     – Y/e 30.9.19 – max claim 6/12 × 30,000   (iii)   (15,000)

                                                                                                         90,000

C/fwd y/e 31.3.22   (iv)   (25,000)

C/fwd   65,000

Tutorial note. Full relief has been claimed in the y/e 31.3.22 because the question stated that maximum reliefs must be taken as early as possible. However, it would be possible in this scenario to restrict the relief in y/e 31.3.22 to £20,000 in keep the relief from the qualifying charitable donation and carry the remaining loss of £5,000 for offset in y/e 31.3.23.

CHAPTER 9 Self-assessment for individuals

Activity 1: Penalties

Kelly's penalty can be reduced from [70] % of the potential lost revenue (for a

deliberate, but not concealed error) to [20] %, with the unprompted disclosure of her error.

Activity 2: Payments on account and balancing payments

	£
2020/21 income tax payable 7,000 – 4,000 =	3,000
The payments on account for 2021/22 are therefore:	
31.1.22 $\frac{1}{2} \times 3,000$	1,500
31.7.22 $\frac{1}{2} \times 3,000$	1,500
The final payment is therefore:	
Income tax liability	8,000
Less PAYE	(2,500)
Less payments on account (2 × 1,500)	(3,000)
	2,500
Capital gains tax liability	1,000
31.1.23 Final payment	3,500

BPP
LEARNING
MEDIA

CHAPTER 10 Self-assessment for companies

Activity 1: Payment of corporation tax

A plc has a 31 March year end and has TTP of £2.1m per year.

	£
Corporation tax due	
2,100,000 × 19%	399,000
Due by instalments on the 14th day of month 7, 10, 13 and 16, counting from the start of the period – ie 1 April 2020.	
14 October 2021	99,750
14 January 2022	99,750
14 April 2022	99,750
14 July 2022	99,750

CHAPTER 11 Chargeable gains for companies

Activity 1: Unindexed gain calculation

Complete the table showing Rose plc's unindexed gain

	£
Proceeds	38,500
Less selling expenses	(1,500)
Net proceeds	37,000
Less cost	(15,000)
Less legal fees on purchase	(500)
Less enhancement	(3,000)
Capital gain	18,500

Activity 2: Chargeable gain calculation

	£
Proceeds	58,500
Less selling expenses	(1,500)
Net proceeds	57,000
Less cost	(15,000)
Less legal fees on purchase	(500)
Less enhancement	(3,000)
Unindexed gain	38,500
Less indexation on cost ((15,000 + 500) × 1.879)	(29,125)
Less indexation on enhancement expenditure (3,000 × 0.856)	(2,568)
Chargeable gain	6,807

Activity 3: Indexation

JEK Ltd bought an asset for £50,000.

What is the chargeable gain/(loss) if it was sold for:

(a)   £20,000?

£	(30,000)

(b)   £70,000?

£	nil

(c)   £150,000?

£	61,950

Workings (not provided in the CBT)

	£	£	£
Proceeds	20,000	70,000	150,000
Less cost	(50,000)	(50,000)	(50,000)
	(30,000)	20,000	100,000
IA (a) N/A	–		
(b) 50,000 × 0.761 = 38,050			
restrict to 20,000		(20,000)	
(c) 50,000 × 0.761			(38,050)
Indexed gain/(loss)	(30,000)	–	61,950

Activity 4: Rollover relief

The gain taxed on Henry Ltd now is:

£	10,000

.

The base cost of the new building is:

£	165,000

.

Workings (not provided in the CBT)

	£
Disposal of fixed plant	
Proceeds	200,000
Less cost	(150,000)
IA 150,000 × 10%	(15,000)
Indexed gain	35,000
Rollover relief (balancing figure)	(25,000)
Proceeds not reinvested taxed now (200,000 – 190,000)	10,000
Base cost of building = £190,000 – £25,000	165,000

CHAPTER 12 Share disposals

Activity 1: Matching rules for companies

	£
Match same day	1,000
Last 9 days	500
FA85 pool	1,000
	2,500

Same-day sale	£
Proceeds $^{1,000}/_{2,500}$ × 12,500	5,000
Cost	(4,822)
	178

Last 9 days	£
Proceeds $^{500}/_{2,500}$ × 12,500	2,500
Cost	(2,511)
	(11)

FA85 pool	Number	Cost £	Indexed cost £
Aug 1996	1,000	2,750	2,750
Index up to December 1998			
0.008 × 2,750 =			22
	1,000	2,750	2,772
Addition December 1998	1,000	3,250	3,250
	2,000	6,000	6,022
Index up to December 2017			
0.692 × 6,022 =			4,167
	2,000	6,000	10,189
Disposal 1,000/2,000 × 6,000 1,000/2,000 × 10,189	(1,000)	(3,000)	(5,095)
C/f	1,000	3,000	5,094

	£
Proceeds 1,000/2,500 × 12,500	5,000
Cost	(3,000)
Unindexed gain	2,000
IA (5,095 – 3,000)	(2,095)
Indexed gain	0

Total gains	£
Same day	178
Last 9 days	(11)
FA85 pool	0
	167

Activity 2: Bonus and rights issues for companies

Matching rules: The shares were all acquired more than 9 days prior to the date of disposal so they are all in the share pool.

Total gains	£
Proceeds	10,000
Less cost (W)	(2,100)
Less indexation (3,730 – 2,100)	(1,630)
Chargeable gain	6,270

1985 pool working	Number	Cost £	Indexed cost £
1.5.85	500	1,000	1,000
5.8.87 rights			
Index up to August 87			
1,000 × 0.072			72
	500	1,000	1,072
Rights 1:2 @ £5	250	1,250	1,250
	750	2,250	2,322
15.9.89 bonus	750	–	–
	1,500	2,250	2,322
10.3.19 rights issue			

1985 pool working	Number	Cost £	Indexed cost £
Index up to December 2017			
2,322 × 1.724			4,003
	1,500	2,250	6,325
10.3.2019 Rights issue 1:3 @ £6	500	3,000	3,000
	2,000	5,250	9,325
5.9.2021 Disposal 800/2,000 × 5,250 800/2,000 × 9,325	(800)	(2,100)	(3,730)
	1,200	3,150	5,595

CHAPTER 13 Business disposals

Activity 1: Computing capital gains tax payable

What is Mr Dunstable's capital gains tax payable?

£ | 950

Workings (not provided in the CBT)

	£
Capital/ chargeable gain	18,800
Less annual exempt amount	(12,300)
Taxable gain	6,500
Basic rate band	37,700
Taxable income	(34,200)
Basic rate band remaining	3,500

	£
Capital gains tax payable	
3,500 × 10%	350
3,000 × 20%	600
6,500	950

Activity 2: Business asset disposal relief – calculation of capital gains tax

Capital gains tax payable at 10% due to business asset disposal relief is

£ | 1,000

Capital gains tax payable at 10% to utilise the remaining basic rate band is

£ | 513

Capital gains tax on other gains payable at 20% is

£ | 6,574

Workings (not provided in the CBT)

	Eligible gains £	Other gains £
Chargeable/capital gains	10,000	50,300
Less annual exempt amount		(12,300)
	10,000	38,000

	Eligible gains £	Other gains £
	£	
Basic rate band	37,700	
Taxable income	(22,570)	
Basic rate band remaining	15,130	
Eligible gains	£	
10,000 × 10%	1,000	
Other gains		
5,130 × 10% (15,130 – 10,000)	513	
32,870 × 20%	6,574	
38,000		
	8,087	

Activity 3: Disposals eligible for business asset disposal relief

Identify which, if any, are qualifying disposals for business asset disposal relief. Tick the relevant box.

	✓
A partner's share of a business in which the individual has been a partner since August 2014	✓
A freehold factory which the individual uses in his business and has owned for ten years – this is not disposal of the whole/ part of a business (as a going concern)	
Unquoted shares held by the individual in a personal trading company in which he is employed and which he has owned for the previous three years	✓
Quoted shares held by the individual in a personal trading company in which he is employed and which he has owned for the previous three years	✓

Activity 4: Business asset disposal relief – calculating gains eligible for relief

(a) The total net taxable gain eligible for business asset disposal relief is

£ | 700,000 .

The total net taxable gain not eligible for business asset disposal relief is

£ | 67,700 .

Workings (not provided in the CBT)

	£
Eligible gains	
Goodwill	500,000
Factory	300,000
Office block	(100,000)
	700,000
Other gains	
Shares	80,000

	Eligible gains £	Other gains £
Chargeable gains	700,000	80,000
Less annual exempt amount		(12,300)
Taxable gains	700,000	67,700

(b) If the gain on the factory was £9,800,000 then the total net taxable gain eligible for business asset disposal relief is

£	1,000,000

.

The total net taxable gain not eligible for business asset disposal relief is

£	9,267,700

.

Workings (not provided in the CBT)

	£	£
Eligible gains		
Goodwill	500,000	
Factory	9,800,000	
Office block	(100,000)	
	10,200,000	
Less business asset disposal relief		
Max	(1,000,000)	
Gain not eligible		9,200,000
Shares		80,000
Other gains		9,280,000

	Eligible gains £	Other gains £
Chargeable gains	1,000,000	9,280,000
Less annual exempt amount		(12,300)
Taxable gains	1,000,000	9,267,700

Activity 5: Gift relief

The gift relief claim must be signed by: | Bill and Ludovic |.

Bill's chargeable gain on disposal is £ | Nil |. Ludovic's base cost is £ | 7,000 |.

Picklist:

Bill and Ludovic
Bill only
Ludovic only

Workings (not provided in the CBT)

	£
Proceeds (deemed)	25,000
Less cost	(7,000)
	18,000
Gain rolled over	(18,000)
Chargeable gain	Nil
Base cost for Ludovic:	
MV (deemed consideration)	25,000
Less gain held over	(18,000)
Adjusted base cost	7,000

Activity 6: With and without gift relief

(a) If gift relief is not claimed, Julie's chargeable gain is:

£ | 35,000 |

	£
Deemed sale proceeds (MV)	85,000
Less cost	(50,000)
Gain	35,000

and Jack's chargeable gain is:

£ | 10,000 |

	£
Proceeds	95,000
Less cost (MV)	(85,000)
Gain	10,000

(b)   If gift relief is claimed, Julie's chargeable gain is:

£ | 0

	£
Deemed sale proceeds	85,000
Less cost	(50,000)
	35,000
Less gift relief	(35,000)
Gain	0

and Jack's chargeable gain is:

£ | 45,000

	£	£
Proceeds		95,000
Less cost	85,000	
Less gift relief	(35,000)	
		(50,000)
Gain		45,000

Activity 7: Disposal of an unincorporated business 1

Asset	Market value £	Original cost £	TWDV £	Impact
Factory	120,000	100,000		Chargeable gain
Warehouse	90,000	100,000		Capital loss
Plant & machinery	20,000	60,000	5,000	Increase in trading profit
Goodwill	26,000	0		Chargeable gain
Inventory	5,000	6,000		Decrease in trading profit

The factory will be sold realising a chargeable gain of £20,000 (£120,000 – £100,000).

The warehouse will realise a capital loss of (£10,000) (£90,000 – £100,000).

The plant & machinery will not give rise to a capital loss as capital allowances will have been claimed. Instead, as trade has ceased, there will be a balancing adjustment. The proceeds of £20,000 will be deducted from the TWDV of £5,000 and there will then be a £15,000 balancing charge which will increase trading profits.

Inventory is not a chargeable asset. Instead, as MV < cost there will be a £1,000 deduction from trading profits.

Activity 8: Disposal of an unincorporated business 2

Statement	True ✓	False ✓
As Mr A has been trading for at least two years prior to the sale of his business, business asset disposal relief will be available on his gain.	✓	
In order for Mr B to be able to claim business asset disposal relief, he would need to sell his business by 31 October 2023. - Mr B would need to sell his business within three years of the cessation of trade (ie 31 October 2024) for relief to be available.		✓
In order for Mr B to be able to claim business asset disposal relief he would need to sell his business by 31 October 2024 and he would need to be employed by the business. - For an unincorporated business there is no requirement that the owner of the business be employed by it.		✓
Mrs C will be able to claim business asset disposal relief on her gains. - The gains on the rental property will not be eligible for business asset disposal relief.		✓

Activity 9: Disposal of an unincorporated business 3

	£
Proceeds	295,000
Less IT/NICs on adjustment to trade profits	(16,800)
Less capital gains tax on gains @ 10% (W1)	(6,770)
Post-tax proceeds	271,430

(W1) Capital gains tax due	£
Gain on factory (£200,000- £150,000)	50,000
Gain on goodwill (£30,000 - £0)	30,000
Less annual exempt amount	(12,300)
Taxable gains	67,700
CGT @ 10% (BADR)	6,770

Activity 10: Disposal of an incorporated business

Calculate Anton's taxable gain from the sale of his shares.

£	322,700

Taxable gains	£
Proceeds	350,000
Cost	(15,000)
Chargeable (or capital) gain	335,000
Less AEA	(12,300)
Taxable gains	322,700
CGT @ 10% (BADR)	32,270

Calculate the tax that will be charged on Anton's taxable gains assuming all beneficial claims are made.

£	32,270

Calculate Anton's post-tax proceeds from the sale of his shares.

£	317,730

	£
Proceeds	350,000
Less capital gains tax on gain @ 10%/ 20%	(32,270)
Post-tax proceeds	317,730

CHAPTER 14 Tax planning for businesses

Activity 1: Sole trader versus company

Statement	True ✓	False ✓
A sole trader business is a separate legal entity from its owner. - It is a company that is a separate legal entity from its owner.		✓
Profits can be extracted from a sole trade business with no tax consequence. How much profit and how the sole trader/partner extracts it from the business makes no difference to their tax bill because profits are taxed to income tax before any extraction.	✓	
Sole traders pay income tax on their trade profits at 20% - The rate of income tax paid by a sole trader depends on their level of trade profits and their other income. It could be 20%, 40% or 45%.		✓
Companies pay their tax in two payments on account. - Sole traders make payments on account of their income tax and Class 4 NICs. Companies usually make one payment of corporation tax, 9 months and 1 day after the end of the AP.		✓
A sole trader will pay Class 2 and Class 4 NICs.	✓	
A company pays Class 1 employee's NIC on any cash earnings in excess of £8,840 at 13.8%. - Companies pay class 1 employer's rather than class 1 employee's NIC. The threshold and rate are, however, correct.		✓

Activity 2: Extraction of profit 2

	£
Pringle Ltd's TTP	75,000
Less corporation tax @ 19%	(14,250)
Profits available to distribute as a dividend = dividend	60,750
As a higher rate taxpayer Dash will pay income tax at 32.5% on the dividend with no NIC (£60,750 × 32.5%)	(19,744)
After tax dividend kept by Dash	41,006

	£
Pringle Ltd's TTP	75,000
Employer's NIC will be due at 13.8% on any salary that Dash chooses to take from the company. So, the TTP figures represents 113.8% of the salary. Employer's NIC on salary to withdraw (13.8/113.8 × £75,000)	(9,095)
Salary for Dash to withdraw (100/113.8 × £20,000)	65,905
This salary will be taxed on Dash, a higher rate tax payer at a rate of 40% income tax and 2% employee's NICs. Thus 42% tax will be suffered (42% × £65,905)	(27,680)
After tax salary kept by Dash	38,225

Activity 3: Spouse/civil partner tax planning

If William owns the shares, he will pay income tax at 32.5% on any dividend income received.

In contrast, as Isla has no other taxable income her personal allowance is available to utilise against any dividend income. She can earn £12,570 of dividends income tax free. Any dividend income in excess of the personal allowance will be taxed at 7.5%.

Consequently, the couple's income tax liability will be minimised if Isla buys the shares.

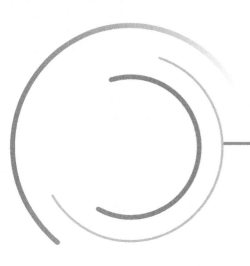

Test your learning: answers

CHAPTER 1 Tax framework

1

	✓
Integrity	✓
Objectivity	✓
Professional competence and due care	
Confidentiality	
Professional behaviour	✓

Integrity: It would not be honest to knowingly reduce profits by including expenditure that was not incurred in the year.

Objectivity: If you agreed to her request because of your job prospects, you are allowing bias to affect your judgement.

Professional behaviour: Submitting a tax return that does not follow tax law is illegal.

2

	✓
True	
False	✓

Tax evasion can lead to fines/imprisonment.

3

	✓
True	
False	✓

A company pays **corporation tax** on its total profits.

4   Each tax year all of an individual's components of income are added together, then a personal allowance is deducted to arrive at [taxable income] .

5

£	4,886

	Non-savings income £
Trading profits	25,000
Property income	12,000
Total income	37,000
Personal allowance	(12,570)
Taxable income	24,430

Tax	£
Non-savings income	
£24,430 × 20%	4,886
Tax liability	**4,886**

CHAPTER 2   Computing trading income

1

	Allowable ✓
Legal fees incurred on the acquisition of a factory to be used for trade purposes	
Heating for factory	✓
Legal fees incurred on pursuing trade receivables	✓
Acquiring a machine to be used in the factory	

Legal fees on the acquisition of a factory are capital expenditure and so not allowable. Heating is a revenue expense and so allowable. Legal fees incurred on pursuing trade receivables are allowable as they relate to a revenue source. Acquiring a machine is a capital expense and so not allowable (although capital allowances will be available for this expenditure).

2

£	700

The cost of staff entertaining is allowable. Gifts of food to customers are never allowable. The entertaining of customers is never allowable.

3

	Allowable ✓	Disallowable ✓
Parking fines incurred by business owner		✓
Parking fines incurred by an employee while on the employer's business	✓	
Parking fines incurred by the director of a company while on company business		✓
Legal costs incurred in relation to acquiring a 10-year lease of property for the first time		✓
Legal costs incurred in relation to the renewal of a lease for 20 years	✓	
Gifts of calendars to customers, costing £4 each and displaying an advertisement for the company	✓	
Gifts of bottles of whisky to customers, costing £12 each		✓

4

	✓
£80 must be deducted from the accounts profit	
£80 must be added back to the accounts profit	
£96 must be deducted from the accounts profit	
£96 must be added back to the accounts profit	✓

The normal selling price of £80 + (20% × £80) = £96 must be added to the accounts profit.

5

£	700

Added back	Deducted
✓	✓
	✓

The movement on the general provision is disallowable (if an increase)/not taxable (if a decrease). This means that the decrease in the general provision of **£700** (£2,500 – £1,800) must be deducted from the accounts profit.

6

£	360

80% × £450 is disallowable for tax purposes.

7

	Taxable trading profits
Zack • As trading receipts do not exceed £1,000 the trading allowance means trade profits will be nil.	0
Mythili • As trading profits do not exceed £1,000 the trading allowance means trade profits will be nil. However, Mythili should elect for the trading allowance not to apply and instead deduct allowable costs, thus giving rise to a trading loss.	(100)
Rohan • As trading profits exceed £1,000 the normal adjustment to profits will apply, meaning Rohan will be taxed on £700 of trade profits. However, as the allowable expenses are less than £1,000, Rohan should elect to instead deduct the trading allowance, which will give lower trade profits of £500.	500
Arthur • As Arthur's trading receipts exceed £1,000 the normal adjustment to profits will apply, giving trading profits of £400. It would not be preferable to elect to deduct the trading allowance instead.	400

CHAPTER 3   Capital allowances

1

£	2,000

A maximum of the original cost is deducted from the pool.

2

£	173,896

Workings

Year ended 30 September 2022

	AIA	General pool	Allowances
B/f		22,500	
Addition qualifying for AIA			
Addition 1.12.21	171,250		
AIA (max. £1,000,000)	(171,250)		171,250
Disposal 1.8.22			
Proceeds		(7,800)	
		14,700	
WDA @ 18%		(2,646)	2,646
C/f		12,054	
Allowances			173,896

3

£	6,620

6 months ended 31 December 2021

	FYA @ 100%	General pool	Allowances
Addition (no AIA)		18,000	
WDA @ 18% × $\frac{6}{12}$		(1,620)	1,620
		16,380	
Addition	5,000		
FYA @ 100%	(5,000)		5,000
C/f		16,380	
			6,620

Note. The AIA and WDAs are time apportioned in a short period. FYAs are not. AIAs and FYAs are not available on a car with CO_2 emissions of 45g/km.

4

	✓
True	
False	✓

There is no AIA or WDA in the final period so a **balancing allowance** arises as follows:

	£
B/f	12,500
Addition	20,000
Proceeds	(18,300)
	14,200
Balancing allowance	**(14,200)**

5

£	1,080

Year ended 30 April 2021

	Private use asset @ 60%	Allowances
Addition	30,000	
WDA @ 6%	(1,800) × 60%	**1,080**
C/f	28,200	

6 (a) **If Barry sells all the plant for £10,000 then he will have a**

balancing charge	of	£	1,200

Picklist:

balancing allowance
balancing charge
Workings

TWDV b/f		7,200
Addition		1,600
		8,800
Disposal		(10,000)
		(1,200)
Balancing charge		1,200

(b)   If Barry sells his plant for £6,000 then he will have a

| balancing allowance | of | £ | 2,800 |

Picklist:

balancing allowance
balancing charge

Workings

TWDV b/f		7,200
Addition		1,600
		8,800
Disposal		(6,000)
		2,800
Balancing allowance		(2,800)

7   **Peter can claim capital allowances for the 9 month accounting period ending 31 March 2022 of**

| £ | 684 |

Workings

Cars are not entitled to the AIA.	
The car will be treated as a special rate item and be entitled to 6% WDA.	
The WDA will be prorated by 9/12 as it is a 9-month accounting period.	
The WDA claimed will be restricted to 80% due to the private use.	
WDA = £19,000 × 6% × 9/12 × 80% =	£684

8   £40,500

£1,800,000 × 3% × 9/12 = £40,500

The qualifying cost for SBAs excludes acquisition fees. The SBA must be time-apportioned in the year of acquisition from the date the building is brought into use.

	True ✓	False ✓
If the contract for the factory is signed in 2021 and the factory brought into use in that year, an SBA will be available for the year ended 31 December 2021.	✓	
If the factory is constructed by 1 March 2021 and brought into use in A Ltd's trade on 1 July 2021 then an SBA of £24,000 is available as SBAs are claimed in full in year of construction/ purchase. - The SBA will only be available from 1 July 2021 and so must be time apportioned.		✓
The eligible cost qualifying for the SBA is £1,000,000. - Land does not qualify for an SBA.		✓

10

	AIA	FYA	Super deduction	General pool	Special rate pool	Private use asset	Total allowances
TWDV brought forward at 1/1/2022				123,000			
Zero emission car		41,000					
Machinery			60,000				
Managing director's car				38,000			
Plant			36,000				
FYA @ 100%		(41,000)					41,000
Super-deduction @ 130%			(96,000)				124,800
Disposal				(15,000)			
				146,000			
WDA @ 18% × 9/12				(19,710)			19,710
C/fwd/ total				126,290			185,510

If Nailsea Ltd were a sole trader, the super-deduction would not be available. Instead, the plant and machinery would be eligible for the 100% AIA thus giving lower total allowances.

In addition, consideration would need to be given to the managing director's car. If this was a car provided to the sole trader a private use adjustment would arise meaning the business could only claim 90% of the allowance. If, however, the car was provided to an employee of the business then the full allowance can be claimed (as for if Nailsea Ltd is a company).

CHAPTER 4   Taxing unincorporated businesses

1

Tax year	Basis period
2020/21	1 May 2020 – 5 April 2021
2021/22	Year ended 31 December 2021
2022/23	Year ended 31 December 2022
Overlap profits	1 January 2021 – 5 April 2021

2   When the trade ceases, overlap profits are deducted from the final tax year's taxable profits.

	✓
True	✓
False	

3

Tax year	Basis period	Taxable profits £
2019/20	1 June 2018 to 31 May 2019	18,000
2020/21	1 June 2019 to 31 May 2020	32,000
2021/22	1 June 2020 to 31 December 2021	30,000

In 2021/22, taxable profits are (£25,000 + £15,000 – £10,000) = £30,000

4

Tax year	Basis period	Taxable profits £
2020/22	1 February 2021 – 5 April 2021	34,000 × 2/17 = 4,000
2021/22	6 April 2021 – 5 April 2022	34,000 × 12/17 = 24,000
2022/23	12 months ended 30 June 2022	34,000 × 12/17 = 24,000

His overlap profits are:

£	18,000

(1 July 2021 to 5 April 2022)

9/17 × £34,000

5 (a) Her taxable profits for 2020/21 are:

£ | 40,000

(1 December 2020 – 5 April 2021)   4/7 × £70,000

   (b) Her taxable profits for 2021/22 are:

£ | 95,000

(1 December 2020– 30 November 2021) £70,000 + 5/12 × £60,000

   (c) Her taxable profits for 2022/23 are:

£ | 60,000

(1 July 2021 to 30 June 2022)

   (d) Her overlap profits are:

£ | 65,000

	£
1 December 2020 – 5 April 2021	40,000
1 July 2021 – 30 November 2021	25,000
	65,000

6

	True ✓	False ✓
If profits are expected to rise, a 31 March year end will delay the time when rising accounting profits feed through into rising taxable profits.		
A 31 March year end is more straightforward than a 30 April year end as it avoids overlap profits.		

CHAPTER 5 Partnerships

1

	✓
The calendar year	
The tax year	
The period of account concerned	✓
The period agreed by the partners	

2 Dave's taxable profits for 2021/22 are:

£	9,450

and Joe's taxable profits for 2021/22 are:

£	8,550

Working

	Total £	Dave £	Joe £
1.1.21 – 30.9.21 (9/12) 1:1	13,500	6,750	6,750
1.10.21 – 31.12.21 (3/12) 3:2	4,500	2,700	1,800
	18,000	**9,450**	**8,550**

3

	Total £	Holly £	Jasmine £
Salary	85,000	5,000	80,000
Division of profits 1:1	115,000	57,500	57,500
	200,000	62,500	137,500

4

	✓
£60,000	
£15,000	
£45,000	
£20,000	✓

2021/22 (year ended 31 March 2022)

Taxable profits on Steve for 2021/22 are £20,000 ($\frac{1}{4}$ × £80,000).

5   The profits assessable on Sase in 2021/22 are:

£	14,000

The opening year rules apply to Sase.

(1 September 2021 – 5 April 2022) $\frac{7}{12}$ × £24,000

The profits assessable on Sase in 2022/23 are:

£	24,000

(Year ended 31 August 2022)

The overlap profits arising for Sase are:

£	14,000

(1/9/21 – 5/4/22)

Workings

Year ended 31 August 2022

	Total £	Abdul £	Ghita £	Sase £
Profits (2:2:1)	120,000	48,000	48,000	24,000

6   (a)

	Total £	William £	Ann £	John £
Y/e 31.10.20	21,000	7,000	7,000	7,000
Y/e 31.10.21	33,000	11,000	11,000	11,000
Y/e 31.10.22				
1.11.21 – 31.12.21(2/12)	6,000	2,000	2,000	2,000
1.1.22– 31.10.22 (10/12)	30,000	0	15,000	15,000
	36,000	2,000	17,000	17,000

(b)

	William £	Ann £	John £
2020/21 (y/e 31.10.20)	7,000	7,000	7,000
2021/22 (y/e 31.10.21)	8,000	11,000	11,000
2022/23 (y/e 31.10.22)	0	17,000	17,000

Ann and John will be taxed on the current year basis of assessment throughout. The cessation rules apply to William in 2021/22, the year he left the business:

1 November 2020 – 31 December 2021 (£11,000 + £2,000 – £5,000) = £8,000

CHAPTER 6 National insurance

1 Acker

£	0	.	00

No Class 2 NICs, as earnings below small earnings exemption of £6,515

No Class 4 NICs due, as profits below annual lower earnings limit of £9,568

2 Bailey

£	4,016	.	38

		£
Class 2 NICs	52 × £3.05	158.60
Class 4 NICs	(£50,270 – £9,568) × 9%	3,663.18
	(£60,000 – £50,270) × 2%	194.60
Total NICs		**4,016.38**

3 Cartwright

£	273	.	98

Class 2 NICs 52 × £3.05 = £158.60

Class 4 NICs (£10,850 – £9,568) × 9% = £115.38

Total NICs = **£273.98**

CHAPTER 7   Computing corporation tax

1

	True	False
A company with a nine-month period of account will calculate capital allowances for nine months and deduct them from adjusted trading profits.	✓	
A company with an 18-month period of account will calculate capital allowances for 18 months and deduct them from adjusted trading profits, and then prorate the answer between the appropriate accounting periods.		✓
A company with an 18-month period of account will calculate capital allowances for the first 12 months, then capital allowances for the remaining 6 months, and deduct them from the relevant prorated trading profits allocated to each accounting period.	✓	
Dividends are not included in the taxable total profits. They are taxed separately.		✓

Capital allowances are calculated separately for each accounting period and then deducted from the prorated adjusted profits.

Dividends are not taxable for the company (for the purpose of the *Business Tax* assessment).

2

	✓
Added to trading income	
Added to net non-trading interest ie a NTL-R credit	
Deducted from trading income	✓
Deducted from net non-trading interest ie a NTL-R debit	

The loan is for trading purposes and is interest **paid**, not received, so it is included as an expense.

3

£	385

Companies make donations gross, so the actual amount given to the charity is deducted from TTP.

4

	✓
1 June 2020 – 31 March 2021 and 1 April 2021 – 31 August 2021	
1 June 2020 – 31 May 2021 and 1 June 2021– 31 August 2021	✓
1 June 2020 – 31 December 2020 and 1 January 2021 – 31 August 2021	
1 June 2020– 31 August 2020 and 1 September 2020 – 31 August 2021	

The first accounting period is always 12 months in length in a long period of account.

5

	Year ended 31.12.21 £	4 months ended 30.4.22 £
Trading profits ($12/16$: $4/16$)	240,000	80,000
NTL-R income (Investment) (accrued for each period)	1,200	400
Chargeable gain (allocate to period made)	0	20,000
Total profits	241,200	100,400
Qualifying charitable donation (allocate to period paid)	(15,000)	0
Taxable total profits	226,200	100,400

6

£	48,450

£255,000 × 19% = **£48,450**

7

£	93,100

£490,000 × 19% = **£93,100**

8

	✓
True	✓
False	

Financial Year 2021 (FY21) begins on 1 April 2021 and ends on 31 March 2022.

CHAPTER 8   Losses

1

	✓
2021/22 only	
2022/23 and/or 2021/22	
2020/21 only	
2021/22 and/or 2020/21	✓

The tax year of the loss is 2021/22. Claims against total income are for this year and/or 2020/21.

2

	✓
True	
False	✓

Trading losses can be carried forward indefinitely.

3

	✓
Against non-savings income	
Against total income	
Against trading income arising in the same trade	✓
Against trading income arising in all trades carried on by the taxpayer	

4   The loss is incurred in 2021/22.

It can be:

(a)   Deducted from total income of £9,000 in 2021/22 and/or from total income of £19,000 in 2020/21; and/or

(b)   Carried forward to be deducted from taxable trading profits of £25,000 in 2022/23 and then in later years.

5   **Martin**

(a)   Martin's first tax year is 2020/21. In his first tax year he's taxed on profits from 1 July 2020 to 5 April 2021. This will be the trade loss of £24,200 for the 9 m/e 5 April 2021.

His second tax year is 2021/22 and he will be taxed on the trade profits of £9,800 for the y/e 5/4/22 under the current year basis.

(b)   The loss of £24,200 for 2020/21 can be claimed against total income for the three preceding years, under opening years loss relief, earliest year first, since the loss is incurred in one of the first four years of Martin's trade.

The loss relief claim will therefore be £21,000 in 2017/18 and £(24,200 − 21,000 = £3,200 in 2018/19.

For 2017/18 this will waste Martin's personal allowance, with the balance of the claim saving income tax at the basic rate of 20%.

For 2018/19 Martin has income subject to income tax at the higher rate of 40%, so the claim will save tax at the higher rate.

Alternatively, Martin could have carried the trading loss forward against future trading profits, but the trading profit of £9,800 for 2021/22 is covered by the personal allowance, and there is no information regarding future trading profits.

(c) The opening year loss relief claim will therefor save Martin the most tax as well as generating a cash flow saving due to a tax refund.

Tutorial note

A claim for loss relief against total income for 2020/21 and/or 2019/20 is not possible since Michael does not have any income for either of these years.

6   **Sylvie**

(a) As Sylvie ceased trading on 31 December 2021 2021/22 will be her final tax year. In her final tax year she will be taxed on any profits not yet taxed less her overlap profits.

Her penultimate tax year was 2020/21 and she would have been taxed on the profits of the y/e 31/12/20 under the current year basis.

Her trade profits of 2021/22 will therefore comprise of her trade loss of the y/e 31/12/21 £24,300 plus her overlap profits of £3,400. This gives a total 2021/22 trade loss of £27,700.

(b) The terminal loss is the loss of the last 12 months of trade plus the overlap profits. As Sylvie prepares accounts for a final 12 month period her terminal loss will be the unused overlap profits brought forward added to the loss for the year ended 31 December 2021.

So the terminal loss is also £(24,300 + 3,400) = £27,700.

The terminal loss claim is against trading income for the year of the loss (2021/22 – nil) and the three preceding years, latest first.

The terminal loss claim will therefore be for £3,500 in 2020/21, £18,000 in 2019/20 and £(27,700 – 3,500 – 18,000) = £6,200 in 2018/19.

The property business profits are sufficient to utilise Sylvie's personal allowance for each year, so the loss relief claims will all save income tax at the basic rate of 20%.

Alternatively, Sylvie could have initially claimed loss relief against her total income for 2021/22 and/or 2020/21, but this would have wasted her personal allowance in those years.

(c) As the current year and/or prior year claims would waste personal allowance the terminal loss claim will save more tax and avoid any wastage of the personal allowance.

7   (a) The amount of trading loss remaining to be carried forward at 1 April 2023 (assuming that all possible earlier loss relief claims against total profits are made) is:

£	(85,000)

(£320,000 – £60,000 – £175,000)

	Year ended 31 March	
	2021 **£**	**2022** **£**
Trading profit	170,000	0
Interest	5,000	60,000
Capital gain £(12,000 – 20,000)	0	0

		Year ended 31 March	
		2021 £	2022 £
Total profits		175,000	60,000
Less:	Current period loss relief	0	(60,000)
	Carry back loss relief	(175,000)	0
Less Qualifying charitable donation		0	0
		0	0
Unrelieved qualifying charitable donations		5,000	5,000

(b)   The amount of capital loss remaining to be carried forward at 1 April 2023 is:

£	(8,000)

(£20,000 − £12,000)

8

	✓
£Nil	
£2,000	✓
£4,000	
£3,000	

		Year ended 30.9.20 £	Six months 31.3.21 £	Year ended 31.3.22 £
Trading profit		4,000	6,000	0
Less:	Current period loss relief	0	0	0
	Carry back loss relief	(2,000)	(6,000)	0
	Qualifying charitable donation	(1,000)	–	–
Taxable total profits		1,000	–	–

The maximum relief for year ended 30.9.20 is £4,000 $\times \frac{6}{12}$.

9

	True	False
A sole trader's trade loss will be carried forward to offset against the first available trade profits of the same trade if no other claim is made.	✓	
A company's trade loss will be carried forward to offset against the first available trade profits of the same trade. • The loss will be offset against future total profits as and when a claim is made.		✓
A company's trade loss is carried forward and can be offset against total profits of future accounting periods.	✓	
A sole trader's trade loss must be offset against current year's total income before being offset against the total income of the prior year. • A sole trader can claim to offset the loss against total income of the prior year and/or the current year. This can be in any order. A company must make a claim to offset its trade loss against total profits of the current period before it can carry back the loss to the prior 12 months.		✓

10

	True	False
A sole trader incurring a trade loss in their second tax year can carry back their trade loss three tax years on a LIFO basis against total income • Opening year loss relief is on a FIFO basis		✓
A company can carry back a trade loss made in it's first accounting period three years on a FIFO basis against its total profits • Companies are not entitled to opening year loss relief		✓
Terminal loss relief is only available to unincorporated businesses • TLR is available to both incorporated and unincorporated businesses		✓
For an unincorporated business terminal loss relief is offset against trade profits only whereas for an incorporated business terminal loss relief is against total profits	✓	

These facts can be obtained by use of the reference material.

CHAPTER 9 Self-assessment for individuals

1   The due filing date for an income tax return for 2021/22, assuming the taxpayer will submit the return online is:

31/01/23

2   The 2021/22 payments on account will be calculated as

1	50%

of the income tax payable for

2	2020/21

and will be due on

3	31 January 2022

and

4	31 July 2022

3   £100 penalty for failure to deliver return on time.

Possible £10 per day penalty from 1 May 2023 until date of filing.

5% penalty on tax paid late. Interest on tax paid late.

4

	✓
31 January 2023	
31 March 2023	
6 April 2023	
28 January 2023	✓

A year after the actual filing date, because Susie filed the return before the due filing date (31 January 2022).

5   Jamie's 2021/22 payments on account will each be

£	6,000

and will be due on

31/01/22

and

31/07/22

Jamie's balancing payment will be

£	4,000

and will be due on

31/01/23

6

£	0

No penalties for late payment are due on late payments on account.

7   (a)

	✓
30 September 2022	
31 October 2022	✓
31 December 2022	
31 January 2023	

Paper returns must usually be submitted by 31 October following the end of the tax year.

(b)

	✓
31 January 2023 and 31 July 2023	
31 January 2022 and 31 July 2022	✓
31 October 2022 and 31 January 2023	
31 July 2022 and 31 January 2023	

Payments on account are due on 31 January in the tax year and 31 July following the end of the tax year.

8

	✓
£5,100	
£3,400	
£1,020	✓
£2,380	

30% × PLR = **£1,020**

PLR = £17,000 × 20% = £3,400

CHAPTER 10 Self-assessment for companies

1

1 June 2022

(12 months after the actual filing date)

2

£	100

(The return is less than 3 months late)

3

	✓
14 July 2021	
1 October 2022	✓
31 December 2022	
1 January 2023	

Girton Ltd is not a large company, so all CT is due nine months and one day after the end of the accounting period.

4

	✓
14 July 2021	
14 April 2022	✓
1 October 2022	
31 December 2022	

Eaton Ltd is a large company and is required to pay corporation tax by instalments. The instalments are due in the seventh and tenth months of the accounting period and in the first and fourth months after the accounting period.

5

£	60,000

$\frac{1}{4} \times £240,000$

CHAPTER 11 Chargeable gains for companies

1   Indexation allowance runs from the date | the expenditure was incurred | to

       | December 2017 | .

2

	£
Proceeds of sale	200,000
Less cost	(80,000)
Less enhancement expenditure	(10,000)
	110,000
Less indexation allowance on cost £80,000 × 0.401	(32,080)
Less indexation allowance on enhancement £10,000 × 0.315	(3,150)
Chargeable gain	74,770

3

	✓
Office block	
Freehold factory	✓
Fork lift truck	
Freehold warehouse	

The office block and the freehold warehouse were acquired outside the qualifying reinvestment period, commencing one year before and ending three years after, the disposal.

The forklift truck is not fixed plant and machinery.

4

£	368,900

Land

	£
Sales proceeds	400,000
Less cost	(100,000)
Less IA £100,000 × 0.311	(31,100)
Gain	268,900

£20,000 of the proceeds are not reinvested, so £20,000 of the gain remains chargeable; £248,900 is rolled over.

Replacement land

	£	£
Sale proceeds		500,000
Less cost	380,000	
Rolled-over gain	(248,900)	
Revised base cost		(131,100)
Chargeable gain		368,900

5   If relief for replacement of business assets is to be claimed, reinvestment of the proceeds must take place in a period beginning

12

months before and ending

36

months after the date of disposal.

6   The chargeable gain after rollover relief is:

£	25,000

The gain on the sale of first warehouse is:

	£
Proceeds	400,000
Less cost	(220,000)
	180,000
Less indexation allowance	(40,000)
	140,000
Less rollover relief (balancing figure)	(115,000)
Chargeable gain: amount not reinvested £(400,000 – 375,000)	**25,000**

CHAPTER 12   Share disposals

1

	✓
True	
False	✓

In a rights issue, shares are paid for and this amount is added to the original cost. In a bonus issue, shares are free and so there is no adjustment to the original cost.

2   The matching rules for share disposals by a company are:

(a)   Shares acquired on the same day
(b)   Shares acquired in the previous nine days (FIFO)
(c)   Shares from the FA 1985 pool

3   (a)   **Share pool**

		No of shares	Cost £	Indexed cost £
5.03	Acquisition	10,000	90,000	90,000
6.09	Indexed rise			
	£90,000 × 0.176			15,840
	Rights 1:4 @ £12	2,500	30,000	30,000
		12,500	120,000	135,840
12.17	Indexed rise			
	£135,840 × 0.303			41,160
				177,000
	Disposal $(× \frac{10,000}{12,500})$	(10,000)	(96,000)	(141,600)
		2,500	24,000	35,400

(b)   **Gain on Sale**

	£
Proceeds	150,000
Less cost	(96,000)
	54,000
Less indexation allowance £(141,600 – 96,000)	(45,600)
Chargeable gain	8,400

CHAPTER 13   Business disposals

1   Her chargeable gain on sale is:

£	235,000

	£
Proceeds	560,000
Less cost	(325,000)
Chargeable gain	235,000

2   Martha's CGT liability for 2021/22 is:

£	2,380

	£
Chargeable gains	24,200
Less annual exempt amount	(12,300)
Taxable gains	11,900
CGT on £11,900 @ 20%	2,380

3   Ian's CGT liability for 2021/22 is:

£	177,540

	£
Gains	1,400,000
Less annual exempt amount	(12,300)
Taxable gain	1,387,700
CGT:	
1,000,000 @ 10%	100,000
387,700 @ 20%	77,540
	177,540

4   Jemma's CGT on the disposal, assuming she has already used the annual exempt amount for 2021/22, is:

£	7,000

	£
Proceeds of sale	80,000
Less allowable cost	(10,000)
Taxable gain (no annual exempt amount available)	70,000
CGT @ 10%	**7,000**

5

	✓
True	
False	✓

Jewellery is not a qualifying asset for gift relief purposes. It is not used in Sara's trade.

6   If gift relief is claimed, the gain on the gift by Tommy is:

£	0

	£
Market value	200,000
Less cost	(50,000)
Gain	150,000
Less gift relief	(150,000)
Gain left in charge	0

and the gain on the sale by Sinbad is:

£	300,000

	£
Sale proceeds	350,000
Less cost (£200,000 – £150,000)	(50,000)
Gain	**300,000**

7   Sunil's CGT liability for 2021/22 is:

£	1,770

	BADR gains £
Chargeable gains (£50,000 – £20,000)	30,000
Less annual exempt amount	(12,300)
Taxable gains	17,700
CGT due @ 105 (BADR)	1,770

His post-tax proceeds on disposal of his shares are:

£	48,230

	£
Proceeds	50,000
Less CGT on the gain	(1,770)
Post-tax proceeds	48,230

8

Statement	True ✓	False ✓
On a disposal of a sole trade business we compare proceeds to cost to calculate the chargeable gain/ allowable loss. - Each separate category of assets must be considered separately it is not one disposal.		✓
If inventory costing £10,000 is sold for £12,000 it will give a chargeable gain of £2,000. - It would give an increase in trading profit of £2,000 rather than a gain.		✓
A capital loss arises where plant and machinery is sold for less than cost. - A capital loss is not available where capital allowances have been claimed.		✓
A gain equal to the market value of goodwill will arise on disposal of an unincorporated business.	✓	
If a business with assets worth £100,000 is sold for £120,000 this will generate £20,000 of goodwill.	✓	

CHAPTER 14   Tax planning for businesses

1

Statement	True ✓	False ✓
A company must comply with fewer rules and regulations than a sole trader. - A sole trader must comply with fewer rules and regulations.		✓
A sole trader can extract profits from the business with no direct tax consequence.	✓	
Class 1 employee's NIC is paid at 13.8% on any cash salary paid to an employee. - Employee's NIC is at 12%/2%. 13.8% is the rate for employer's NIC.		✓
A company pays its tax in two payments on account (31 July and 31 January). - This is how a sole trader would pay their tax. A small company pays its tax 9 months and 1 day after the end of the accounting period.		✓

2

Statement	True ✓	False ✓
There are fewer NICs due when profits are extracted by way of dividend rather than salary.	✓	
A dividend payment will reduce the company's corporation tax liability. - Dividends are not tax deductible for a company.		✓
When a company pays a salary, the salary and the employer's NIC thereon is tax deductible for the company.	✓	
Where profits are extracted as a dividend the individual will pay income tax at 20%/40%/45% - The tax rates on dividend income are 7.5%/32.5% and 38.1%.		✓
A basic rate taxpayer will suffer a combined total of 32% tax on any salary they receive. (20% income tax + 12% Class 1 NICs)	✓	
A higher rate taxpayer will suffer a combined total of 52% tax on any salary they receive. - They will pay 40% income tax but only 2% NIC so a combined total of 42%.		✓

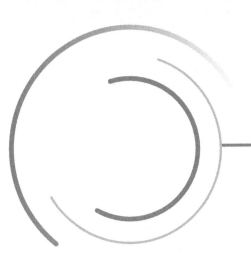

Tax reference material

Reference material

1 Income tax

Trading allowance			£1,000
Personal allowance			£12,570
	Basic rate (0-£37,700)	Higher rate (£37,701 - £150,000)	Additional rate (Above £150,000)
Salary	20%	40%	45%
Dividends	7.5%	32.5%	38.1%
Trading income	20%	40%	45%

- Income tax computations will not be required in the assessment, but the rates may be used in tax planning discussions.

2 Income tax basis period rules

Ongoing business	Current year basis		
Year of commencement	Actual basis		
	Accounting period <12 months ends in the year	Accounting period ≥12 months ends in the year	No accounting period ends in year
	Tax first 12 months of trade	Tax 12 months to accounting date	Actual basis
Third tax year	Tax 12 months to the accounting date		
Final tax year	Tax from end of basis period in previous tax year to the date of cessation. Deduct overlap profits		

3 National Insurance (NI)

Class 2 contributions	£3.05 per week
Small profits threshold	£6,515
Class 4 contributions on trading profits between £9,568 and £50,270	9%
Class 4 contributions on trading profits above £50,270	2%

- Dividends are not subject to NI
- Salaries are subject to:
  - employee NI at 12% between £9,568 and £50,270 and 2% above £50,270
  - employer NI at 13.8% above £8,840 (an employment allowance of £4,000 is available)
- Calculations of NI on salaries will not be required in the assessment but the rates may be used in tax planning discussions.

4   Capital gains tax

Annual exempt amount	£12,300
Basic rate	10%
Higher rate	20%
Business asset disposal relief rate	10%
Business asset disposal relief lifetime allowance	£1,000,000

5   Corporation tax

Rate of corporation tax	19%

6   Capital allowances

Annual investment allowance	£1,000,000
Writing down allowance – assets other than motor cars	18%
Super deduction – expenditure by companies after 1 April 2021	130%
Writing down allowance cars: – CO2 emissions 0g/km – CO2 emissions up to 50 g/km – CO2 emissions over 50 g/km	100% 18% 6%
Small pools allowance	£1,000
Structures and buildings allowance	3%

7   Disallowed expenditure

Type of expense	Disallowable in calculation of trading profit	Notes
Fines and penalties	Fines on the business Fines on directors/owners	Employee fines are not disallowed if incurred in the course of their employment.
Donations	Political donations Donations to national charities	Donations to local charities are allowable (these will only be examined for unincorporated
Capital expenditure	Depreciation Loss on disposal Capital items expensed	Capital allowances may be available.

Type of expense	Disallowable in calculation of trading profit	Notes
Legal and professional	Relating to: – capital items – purchase/renewal of a long lease – purchase of a short lease (50 years or less) – breaches of law/regulations.	Legal fees on the renewal of a short lease (50 years or less) are allowable.
Entertaining and gifts	Customer gifts (unless <£50 per annum, not food, drink, tobacco, or cash vouchers and contains business advertising). Customer/supplier entertaining.	Staff gifts and staff entertaining are allowable.
Cars	Depreciation. Private use by owners. 15% of lease cost if leased car >50g/km CO_2 emissions.	
Private expenditure of owner (unincorporated businesses only)	Goods taken for own use. Salary of owners. Private use % by owners. Private expenditure, e.g., class 2 and 4 NICs, legal and professional fees for personal expenditure.	Reasonable salaries of family members are allowable.

8   Trading losses

Loss option	Sole trader/Partner	Company
Carry forward	Against future profits of the same trade only. Applies automatically to first available profits. Applies after any other elections or if no elections are made.	Losses not relieved in the current accounting period or previous 12 months are carried forward and an election can be made to set against total profits in future periods.
Current year/carry back	Against total income in the current and/or previous tax year in any order. If opted for in either year, the amount of loss used cannot be restricted to preserve the personal allowance. Make claim by 31 January 2024 for 2021/22 tax year.	Can elect to set trading losses against current accounting period 'total profits'. Qualifying charitable donations will remain unrelieved. If the above election is made, can also carry back trading loss to set against 'total profits' within the previous 12 months. Claim within 2 years of the end of the loss-making period.

Loss option	Sole trader/Partner	Company
Opening year loss relief – loss in first four years of trade	Against total income of the previous three tax years on a FIFO basis. If opted for, losses will be used to reduce total income as much as possible in each year and cannot be restricted to preserve the personal allowance. Make claim by 31 January 2024 for 2021/22 tax year.	N/A
Terminal loss relief	Against trading profits of the previous 3 years on a LIFO basis. Claim within 4 years from the end of the last tax year of trade.	Against total profits of the previous 3 years. Claim within 2 years of the end of the loss-making period.

9 Chargeable gains – Reliefs

Relief	Conditions
Replacement of business assets (Rollover) relief	Available to individuals and companies. Examinable for companies. Qualifying assets (original and replacement) – must be used in a trade and be land and buildings or fixed plant and machinery. Qualifying time period – replacement asset must be purchased between one year before and three years after the sale of the original asset. Partial reinvestment – if only some of the sales proceeds reinvested then the gain taxable is the lower of the full gain and the proceeds not reinvested.
Gift relief (holdover relief)	Available to individuals only. Qualifying assets – assets used in the trade of the donor or the donor's personal company, shares in any unquoted trading company or shares in the donors personal trading company. A personal trading company is one where the donor has at least 5%.
Business asset disposal relief	Available to individuals only. Gain taxable at 10%. £1m lifetime limit For 2021/22 a claim must be made by 31 January 2024. Qualifying assets: – the whole or part of a business carried on by the individual (alone or in partnership). The assets must have been owned for 24 months prior to sale – assets of the individual's or partnership's trading business that has now ceased. The assets must have been owned for 24 months prior to cessation and sale must be within 3 years of cessation – shares in the individual's 'personal trading company' (own at least 5%). The individual must have owned the shares and been an employee of the company for 24 months prior to sale.

10 Payment and administration

	Sole trader/Partners	Company
Filing date	31 October following the end of the tax year if filing a paper return. 31 January following the end of the tax year if filing online. Amendments can be made within 12 months of filing.	Filed on the later of 12 months after end of AP or 3 months after the notice to deliver a tax return has been issued. Company can amend return within 12 months of the filing date.
Payment date	31 January following the end of the tax year. If payments on accounts are due: • first POA – 31 January during tax year • second POA – 31 July after tax year • balancing payment – 31 January after tax year. POA's are each 50% of the previous years income tax and class 4 NICS due by self-assessment. POA's are not required for capital gains or class 2 NICs. POA's are not due if prior year tax payable by self-assessment is less than £1,000 OR if >80% of prior year tax was collected at source.	Small companies (annual profits less than £1.5 million): 9 months + 1 day after end of the accounting period (AP). Large companies (annual profits greater than £1.5 million) must estimate the year's tax liability and pay 25% of the estimate on the 14th day of each of the 7th, 10th, 13th and 16th month from the start of the accounting period.
Interest	Charged daily on late payment	Interest charged daily on late payment. Overpayment of tax receives interest from HMRC. Interest is taxable/tax allowable as interest income.
Penalties for late filing	£100. After 3 months, £10 per day for up to 90 days. After 6 months, 5% tax due (or £300 if greater). After 12 months, 5% tax due (or £300 if greater) if not deliberate. After 12 months, 70% of tax due (or £300 if greater) if deliberate and not concealed. After 12 months, 100% tax due (or £300 if greater) if deliberate and concealed.	£100. After 3 months, £100. After 6 months, 10% of unpaid tax. After 12 months, 10% of unpaid tax.

	Sole trader/Partners	Company
Late payment	30 days late – 5% of tax outstanding at that date. 6 months days late – 5% of tax outstanding at that date. 12 months late – 5% of tax outstanding at that date.	N/A
Notify of chargeability	5 October following the end of the tax year	Within 3 months of starting to trade.
Enquiry	Within 12 months of submission of return. Penalty for failure to produce enquiry documents = £300 + £60 per day.	Within 12 months of submission of return. Penalty for failure to produce enquiry documents: £300 + £60 per day.
Record retention	Five years from filing date. Penalty for failure to keep records is up to £3,000.	Six years after the end of the relevant accounting period. Penalty for failure to keep proper records is up to £3,000.

11 Penalties for incorrect returns

Type of behaviour	Maximum	Unprompted (minimum)	Prompted (minimum)
Careless error and inaccuracy are due to failure to take reasonable care	30%	0%	15%
Deliberate error but not concealed	70%	20%	35%
Deliberate error and concealed	100%	30%	50%

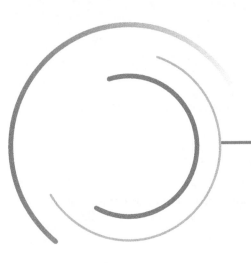

Bibliography

AAT (2017) AAT Code of Professional Ethics. [Online.] Available from: https://www.aat.org.uk/prod/s3fs-public/assets/AAT-Code-Professional-Ethics.pdf [Accessed 11 January 2022].

Contains public sector information licensed under the Open Government Licence v3.0. www.nationalarchives.gov.uk/doc/open-government-licence/version/3/.

HMRC (2015) *Tackling tax evasion and avoidance.* [Online.] Available from: https://assets.publishing.service.gov.uk/government/uploads/system/uploads/attachment_data /file/413931/Tax_evasion_FINAL__with_covers_and_right_sig_.pdf [accessed 11 January 2022].

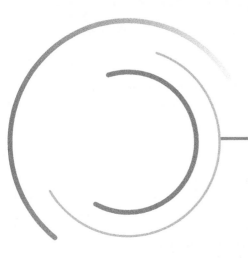

Index

Index

A

Accountancy expenses, 23
Accounting period, 101, 105, 150
Additional rate, 8
Adjustment of profits, 17, 28
Agent, 141
Agent vs Principal, 141
Amortisation, 21
Annual exempt amount (AEA)/annual
exemption, 189
Annual investment allowance (AIA), 38, 54
Appeal, 137
Augmented profits, 152

B

Badges of trade, 211, 218
Balancing allowance, 43, 54
Balancing charge, 43, 54
Basic rate, 8
Basic rate band, 190
Basis period, 61, 70
Bonus issues, 179
Bonus shares, 183
Business asset disposal relief (BADR), 191

C

Capital allowances, 19, 37
Capital expenditure, 18, 37, 54
Capital gains calculation, 188
Capital gains tax (CGT), 162, 190, 200, 202
Capital losses, 124
Careless, 136
Carry back loss relief, 127
Carry forward loss relief, 127
Case law, 5
Cessation, 43
Chargeable gains, 98
Choice of business structure, 212
Choosing loss relief, 124
Class 2 contributions, 92
Class 2 NICs, 138
Class 4 contributions, 92, 138
Closure notice, 141
Companies, 4
Company tax returns, 150
Compliance checks, 141, 151
Corporation tax, 162
Costs of registering trademarks and
    patents, 21
Costs
    disposal, 163
    original purchase price, 163

Current

Current year basis of assessment, 61, 70, 78
Current year loss relief, 120, 127

D

Date, 150
Deliberate, 136
Deliberate error, 136
Depreciation, 21
Disallowable expenditure, 28
Disallowed expenditure, 18
Discovered, 136
Disposal of an incorporated business, 202
Disposal of an unincorporated business, 199
Disposals, 41
Dividend income, 99

E

Enhanced capital allowances for companies,
    48
Enhancement expenditure, 163, 170, 188
Enquiries, 141
Entertaining, 22
Entrepreneurs' relief, 205
Ethics, 5
Expenditure wholly and exclusively for trade
    purposes, 28
Extraction of profit, 214

F

Filing due date, 143
    companies, 150, 157
Filling due date, 137
Finance Act, 4
Financial year, 103, 105
Fines, 21
First year allowance (FYAs), 54
First year allowances (FYAs), 39
Fiscal year, 61, 70
Fundamental principles, 5

G

General provisions, 19
Gift relief, 196, 205
Gifts, 22
Goods taken from stock, 20

H

Higher rate, 8
HMRC (FY), 5

I

Incidental costs of disposal, 163
Incidental costs of obtaining loan finance, 21
Income tax, 7, 162
Income tax liability, 8
Incorporated businesses, 4
Indexation, 177
Indexation allowance, 188
Inline eXtensible Business Reporting
    Language' (iXBRL), 150
Interest, 23, 98, 143
Interest on late paid tax, 140, 154
Interest on over paid tax, 140
Irrecoverable debts, 22

K

Keeping records, 150

L

Large companies, 152, 157
Late filing, 137
Leasing costs of car, 23
Legal and professional charges, 22
Lifetime limit, 194
Loan relationship, 98
Long period of account, 97, 101, 154
Low emission cars, 39
Lower earnings limit (LEL), 89

M

Main pool, 38

N

National insurance contributions (NICs), 200
National Insurance Contributions (NICs), 89
Net income, 7, 12
Non-trading loan relationship (NTL-R), 98
Notice to make a return, 134
Notification of chargeability, 150

O

Opening year rules, 62, 78
Operative events,176, 180, 183
Overlap profits, 64, 66, 70

P

Partial closure notice, 141, 152
Partnership, 75, 82, 83
Partnerships, 4
Payment of corporation tax, 152
Payment of income tax, 138
Payment on account, 138, 143
Penalties, 21, 136, 140, 151
Penalties for error, 136

Penalties for failure to keep records, 151
Period of account, 38, 47, 54, 101, 105, 150
Personal allowance, 7
Plant, 54
Political donations, 22
Post-tax proceeds, 201, 202
Potential lost revenue (PLR), 136
Principal, 141
Private expenditure, 20
Private use adjustments, 97
Private use asset, 47, 54
Professional behaviour, 5, 12
Professional competence, 5, 12
Profit-sharing agreement, 76
Prompted, 136
Property business income, 98

Q

Qualifying assets, 167
Qualifying charitable donations, 99, 105

R

Redundancy payments, 23
Repair expenditure, 19
Repayment interest, 143
Retail price index (RPI), 164
Retention of records, 135
Revenue expenditure, 18, 37, 54
Rights issues, 180, 183
Rollover relief, 166, 205
Royalties, 22

S

Small Profits Threshold, 89
Sole traders, 4
Special rate pool, 45
Spouse or civil partner tax planning, 216
Statue law, 4
Statutory Instruments, 4
Structures and buildings allowances (SBAs),
    50
Subscriptions, 22
Super-deduction, 48

T

Tax avoidance, 5, 12
Tax evasion, 5
Tax liability, 8
Tax planning, 5, 12
Tax Written-Down Value, 40
Tax year, 12, 61, 70, 189
Taxable gain, 189
Taxable income, 7, 12, 190
Taxable total profits (TTP), 105
The tax return, 134

Total income, 7, 12
Trading losses, 112, 127
   companies, 119
   individuals, 112
Trading profits
   companies, 97

U

Unincorporated businesses, 4
Unprompted, 136

Upper earnings limit (UEL), 89

W

Wholly and exclusively, 18
Writing down allowance (WDA), 39, 54

Y

Year of assessment, 70